FOOTBALL GENTRY
The Cobbold Brothers

Brian Scovell is a freelance sports writer and the author of twenty previous publications, including books on Dickie Bird, Trevor Brooking, Lawrie McMenemy, Gary Sobers, Brian Lara and Bobby Robson.

FOOTBALL GENTRY
The Cobbold Brothers

BRIAN SCOVELL

TEMPUS

First published 2005
Reprinted 2006

Tempus Publishing Limited
The Mill, Brimscombe Port,
Stroud, Gloucestershire, GL5 2QG
www.tempus-publishing.com

British Library Cataloguing in Publication Data.
A catalogue record for this book is available from the British Library.

ISBN 0 7524 3464 0

Typesetting and origination by Tempus Publishing Limited
Printed in Great Britain

DEDICATION AND ACKNOWLEDGEMENTS

This happy book is dedicated to my wife Audrey Esther Scovell who sadly died of cancer of the liver at the age of fifty-eight on Christmas Day 2000. Audrey didn't have the joy of meeting John Cobbold, who died at fifty-six, and his brother Patrick but she heard plenty about them from me and she would have loved their sense of fun and eccentricity. Unfortunately, she wasn't a football enthusiast. She was an artist, an opera and classical music lover and a much-loved humanitarian.

I first reported a match at Portman Road in 1961, where I first met Alf Ramsey. I was working for the *Daily Sketch* before it merged with the *Daily Mail* and I spent many pleasurable hours with these amazing, unique brothers. I thought someone would write a book about them but John was about to start talking into a tape recorder with a view to giving the material to a writer when he died in 1983.

Late in 1999 David Sheepshanks told me that Harold Smith, the club's oldest serving director and now vice-president, wanted to write his memoirs, much of which would be about the Cobbolds. I went to see Harold in his house, close to the former homes of Sir Alfred and Sir Bobby Robson and he was in remarkable form, recalling many hilarious stories about his former chairmen. Soon it became clear that no publisher would buy a manuscript about a director. A few egocentric chairmen like Bob Lord and Doug Ellis had written books, but not directors.

Instead I suggested to David Sheepshanks that I ought to interview as many people about the brothers for a funny book about the Cobbolds for a wider audience. There is always humour in football, although little of it is written about, especially in books. David was very enthusiastic and I was ready to begin the necessary research. I was scheduled to retire at the end of 2000, ending my forty years at Associated Newspapers, and it would have been a good way to keep busy along with my other sidelines.

On 8 November that year George Best's liver consultant Professor Roger Williams told Audrey that she had a huge tumour and that 'it might be tricky'. Within a month we knew she wouldn't last the year.

Pain-killing tablets, the wrong ones, poisoned her bloodstream and she went into a coma and never came out of it. At 5 a.m. on Christmas Day it was my turn to relieve my son at Audrey's bedside in room 147 at Cromwell Hospital. He said, 'I'm fine, you have a couple more hours' sleep in the next room and I'll wake you.' Even though the TV was still on, I was soon fast asleep.

Suddenly I was woken by the sound of the voice of John Motson, an Ipswich fan, shouting 'And Ipswich have scored!' It was *Match of the Day* replayed from the previous night. It was like an alarm call and I went next door and said, 'Gavin, I'll take over. I just want to say a few words to Mummy.' Audrey had worked as a production assistant at ITN in the days of Reginald Bosanquet, Andrew Gardner and a young Sir Trevor McDonald and she often timed the news programme down to the second. Without planning my little speech, I told her how much we loved her and always would, how much she had done, not just for us but for so many other people around the world, tracing from the moment when we met on 16 March 1963 when I first saw her standing on the other side of the room on a dance floor at the Addiscombe Cricket Club and looking so stunningly beautiful.

As I came close to the end of what I wanted to say, a single tear ran down her cheek. Hearing is the last of the senses and I knew she had heard. I finished by saying, 'you will be swept to the highest peaks of Heaven by a tide of love,' and she stopped breathing. It was almost like a miracle. Such timing! I wrote the Address at her memorial service at Brompton Oratory, read by Sir Trevor McDonald, and I wrote: 'We felt no despair or agony over her departure but almost a feeling of joyousness and celebration. Her next task, spreading happiness, has already started in another place.' Sir Trevor added the words 'a better place'.

I knew I had to press on with writing this book. It proved to be a form of therapy, as though she had planned that I should busy myself working on a labour of love. And that is what happened. It was difficult to convince many of my previous publishers that this would sell outside East Anglia and I am eternally grateful to James Howarth and Holly Bennion at Tempus for publishing *Football Gentry*.

So many hundreds of people have helped me and I apologise in advance if anyone is overlooked in this acknowledgement. Firstly, I have to thank

David Sheepshanks from the bottom of my heart because his support and encouragement were so vital. He presides over a club which is like an oasis in English football. It was moulded by these two Corinthians, Mr John and Mr Patrick, as they were called, and their spirit lives on. The hospitality is unequalled and the welcome is unsurpassed. Portman Road is THE place everyone wants to go. It is a decent club run by decent people.

Major Philip Hope-Cobbold, a club director, has been a tremendous help, giving me the run of Glemham Hall where his uncles lived. John Kerr, the previous chairman, has provided much assistance along with the other directors Richard Moore, Roger Finbow and my good friend Richard Ryder, who subsequently left the board and is now a vice-president. I should also mention the wives, including Mona Sheepshanks because when I started out at this difficult time in my life I felt their love reaching out and it helped me through the tough times. Lady Victoria Ramsey, whose husband died in 1999, was very kind in lending me some pictures of Alf and I marvel at the wonderful way she conducts her life.

Alesha Gooderham was Head of Communications at the time, before she left to concentrate bringing up her three young children, and was a fantastic, supportive friend who bought smiles and happiness to the place. I will never forget her. Pat Godbold was a phenomenon, providing an immense amount of assistance including telephone numbers of ex-players all around the world and also organising the 1962 and 1982 celebration dinners at the club. She was deservedly honoured last year after reaching the milestone of fifty years at the club.

David Rose, who was secretary of the club for forty-three years, was a boon to me during this period. He is now a consultant to the club and still comes up with answers. Other members of the club who were helpful were Terry Baxter, who is Head of Communications, Ann-Marie Williams, Mike Noye, Geoff Sheppard and an old mate, Trevor Kirton, the former kit man who is now Stadium and Facilities Manager.

I have to thank the late 10th Duke of Devonshire and the Duchess, who was kind to receive me at Chatsworth House and let me hear 'Jailhouse Rock' played when she answered the telephone. The Earl of Stockton, grandson of Lord Macmillan, proved helpful. One of the most informative and friendly of my contacts was Major Andrew Napier, who was Patrick Cobbold's best friend. Jack Bayfield, the Cobbolds' head

gamekeeper, provided some wonderful anecdotes and Mr John's chauffeur and friend Roger E. Nightingale did likewise. Bishop John Wain,
Ken Bean, John Eastwood, Richard Cobbold, Mike Hollingsworth and
Michael Stowe of the Good Samaritans provided much local background
information. Many journalists who knew the Cobbolds came up with
much valuable material, one in particular being Dave Allard, who is one
of the most respected football journalists in the country and has reported
on Ipswich FC for more than thirty years. They number the semi-retired
Tony Garnett, the doyen of Ipswich, and several from Fleet Street, including Ken Jones and Patrick Collins.

Others who assisted were the late Sir Bert Millichip, chairman of
the FA, the former FA doctor Neil Phillips, Jack Wiseman, a long-
serving director of Birmingham City, Don Howe, Bob Wilson, Lawrie
McMenemy, John Motson, Peter Hill-Wood, the Arsenal chairman and
Ken Friar, the former secretary of Arsenal, now consultant. When Patrick
Cobbold died in 1994 around 300 players had appeared for the club
since it was formed. With the help of Pat Godbold, I contacted many of
those who played between 1948-1994 and they were eager to help. They
obviously loved the Cobbolds. The ones who assisted, in alphabetical
order, are Terry Austin, Bill Baxter, Kevin Beattie, Keith Bertschin, Alan
Brazil, Joey Broadfoot, Frank Brogan, George Burley, Terry Butcher, Larry
Callaghan, Frank Clarke, Ian Collard, John Compton, Ray Crawford,
Dermot Curtis, Mich D'Avray, John Elsworthy, Tom Garneys, Eric Gates,
Bryan Hamilton, Geoff Hammond, Colin Harper, Ken Hancock, Danny
Hegan, Bobby Hunt, Allan Hunter, Derek Jefferson, David Johnson,
Mick Lambert, Cyril Lea, Jimmy Leadbetter, Jackie Little (who was a
star!), Steve McCall, Mick McNeil, Paul Mariner, Mick Mills, Doug
Millward, Doug Moran, Peter Morris, Arnold Muhren, Andy Nelson,
Kevin O'Callaghan, John O'Rourke, Roger Osborne, Aled Owen, Ted
Phillips, Trevor Putney, Jimmy Robertson, Laurie Sivell, Kevin Steggles,
Alan Sunderland, Brian Talbot, Frans Thijssen, Robin Turner, Colin
Viljoen, John Wark, Trevor Whymark and Charlie Woods.

I am grateful to the Suffolk Records Office and Terry Hunt of the
East Anglian and his staff. Again, apologies if anyone is left out. I enjoyed
every minute of this adventure and I think Audrey would approve.

Brian Scovell, Bromley, Kent, December 2004

I WOULD PREFER A LARGE GIN AND TONIC

An introduction to the Cobbold family and friends

The VIP Room and the Royal Box at the old Wembley Stadium are long since gone and neither was renowned for laughter and fun. But on 6 May 1978, when the 50th FA Cup final between Arsenal and Ipswich was staged, things were much different. Among the guests was Lady Blanche Cobbold, daughter of the 9th Duke of Devonshire and brother-in-law to Harold Macmillan, later the Earl of Stockton, the former Prime Minister. Also present were the two sons of Lady Blanche, John Cavendish Cobbold, the chairman of Ipswich Football Club and Patrick Mark Cobbold, a director who later succeeded him as chairman. They were Old Etonians and their family married into aristocracy.

Denis Hill-Wood, the chairman of Arsenal, was also an Old Etonian (like his son, Peter, the current chairman of the club) and originated from similar stock. The Hill-Woods came from humble origins, before becoming rich businessmen during the industrial revolution in the mid-1700s. Denis's father, Sir Samuel, was a Lancastrian businessman whose surname was plain Hill before he changed it to Hill-Wood. The Hill-Woods and the Cobbolds were close friends and a lunch meeting between their fathers in 1936 led to the formation of a professional football club at Ipswich.

At Wembley that day the wine flowed and so did the conversation. John Cobbold was a rake in the nicest sense, a joker and a wit. His brother, Patrick, was quieter but he, too, liked a good story and a laugh. After lunch in the huge banquet room under the Twin Towers, the chief guests crossed the wooden floor to the Red Room, which was known as the VIP Room, and an official of the FA approached Lady Blanche, who was eighty, and said 'Ma'am, would you like to meet the Prime Minister, James Callaghan?' Lady Blanche looked at him with a stern expression and replied 'I would prefer a large gin and tonic.' John Cobbold burst into uproarious laughter, rolling backwards and forwards. Patrick guffawed and so did the other directors. The Hill-Woods and the other Arsenal notables were convulsed with laughter and James Callaghan (who died in the summer of 2005 at ninety-three) joined in the fun. Princess Alexandra, the chief guest who later presented the FA Cup to Mick Mills, the Ipswich captain, laughed too. One of the few people not to laugh was Professor Sir Harold Thompson, the chairman of the FA. He was reputedly a snob and was universally disliked. A few months after he was snubbed by Lady Blanche, Callaghan fell from power.

Sir Bert Millichip, who took over from Thompson as chairman three years later, told another hilarious story about Lady Blanche, who died on the night of the Great Storm on 17 October 1987. Hurricane winds gusting 100mph swept across England, killing nineteen people, uprooting an estimated 15 million trees and causing damage estimated at £1.8 billion. 'She went with a bang,' Patrick said. Many of the trees, some dating back to the seventeenth century, were felled in the grounds of Glemham Hall. Philip Hope-Cobbold, a nephew of the brothers, now the master of Glemham, said 'that probably contributed to her death.'

Sir Bert said 'I was following Lady Blanche down the steps to the Royal Box to escort her to her seat and to my astonishment I noticed that her knickers was slowly falling down her legs and ended up around her ankles. John Cobbold was coming down the steps behind her and he bent down and picked up the knickers and shoved them into his pocket. She carried on as though nothing had happened. I think we were the only three people present who saw it happened and I had to chuckle.' Sir Bert died on 18 December 2002 at the age of eighty-eight and was considered the most honest and compassionate of the leading football administrators. Steve Curry of the *Daily Mail* said of him 'he had Corinthian values.'

In the late 1970s nearly all the football clubs banned women from going to the directors' boxes at football grounds and the ban even applied to Ipswich FC. 'You can't expect to see women jabbering away when I am telling dirty jokes,' said John Cobbold. Wembley, of course, was exempt from the ban because the chief guest was often a member of the Royal Family, including Her Majesty Queen Elizabeth II, the late Princess of Wales or, as was the case during the fiftieth cup final, Princess Alexandra. At home matches Lady Blanche had to sit in the stand at Portman Road, some distance away from her sons. The restriction was lifted four years after John Cobbold died in 1983.

Lady Blanche was called 'Mama' by her sons, but behind her back she was sometimes referred to as 'The Old Grey Mare.' Widowed in 1944, she was grey haired – almost gaunt-looking in her later years – although she appreciated a good joke. Major Andrew Napier of the Coldstream Guards was in charge of The Coldstream Guards Band which played at Wembley at the cup final. Earlier, John Cobbold spoke to him and arranged that 'The Old Grey Mare Ain't What She Used to Be' should be played when Lady Blanche appeared in the Royal Box. As she made her way down the steps, only a handful of people were in on the joke. It provoked a lot of amusement when the band struck up, with the Cobbold brothers leading the laughter. Major Napier was Patrick Cobbold's best friend. 'He was the best man at our wedding,' said the Major.

Harold Smith, at eighty-six, was one of the longest-serving Ipswich directors and is now a vice president, and he recalled an incident when Lady Blanche was driving to the ground and a tyre burst. 'She got out of the car, took out the jack from the boot and proceeded to change the tyre on her own,' he said. 'Not many women would do that, particularly at her age. She was a very tough nut.'

The Cobbolds were among the last of the Corinthians, who espoused fair play and sportsmanship, and the Hill-Woods shared their beliefs. Around the late 1970s these qualities had almost disappeared. Directors were more concerned about money than ideals and players cheated, kicked and spat as football became more confrontational and increasingly unsavoury. There was always hooliganism – named after an Irish family called 'Holligan' which lived in the Elephant & Castle in the 1880s – but it now erupted into social disorder that required legislation to curb it. Opposing sets of supporters often fought each other, forcing the police to impose strict segregation. In other sports, particularly cricket, rival supporters sat together and clapped both sets of players, not just their own team. Even today, football crowds are still segregated, as though they loathe each other.

The original Corinthians came from Corinth, a town fifty miles west from Athens that was destroyed in 146 BC by the Roman general Lucius Mummius. It is now a town of 30,000 inhabitants. The sporting creed of the Corinthians originated from a letter written by Saint Paul to the people of Corinth in AD 53-4, when he wrote that 'no gift to God, whether it be the gift of tongues, faith that moves mountains, or knowledge of mysteries has meaning unless it is accompanied by Love.'

Towards the end of the nineteenth century, a group of public schoolboys in England, mainly from the aristocracy who loved sport and especially football, formed an amateur side called the Corinthians. Bryon Butler's book *The Official History of the Football Association* tells us that 'they were amateurs to a man and when they pulled the white shirt on they stood apart. They were hugely successful, beating the professional sides and they showed dashing artistry, progressive passing and intelligent manoeuvring but there was much more to it. They were a symbol of fair play and selflessness. They stood for an ideal. They championed the highest standards of sportsmanship.' One of their rules was 'the club shall not compete for any challenge cup or prizes of any description.'

In 1933 G.N. Foster, one of the Corinthians, persuaded Herbert Chapman, the Arsenal manager, to launch a coaching scheme for boys for the first time and planned to start a football school devoted to the best young players. Chapman said 'I shall consider the scheme to be a failure unless the FA start coaching for boys of all classes.' A few months later he died of a common cold. Another generation went by before coaching was introduced into schools. On the Continent, boys were coached in the 1930s and the inventors of the game were the last major country to enter the World Cup, in 1950, a few years before the FA coaching scheme was started.

Today, no-one would expect football at the most exalted levels to be run by amateurs or played by amateurs. To reach the highest standard you need to be paid, but nowadays the pendulum has swung too far from sportsmanship and decency towards greed, selfishness and nastiness. Football is a business today and is no longer a sport. It is dominated by avarice and those who run it – some of the chairmen of the Premiership can be compared with Canadian geese. When these large birds arrive at the Royal Parks in London they gobble up every particle of food, leaving the rest of the bird life to struggle to survive.

In the 2001/02 season, Arsenal's wages bill totalled £61 million, higher than Manchester United's and 280 times the salaries paid to their players forty years earlier. The fall of the value of the pound through inflation is many, many times less than 280 times. One player, Sol Campbell, was paid £100,000 a week. Ipswich was a prudent club under the Cobbolds, but when their successors were paid millions of pounds by BSkyB for TV rights in the Premiership, their finances went into disarray. The chairman David Sheepshanks and his directors sanctioned contracts for players which enabled some of the players to be paid £20,000 a week. And they weren't really stars. Relegation followed, forcing the club to go into administration in a bid to avoid bankruptcy. It was a harsh lesson to learn. John Cobbold, who loved boating, used to say 'steady as she goes'; the directors of many clubs crowded too much sail on their masts and their ships nearly sank.

Peter Hill-Wood, Arsenal's long-serving chairman, said 'If someone had told me in 1962 that one day we could be spending £61 million on wages, I would have said they were off their heads.' When Bobby Robson led Ipswich to victory in the 1978 FA Cup final (then unsponsored), he was paid a bonus of £5,000 and thought it was a fortune.

The Cobbolds were not the only eccentrics in the Ipswich club and one notable absentee at the national stadium on that sunny day in May 1978 was the man who had graced Wembley in 1966 when he was the only England manager to win the World Cup. Sir Alf Ramsey was manager of Ipswich between 1955 to 1963, winning the Second and First Divisions in successive seasons. He was invited to the 1978 cup final but turned down the invitation. Invariably he ignored Robson, despite living close by in the same road in Ipswich, no more than five hundred metres apart. 'There was an open invite to go to Portman Road but he hardly ever came,' said Robson. 'Whenever he was sent a ticket he still didn't come. I am sure it wasn't personal. Alf never really recovered from being sacked by the FA and didn't like to mix with them.'

'After I was appointed England manager in 1982 I bumped into him in the boardroom at Chelsea and said "come on Alf, I've got a car here and I can drive you home to the door." Alf replied "I've come here by train and I shall return by train."' When Ramsey, an intensely private man, died in 1998, a local newspaper reporter rang to check the news. Lady Ramsey declined to confirm the story and it was several hours later before the news was confirmed. She wanted to keep his death quiet until the funeral was held.

Ramsey died of that pernicious disease named after the Austrian doctor Alzheimer. A few days before he died, his friend Pat Godbold, the PA to so many people in her fifty years at Ipswich FC, went to see him and he didn't recognise her. Earlier he had been in a public ward at the Heath Road Hospital in Ipswich and the people running the FA were criticised for not paying to move him into a private ward. It was a sad end to a great footballing life.

During his long and distinguished career, Ramsey had an encyclopaedic memory of the game and its players. Alan Sunderland, the former Ipswich and Arsenal striker, met him at his local golf course after he had retired and tried to start up a discussion about football. 'I am here to play golf and I do not want to talk about football,' he said. He continued, saying 'I know all about your career. I gave you your first and only cap for the under-21 side and I can tell you the names of the eleven.' Sunderland said later 'He was spot on. He had an incredible memory.'

In the days up to the 1978 cup final, the Cobbolds insisted that it should be a jolly trip to London. When he met some of the Arsenal directors at the semi-final a month earlier, he suggested that the two clubs should hold a joint banquet. 'It was too late,' said Ken Friar, the long-serving secretary. 'But it would have been a great night.' The

Cobbolds rarely intervened in the club's business. 'Our job is to open the bottles of wine and pour it out in the right glasses,' they used to say. On the Monday before the game, when the final tickets were about to be sold at Portman Road, John Cobbold turned up at the offices and produced several cardboard boxes to collect the banknotes which had been handed over by the lucky purchasers. 'He got them mixed up and we had to start again,' said one official. His brother Patrick was with him and he ended up sitting on the floor counting the notes.

Three days before the game, the players and officials set off in the team coach for the Sopwell House Hotel in St Albans – an interesting building, which has a mixture of Tudor, Georgian and neo-Georgian architecture, surrounded by beautiful gardens. Prince Louis Battenberg, the German aristocrat who was the First Sea Lord in charge of the British Navy in the First World War, lived there for some years, as did his son, Lord Mountbatten. These days the hotel is frequently used by football clubs, including the England team.

On the way to the hotel, the bright blue Ipswich coach made a detour off the A12 to collect the players' cup final suits. The players had been measured up but when they arrived at the shop and started to try on their new finery, most of them discovered that the suits were ill fitting. 'Christ, I look like Norman Wisdom,' said Paul Mariner. The Cobbolds hooted with laughter. 'The girls had swapped the names round,' said one of the players. Clive Woods, who was later voted the Man of the Match after the game, said 'We were a group of lads on holidays, not preparing for the game of our lives.'

Some of the players were injured after playing so many matches in a short space of time, as were some of Arsenal's, but Robson's men were in a better mental state. Kevin Beattie said 'I was only 80 per cent but the gaffer wanted me to play. I had two cortisone injections before the game and another at halftime to kill the pain. I wouldn't have got through without them.' He is a cheeky man and, the day before the match, FA secretary Ted Croker advised the players on the procedure and etiquette at the event. Beattie was told to be wary about shaking hands too firmly when he was presented to Princess Alexandra.

Beattie said 'When I was interviewed at lunchtime by John Motson, who is a great Ipswich supporter, I said it was all right, I would be gentle with her. But when the teams were presented, she went down the line to shake hands with the players and, when it was my turn, she told me "Mr Beattie, I saw you on TV earlier." I went as red as a beetroot!'

Some of the players were wakened at the hotel the night before the big match by loud noises, caused by a former member of staff who had returned with a grudge against some members of staff. 'Most of us slept through it,' said Mills. Anyone hoping to have a lie-in were woken by the noise caused by Allan Hunter's fitness test on the lawn at 8.30 a.m. A week before, the Northern Ireland centre half (a very tough character who was respected by all his opponents), had had fluid taken from a knee and was unable to train. 'I wanted it decided as early as possible,' he said. 'If I wasn't going to play, I wanted to get drunk.' He did some sprints and turns and, as the trainer gave him the thumbs up, he let out a mighty roar.

Most of the Ipswich players were gamblers, usually sending their bets out from the dressing room before matches. In those days, the FA banned players from backing on their own team, or opponents, but the Ipswich squad carried on as normal and Mick Lambert, the left-winger, collected the money. Robson revealed in his latest autobiography 'I gave him £20 to put on. The odds against us were 5-2, ridiculous, and I thought it would show my confidence in the players. I couldn't see us losing.'

He was right. Arsenal's players were subdued and their key man, Liam Brady, was clearly unfit. It was not a great final but a memorable one and it provided an unlikely hero in Roger Osborne, a twenty-eight-year-old midfield player who was born in Otley, a village in Suffolk. He was a retiring, nice man and an honest guy. He was signed by Ipswich after he came along to watch a friend who had been given a trial. One of the coaches said 'we went to see the wrong guy!'

Osborne had been dropped for the semi-final to make way for Colin Viljoen, the South African who was known as 'Ace' because he was thought to be the top man. Viljoen was out injured for weeks and Robson wanted his top man back. The other players wanted Osborne in the cup final line-up and several of them deliberately sabotaged

Viljoen's chances, declining to pass the ball to him. Ipswich lost 6-1 at Aston Villa on 29 April, the last game before the final and Robson was furious. 'It's player power and I am not giving way to it,' he said.

Later in the week, however, he did, and Osborne was named in the side. Viljoen stayed at home and didn't watch the game on TV. Rain had fallen through the night and so much water lay on the pitch in the morning that there was a danger of the game being called off. Pumps had to be used to remove the surface water and fortunately the sun came out. At lunch, an excited and talkative chairman Cobbold said 'The going is heavy and that will suit the Suffolk punch!' (The horse on the club's badge is known as the Suffolk Punch.)

Players like Brian Talbot, who later signed for Arsenal, John Wark and Osborne out-ran the Arsenal players and Osborne was in the right place to send a 77th-minute, left-foot shot past Arsenal goalkeeper Pat Jennings to win the game 1-0. His fellow players jumped on him as he collapsed to the sodden Wembley turf. Suddenly, everyone realised he was in a bad way as he lay still. Both trainers ran on to try to revive him with their wet sponges. A message was relayed to Robson that the goalscorer couldn't go on and he sent on Lambert, the bookies' runner, to take over. 'It was emotion and excitement mixed in with exhaustion,' said Osborne. 'I didn't really want to go off but it made sense to send on a fresh player.' He was the first person to score a winning goal in a Wembley final and not kick the ball again in the same match.

Cobbold was one of the first to hug Robson and his players and he ordered champagne, and more champagne. The drink kept flowing for hours, setting records for alcohol consumption at a cup final, before the team coach left for a West End hotel to attend the banquet. The players, and most of the officials, stayed up drinking through the night and, when they staggered out in mid-morning to board the coach, they were ready for sleep. On the drive up the A12, before it was a dual carriageway, Cobbold ordered Trevor Kirton, the coach driver, to stop at one of his pubs, the Army & Navy at Chelmsford, a Tolly Cobbold establishment, to show off the FA Cup. The regulars were astonished to see the chairman walking through the doors carrying the trophy. 'Drinks all round!' he shouted. Throughout his career he was always the first to call for a round of drinks. He was the most generous of men.

Back in Ipswich, the party transferred to an open-top bus and an estimated 100,000 people, (80 per cent of the town's population) turned up to greet them. This was the high point of Cobbold's life. Presiding over a football club was the ultimate fun for him. He shied away from difficult decisions, leaving the work to his various managers and officials. He was lucky to have lived through that time. In today's more ruthless era, a Cobbold would probably not have survived.

Up to that time, the Football Association kept the FA Cup in a vault without releasing it until the following year's event, but Robson persuaded them to loan it to him occasionally. 'As you can imagine, the authorities had a really tight security operating but I did things with it I wasn't supposed to do,' he said. 'I often brought it back to the North East, sometimes in secret. I had to show it to my own folk.

'It meant a hell of a lot to me. I took it to Langley Park, my birthplace, to Durham, to Newcastle and, because of the fine tradition of Newcastle Football Club, it felt like bringing it back home. The cup was actually locked in an Ipswich police station, under severe scrutiny but you could take it out for trips, albeit with security. I took the bloody thing all over with me.

'At one stage, I had it for a couple of days. I signed for it and promised to take care of it – I'd always have a bobby with me at functions – and I took it to my village, the old school, the local pub. When it was all over, I put it in the boot of my car, arrived back in Ipswich too late to return it, and stuck it underneath my bed. I actually slept on top of the FA Cup.'

The wealth of the Cobbolds came from a brewery founded in 1723. Thomas Cobbold, a maltster by profession, launched his brewery business in Harwich. One of his descendants, named Thomas Clement Cobbold, was a long-serving MP for Ipswich and he inaugurated the Ipswich Association FC in 1878. A third Cobbold, Captain John Murray Cobbold, turned the club into a professional side in 1936. The Captain's mother, Lady Evelyn Murray, daughter of the 7th Earl of Dunmore, was one of the great characters in the family. She became a Muslim (being the first titled lady in England to do such a thing), was the first woman to cross the Libyan Desert on foot and the first Western woman, it is believed, to go on a Hajj to Mecca.

Jean, a daughter of Captain Cobbold, was a chauffeur to Sir Drummond Inglis, one of Field Marshal Bernard Montgomery's aides in the Second World War, and her poodle used to sleep in Monty's kitchen when he was stationed in Brussels. She took part in the D-Day landings, served at Arnhem, and was one of the first ATS personnel to arrive in Berlin at the end of the war. The Cobbolds often went fishing, shooting and hunting on their estates and lived in two fifteenth-century country houses, Glemham Hall near Woodbridge and Capel Hall near Felixstowe. They also had vast estates in Scotland, which were eventually sold for practically nothing. The stories about them are legion.

One of the finest anecdotes was about the monkey John Cobbold introduced to the Blackpool directors as a member of the Ipswich board. The team coach arrived ahead of schedule and, as it was a pleasant day, Cobbold stopped for a walk with some of his colleagues on the promenade, near to the Tower. 'I saw this chap sitting in the gutter and I started talking to him about his monkey,' he said. 'The monkey couldn't understand what I was saying. The man was trying to sell it to me for a fiver. After a while, I thought it was a good wheeze to buy it and take it to the game. I handed over the fiver and I took the pesky monkey off with its collar and chain. I took it to the ground and carried it into the boardroom. "This is our new director!" I said. Their directors thought it was rather amusing. Then, of course, this blasted monkey slipped its collar, shot across the tea table, upsetting several cups and glasses, and disappeared. It was obviously trained to do this and return to its owner. It was a good way of making a fiver.'

There have only been eight chairmen of Ipswich Town FC since 1936 and five of them were Cobbolds, a record of family patronage unequalled in football anywhere in the world. Some of their predecessors were Conservative MPs for Ipswich and were appointed to the office of High Sheriff of Suffolk. In those seventy-six years, there have only been twenty-nine directors, a third of them being Cobbolds, and John

Cobbold boasted that the club never sacked a manager. 'I wouldn't know how to do it,' he said. After he handed over the chairmanship to Patrick, however, two of the ten managers, John Duncan and John Lyall, left in circumstances suspiciously close to dismissal and Mick O'Brien, Bobby Ferguson and George Burley had to leave.

Lady Blanche was a central figure of the story of the Cobbold brothers, John and Patrick. She taught them manners and insisted they had to dress properly for dinner. Once she was wakened by the ringing of the telephone at 1.30 a.m. at her bedroom in Glemham Hall and she said 'Who is it? What do you think you are doing, waking us up at this hour!' A booming voice said 'This is the Prime Minister speaking.' It was in the middle of the Second World War and Sir Winston Churchill was a close friend of her husband, the Captain. They often went shooting together and Lady Blanche and her children often came along.

There were several burglaries at Glemham Hall and one of the employees recalled 'one day these men got in and Lady Blanche grabbed hold of a stick and chased them out the door. She was a game old bird!'

TWO

OFF ON JOLLIES

Exploits away from home

The best moments for the Cobbolds were when they went on 'jollies' – trips abroad for friendly matches. Other, more serious, trips for competitive matches were treated in almost the same way by the brothers, like school outings. The end-of-season visits were often hilarious occasions. The home club or association would pay a percentage of the proceeds to Ipswich to cover their expenses. It was a 'working' holiday with plenty of drinking, golfing and wenching... and the wives were left behind.

One England international told a story about one of the senior officials, now dead, hiring a prostitute and, when she visited his hotel room, some of the players queued to look through the keyhole of the door. After minimal talk, because she was unable to speak much English, she stripped off and clambered on to his inert, unclothed body. After a lot of fumbling and grunting she provided the service he had paid for and the man kept repeating 'Oh that's lovely'. The players took turns to be peeping Toms, suppressing their laughter for fear of interrupting the act. Afterwards the players called him 'Oh that's lovely' for the rest of the tour. The next evening the players teased him about his lie ins. 'It's too good to hurry,' he said.

In their beach bar soirees, the directors enjoyed reminiscing about past funny stories and one of Mr Patrick's favourites was about a chairman of a Football League who boasted his club was the first to allow women in his boardroom. 'He said it was 1981, a long time before we let women in,' said Patrick. 'His lady was of Oriental disposition and was sitting there breastfeeding a baby. I said to our directors "It's all very well ladies being admitted but letting boat people in is something else!"'

On a trip to Bermuda to play a Bermuda XI, the local FA agreed to pay Ipswich 50 per cent of the proceeds – around £10,000 if the ground was full. That would have been enough to pay for the travelling expenses and meet the costly drinks bill. Robson put out his best side and, although the players were tired after so many nights, they won 5-0. Afterwards he met the treasurer of the Bermudan FA in the directors' room and, following an exchange of pleasantries, the treasurer pulled out a cheque from his briefcase and gave it to Robson. Robson looked at the amount and it appeared to be 66,000 US dollars. Then he looked at it again.

'Is that 66,000 or 66.000?' he asked. 'Sixty-six dollars,' said the treasurer. 'Hang on,' said Robson. 'It was a full house and it should have brought in 130,000 dollars. We agreed 50-50 so where is the remainder?' The treasurer looked at him and said 'There was a terrible accident, Bobby. Ipswich were such a draw that the supporters stormed into the ground, climbing over the turnstiles. No-one paid. That is all that's left. I'm sorry.'

'Come off it man,' said an angry Robson. 'You can't pull the wool over me.' 'It's true,' said the treasurer. 'I can do nothing.' Eventually Robson had to leave. He joined the players in the coach and sitting behind him was Murray Sangster, one of the directors. 'How's that cheque?' asked Sangster. Robson told him and he laughed.

When Robson met John Cobbold back at the hotel he told him 'Bad news chairman, they've only paid us sixty-six dollars.' Robson started to explain and feared an outburst, but instead Cobbold said 'Well Bobby, if we hadn't come we wouldn't have had that sixty-six dollars. Come and have a drink.'

One of the players, Keith Bertschin, a striker on the Ipswich staff between 1973 and 1977, was renowned for scoring his first League goal with his first touch of the ball on debut. 'I scored against Arsenal after just fifteen seconds,' he said. 'The chairman, Mr John, said to me "Very good, Bertschin, good to have you on board!"

'In 1975 I went on my first trip with the club to Martinique and we were in the bar of a swanky hotel by the beach. I was just nineteen and Patrick Cobbold was drinking and a bit cheekily I said "What's that drink?" He said "Crème de menthe, it's very nice, you should have one. You'll enjoy it." So I had one, perhaps one or two and he said "it won't harm you". It was amazing really. I was young, on my first trip and he treated me like an equal. I never forgot that. He wasn't aloof, just a very friendly and sociable man with a posh accent. He was a great chap.'

Another player, the goalkeeper Laurie Sivell, who was born in Lowestoft and spent all his playing career with Ipswich (between 1969 and 1984), recalls similar stories. 'The directors used to assemble in the bar after tea for joke sessions, led by the chairman,' he said 'and after a succession of drinks Mr John wasn't fit to walk up to his room. Allan Hunter was deputed to pick him up and give him a pick-a-back up the stairs. You can't imagine the chairman of any other club would allow that. He loved a joke and a giggle. One day the chairman said to me "you look ill". I said "well you gave it to me, filling me with cocktails".'

Another young recruit who was indoctrinated into drinking by the Cobbolds was Dale Roberts, who fought a courageous battle against cancer while still carrying out his duties as assistant manager under

George Burley. 'You've got to stay positive,' he said. 'I only had eight days off while I was on chemotherapy.' He was born in Newcastle and was two years younger than Butcher. He was eighteen when he was chosen for the end-of-season trip to Martinique. 'Before that I'd only had a few lagers,' he said. 'The trip lasted seventeen days and it was a long one – too long. It was a great hotel but there wasn't much to do. The chairman and Patrick saw it as a chance to catch up on their drinking. I was sharing a room with George (Burley) and our room was three up from Mr Patrick's. The first day I heard this knock on the door and Mr Patrick invited me to his room to join with some of the other players for a welcome drink. There was a bar packed full of all different types of bottles. He was very friendly and amusing and offered me a bottle of Drambuie. "Try that," he said. "Take a swig, won't do you any harm." I took a sip and it was sickly stuff but he said it would do me good. By the time I came out of his room to go down for dinner I was in a right state. I got in the lift but when it reached the bottom I was spread out on the floor and had to be helped up. I couldn't remember much about it after that.' Sadly, Dale Roberts died on 4 February 2003 at the age of forty-six.

The trip to Martinique was an odd one. Two friendly matches were played and one of them was played in another French-owned island. Despite the condition of the players after such heavy drinking bouts, the games were won by Ipswich against a Martinique FA Xl. 'The crowd were a bit hostile,' said Roberts. 'They threw stuff on to the pitch and it wasn't pleasant.' No other English club would spend seventeen days in Martinique. 'The Cobbolds liked the West Indies,' said Roberts. 'But that time they took it too far. Everyone spoke French. And the beaches had black sand.'

After a week the players complained about the lack of entertainment. 'It was boring,' said one. 'We've got another couple of weeks and all we do is booze. There's no crumpet.' The next night they gathered round the pool and discussed the shortage of girls. They decided to confront Robson. 'If there's no women, we're off back home,' said one. Robson said 'I can't do anything about it. You're having a nice break in the sun, just get on with it.' The crumpet rebellion collapsed.

'Harry's Niterie' was known throughout Barbados and on one of the club's trips there Allan Hunter was woken at 2.30 a.m. by a telephone call from John Cobbold. 'You promised me you would take me to Harry's place, whatever it's called,' he said. 'Mr Chairman,' said Hunter. 'I'm in bed, fast asleep.' 'Nonsense,' said Mr John. 'Get your shorts on.' So Hunter got up and dressed and came down. He called for a taxi and off they went to the beachside bar. 'We had a good night,' he reported at breakfast. Now it is closed. Barbados still has standards.

Bobby Hunt, the Ipswich striker of the 1967 to 1970 period, a member of the footballing Hunt family from Colchester, had many hilarious sessions with John Cobbold. 'He was an outrageous character,' he said. 'One of the boys really. On a trip to Cyprus I tried to reciprocate and buy him a drink. "Do you want whisky?" I said to him. "Just the bottle," he said. A few days later, when he'd had a few, he was sitting round the pool at the hotel and said to us "have you ever seen whisky floating?" He assured me that it was a bit difficult. He dived in, came to the surface and floated along with his back. "That's whisky floating!" he shouted.'

Terry Butcher, the England centre half, was Ipswich Town's most capped player with 77 caps. Though he was born in Singapore in 1958, he grew up in Lowestoft and first saw a game at Portman Road when he was eight. 'I loved the club and still do,' he said. 'It's unique. My Dad took me and I used to stand on a soapbox which he brought along. We used to travel all over and on 27 May 1975 we were at the third FA Cup replay against Leeds and we won 3-2. It was so late and we couldn't get back home to Ipswich.

'I hardly drank, but the people who got me going were John and Patrick Cobbold. My first foreign trip was in 1977, the year of the Queen's Silver Jubilee, and I remember being in a hotel in Waikiki Beach in Honolulu. The players were summoned to the bar and Mr John gave me a glass of Mitizz, a pretty potent cocktail. After a few drinks I was away and the directors were well on the way to being legless. I don't think it would happen at any other club. On the same tour, I was introduced to vodka in Tampa and that almost knocked me out.

'Patrick took us to a Japanese restaurant and got us to drink sake, the Japanese drink made from rice.' It was an educational tour in how to learn to drink alcohol. 'It was great for team spirit,' said Butcher. Patrick Cobbold's sense of fun was similar to his brother's. On another visit to Barbados, the Ipswich party were waiting at the airport to board a plane to Trinidad. An American jumbo jet was preparing to come in to land and Robson said 'I wonder where that plane has come from?' 'From the sky, you dolthead,' said Patrick.

Mick Mills, Butcher's England colleague, was a veteran of many trips to the Caribbean and Europe and was a few years older than Butcher, Roberts and the younger signings. As captain he was also more restrained in his social habits. Mills was the last Ipswich player to be capped for England by Ramsey. Short, stocky and unbending, he was signed from Portsmouth when their youth scheme was abandoned. Mills made his debut against Yugoslavia and Robson later chose him as his captain at Ipswich at the age of twenty-one. Mills had a moustache (and still has one). An oddity about Ipswich at this time was that so many of their players looked like soldiers in Queen Victoria's redcoats. Others with moustaches were the Dutchman Frans Thijssen, the FWA Player of the Year in 1981, John Wark, a former PFA Player of the Year, Robin Turner, Mich D'Avray and Kevin Steggles.

When Robson was fêted at the club's twentieth anniversary dinner to commemorate the winning of the UEFA Cup in 1982, Mills rose to his feet and spoke in heart warming terms, without notes, about his old manager. He wasn't down on the list of speakers but stood up to reply on behalf of his players.

Another player, Les Tibbott, a Welshman from Oswestry, soon realised that his chairman was different to the average football club chairman on the day the home tie against Real Madrid was played in a vital UEFA Cup game. 'I was in the squad but didn't play,' he said. 'Mr John and the directors had a good lunch with the Spanish directors and a couple of hours before the kick-off I saw him looking out from a window overlooking the practice pitch. Someone was walking by who knew him and shouted out "Hi Mr Chairman, how are you?" Mr John looked at him for a moment and smiled, waving his hand. He shouted back "I'm fine, f—— off!" I don't think the man heard it.

'When I was in the Youth side we had a tough game against Aston Villa, a semi-final in the FA Youth Cup and just before half-time I was in a tangle with a Villa player and threw a right hander. It wasn't too bad. Handbags at a couple of yards. But in the dressing room Bobby Robson gave me a right bollocking. He didn't like players putting themselves in danger of being sent off. Afterwards I bumped into Mr John and was he was beaming. "That's the best right hander I've seen for many, many years," he said. "Well done!'"

By 1973 Robson was emerging as being one of the outstanding young managers in the country and was sought by a number of big clubs. Everton was the first. He wasn't on a contract and when he heard about the offer, John Cobbold asked to speak to him. 'I'm offering you a contract for ten years,' he said. Robson was taken aback. No manager had ever been offered a ten-year deal. He rejected Everton's overtures. Next it was Derby County. Brian Clough had quit and Derby's loquacious Sam Longson said 'Money is no object but I want a quick decision.' Robson was known to be cautious about making quick decisions and nothing happened.

The following year Robson took a mysterious call from someone who claimed he represented the West Riding Referees Association. Although he was usually too busy to take such calls, he answered that one. In those days only the club secretary David Rose and his secretary Pat Godbold, who worked for him, handled calls to the main office. Tony Collins, one of Don Revie's assistants, was on the line to Robson's private number. 'Don wants to speak to you,' he said. Revie was steeped in crookedness by this time.

Collins handed over the telephone to Revie and Revie said 'We want you here,' he said. 'It's made for you.' Leeds were champions and their directors gave him forty-eight hours to make up his mind. Again Robson vacillated and decided to stay on. Cobbold took him out for a drink and congratulated him for making the right decision. In 1976 Barcelona offered Robson three times as much money as Ipswich was paying him and Cobbold left it up to him – except that the club wanted £200,000 compensation for the remaining of his ten-year contract. Barcelona refused. So Robson stayed on. Sunderland also came on and he rejected them, too.

★

The Cobbolds were like mischievous schoolboys on these away days and Robson recalled an incident in the restaurant of a train, the usual mode of travelling on long journeys before clubs decided to go on their own coach with TV, videos and a toilet to avoid the fans. Mr John was one side of an aisle sitting with Robson and his brother Patrick was sitting opposite with another director Willie Kerr, the Scots farmer who had a sharp sense of humour. Robson noticed that John was breaking bits of a roll, soaking them in water in a pitcher and throwing them at Patrick. Mr Patrick followed suit.

John started poking the bread into a butter dish and hurled a large, greasy lump across the aisle, hitting Patrick on the side of his cheek. 'You're potty,' Robson told them. By now they were laughing, their shoulders bouncing up and down. John used to titter when he was amused. This time he was in full voice.

Willie Kerr shared the Cobbold's love for imbibing and on a walk down Las Ramblas, the main boulevard in Barcelona, he said to the other directors 'I fancy buying a new pair of shoes. The shoes in Spain are great value for money, you know.' So he went into a high class shop, accompanied by several other directors, and started trying on shoes. There was an interminable delay as he tried a succession of shoes and then discarded them. The shop assistant was becoming irritable. Closing time was approaching. 'Come on Willie,' said another director. 'We've got other and better things to do, including having a drink by the pool.' Eventually the slightly tipsy Kerr picked up a shoe, tried it for size, and pronounced 'that's a wonderful fit. I'll have them.' The shop assistant said rather crossly 'Sir, that is your shoes, you were wearing them when you came in.'

Kerr was renowned for being reluctant to buy rounds of drink and was continually ribbed over it. One player said 'we used to stop on long coach journeys back from the North for something to eat and have a drink or two and on one occasion we got back on the coach, Allan Hunter took the mike and said he had an important announcement. Allan said "Gentlemen, one of the directors, Mr Willie Kerr, has been charged with a serious offence. It is breaking into his wallet. But as it was his first case, the magistrates have put him on probation." The Cobbolds led the boisterous laughter.'

On the Barcelona trip, Trevor Whymark, one of the strikers, had an unusual mission. The temperature was in the high eighties and, along with the players, he was sunning himself around the hotel swimming pool. 'John Cobbold turned up wearing a heavy, woollen jersey, an old pair of brown, khaki shorts, long, woollen socks and brown brogue shoes,' said Whymark. 'It was an amazing sight. Everyone was laughing and he explained "Lady Blanche is a bit worried about my state of health. She reckons it gets cold in the night so I'm going to commission a photograph to send her to prove that I'm properly dressed! You're the man to take the picture." I lined him up and took a few shots. It was such a funny sight. He wasn't Charles Atlas, he didn't have a well honed body. It wasn't cold at night: the temperature hardly dropped under sixty-five degrees. The players made jokes about his appearance and he took it like a gentleman. He was an educated man with a different background to the rest of us but he loved talking to anyone, at any level.'

Lady Thatcher once praised Whymark's performance in the FA Cup final in a BBC interview. Unfortunately for the Prime Minister, Whymark didn't play. David Geddis took his place.

Bobby Ferguson, like Robson a Geordie from coalmining stock, was the coach until he succeeded him as manager between 1982 and 1987. Robson left to take over the England side with the reputation of being football's finest salesman. In his fourteen years at Portman Road, he sold forty-five players bringing in £2.65 million – not much of a sum compared to the fees paid in the Premiership these days but not inconsiderable then. Robson bought just fourteen players, costing £1.03 million. One of his mistakes came when he considered signing Paul Gascoigne. When he was fourteen, Gascoigne was invited to a trial and Robson decided against him. But perhaps Robson was right.

Bobby Ferguson always had a good relationship with John Cobbold. He said 'Mr John always insisted on good food for the players,' he said. 'It came from the Army background of the Cobbold brothers and their father. They used to say "an Army marches on its stomach, and footballers are the same." On one of these trips to the South of Spain, we were having dinner at a restaurant in Puerto Banus and the brothers played a jape on Bobby Robson, picking out the meat of a lobster and filling it with bread. Later, when the lobster was put in front of him, he looked rather quizzically and Mr Patrick said "How is your lobster, Bobby?" Bobby said "Well, it's a bit bland." It was the signal for the Cobbolds to burst into laughter, their shoulders shaking and heaving.'

In a game at Roker Park, Ipswich were leading 3–2 and holding on in the final minutes by holding up play. Ferguson ordered his players to delay taking throws and one of the new signings, Ian Atkins, took a throw in several yards further down the touchline than it should have been taken. The referee blew the whistle and ordered the throw to be given to a Sunderland player. 'At the time the FA had introduced a law giving the opposition the throw if a player pinched a yard or two,' said Ferguson. 'Mr Patrick said "Bobby, can you take me through this new law?" He hadn't heard of it! Both the brothers were the same. They loved the game but never really mastered the laws.'

Mr John's public school accent and demeanour came to the fore at the end of the 1972/73 season when Ipswich won the Texaco Cup, winning a two-match final against rivals Norwich City. As if football clubs were short of fixtures, the Football League sanctioned yet another competition, a knock out tournament for nine English clubs and seven Scottish clubs. Ipswich were not invited at first but two Irish clubs had to withdraw because of The Troubles which had erupted. Ipswich filled the gap and won the final against Norwich, winning 2–1 at home and 1–0 at Carrow Road. Clive Woods, born in Norwich, scored the Ipswich goal in the second game and that upset the local fans.

On the way back Ipswich fans wrecked two homebound trains after running amok through the streets in Norwich, causing £2,000 worth of damage to shop windows. Several people were taken to hospital and police made twenty-two arrests. It was almost unheard of in East Anglia. Mr John's reaction was typical. 'These people are f——ing creeps,' he said. 'They should be birched. We are disgusted at the antics of a small collection of cowardly creeps. We are not interested in louts and they will be kept away from Portman Road.'

There has always been animosity between the two sets of fans and
it still lingers on. It is a truism that the supporters of nearby clubs
provoke the most hate – Ipswich *v.* Norwich, Arsenal *v.* Tottenham,
Southampton *v.* Portsmouth, Birmingham *v.* Aston Villa, Liverpool
v. Everton, Manchester City *v.* Manchester United and, worst of all,
Rangers *v.* Celtic. Abroad, there are many others examples like Lazio
v. Roma and Inter *v.* AC in Milan.

Ipswich qualified for the UEFA Cup in the 1973/74 season after
finishing fourth, fifteen points behind champions Leeds. After getting
through to the second round, beating Real Madrid 1-0 at home and
drawing 0-0 at the Bernabeu, they were drawn against Lazio, the Italian
club which defamed the name of sport three years earlier.

In 1970 the Italians attacked Arsenal players in a restaurant after a
celebration dinner following a Fairs Cup tie in Rome and Lazio – a
Serie B club at the time – was later banned from European competi-
tions for two years. Relations between the two sets of players were
tetchy after the game and some taunts were hurled at some of the
Italian players over the dinner table. Suddenly Ray Kennedy, a placid
Northerner, was knocked off his chair and punched. Players from both
sides joined in. Others tried to intervene to keep them apart and as
the players spilled out on to the road, more fighting erupted. Bob
McNab, now coaching in California, was floored and the late George
Armstrong was trapped against the team coach. Lazio officials threatened to boycott the second leg at Highbury but UEFA warned them
that there would be serious consequences and when the game was
played Rudi Glockner, the World Cup final referee in 1970, cautioned
five Italians and no Arsenal player was punished.

Lazio had barely been allowed back into European competition
before Ipswich confronted them in the Olympic Stadium in Rome
on 7 November 1973. As Cobbold said 'We'd won the first leg 4-0,
with Whymark scoring all four goals and we expected a quiet night.
But they were at their tricks again, kicking and spitting. They didn't
behave like gentlemen.'

A brutal kick left Ipswich striker David Johnson writhing on the
ground in the first match. An opponent's boot caught him on the

testicles and blood splattered all over his shorts. Robson said 'It was a deliberate assault. It was an appalling injury.' Johnson, a cheery Liverpudlian, needed several stitches in his scrotum and his penis and for several days later he was unable to walk properly. 'It was an over the balls tackle,' he joked. The following week he was at the club when some of the directors were in the boardroom starting a meeting.

Mr John spotted Johnson through the window and rushed to the door to ask about his injury. 'Come in David,' he said. 'How is the injury progressing?' 'Here,' said Johnson with a smile, unzipping his fly, 'have a look for yourself!' 'Goodness me!' said Mr John. 'Put that thing away!' The chairman let out a loud noise and left. 'The board meeting had to be cancelled,' said Johnson. Harold Smith, one of the directors, said 'What you need is a transplant.' 'Not one from any of those buggers,' said Johnson.

Johnson insisted on coming for the return match although he was still very sore. Robson warned his players not to be involved with the home fans and keep their distance. 'It was my first experience of Italian football and I didn't like it,' said the manager. There was an explosive atmosphere in the ground, which had hosted the 1960 Olympic Games. A Union Jack was torn off a flagpole and burnt. One of the worst scenes was when Clive Woods was hacked down and the Dutch referee Leonardus van der Kroft awarded a penalty kick.

A Lazio player picked up the ball and kicked it over the running track, over a fence and high into the stand. The ball was eventually returned and, as Colin Viljoen placed the ball on the spot, another Lazio player squared up to him. Viljoen put the ball back yet again, before another opponent kicked the ball away. The referee had lost control and was terrified to issue any cautions. Lawlessness took over. After Viljoen converted the spot-kick, the Ipswich player was chased by a Lazio assailant, attempting to strike him. The Italian was still pursuing Viljoen when the referee signalled the restart.

Another Lazio thug turned on Woods, accusing him of taking a dive. Woods was white faced, petrified by fear. Robson rushed to the touchline shouting to a linesman as he pointed to Woods 'here, get that man off!' Woods ran towards the dugout. Johnson was on his feet. He was changed, but Robson hadn't intended to use him. 'I'll go on,' said Johnson. 'I'll be all right.' Robson patted him on the back and the centre forward went on for action. At that moment a Lazio substitute stepped in front of Johnson and spat into his face. Johnson wiped the spittle off by the back of his hand. 'F—— you,' he said. As the final whistle sounded, the Ipswich players sprinted for the tunnel, just ahead of the running Italians. Robson came to Johnson with an arm round him. 'Let's get out of here!' he shouted.

Allan Hunter was in the middle of the fracas outside the door of the away team dressing room and David Best, the Ipswich goalkeeper, was kicked and punched by Guiseppe Wilson, the English-speaking Lazio defender. It was a rare example of the English running away from the Italians but, as Robson later said, 'If we'd stood our ground and taken them on we would have been banned by UEFA as well.' As his players managed to get in the door, Robson bolted it. There was no police, no security. Several of his stronger, tougher players stood near the door to hold it up if it had caved in. There was a crate of lemonade in the corner of the room and Robson pointed to the bottles. 'Take one each,' he ordered. 'If they get in here, make sure you don't miss. It's every man for himself.'

In his first autobiography entitled *Time on the Grass* Robson said 'Lazio's players were furious and vengeful at having lost. They were more like demented animals, a pack of wolves, than a group of human beings. For the first time in my years in football I felt fear for my safety and the safety of my players. It was the worst moment of my life. If that door had been broken down, I dread to think what the outcome would have been. It would have been them against us. Fortunately the door stood firm.'

The door was locked and bolted for two hours before the Ipswich party eventually left. But still some of the Ipswich fans were stoned and when the team coach drove off, the players hid under their seats. Robson and the directors were warned that several hundred Lazio fans were waiting outside the team hotel so the coach took the party to a quiet restaurant outside the city. It was 3.30 a.m. before they arrived at the hotel. As the players walked into the foyer a smiling Mr John said to Robson 'Come and have a drinky-poo. You deserve it – a stiff one!'

At the UEFA Disciplinary Committee hearing, Lazio were fined £1,000 and banned for a further year. 'It should have been life,' said Cobbold. Happily, Johnson made a full recovery and was soon back playing again. He was asked what was he doing after his retirement. He replied 'as little as possible.' He explained 'I go to every home game, do a bit of speaking and a bit of corporate entertaining. It's a great life.' It's become a good job for ex-footballers. They are paid for their name and the supporters love it.

Twenty-eight years later, Ipswich encountered a different approach at the UEFA Cup third-round match against Inter of Milan. Ipswich won 1-0 in the first leg but no-one really expected them to progress further, especially as the Italian striker Christian Vieri was back in action along with Ronaldo. Defensive mistakes by Titus Bramble, the twenty-year-old England under-21 centre half (who has been compared to Kevin Beattie – a little prematurely), let Vieri score three goals in a 4-1 defeat. The 85,000 capacity of San Siro attracted a modest crowd of 25,000 and 8,000 were Ipswich supporters. 'We could have had many more,' said Paul Clouting, the Director of Commercial Affairs. 'Inter limited us to 8,000. The Italian police turned up mob handed, fearing trouble, but instead it all went off magnificently. There was no trouble at all and the chief of police said they were a credit to English football and had set an example to Italian football. It was a family crowd with youngsters with their parents and the total included twenty or so fans who were in wheelchairs.'

The Ipswich contingent were asked to stay in their seats until the other parts of the ground were cleared and the delay lasted almost an hour, totally unnecessarily. But they stood and chanted and cheered, calling for the directors and Beattie, whom they spotted after his radio work. Sheepshanks and the other directors came round to the other end to speak to them and it was one of the rare instances of club officials going to fans to thank them for supporting a team which had just been thrashed by a team top of Serie A.

'I felt a bit embarrassed but the feeling for the club was such that it brought a tear to my eye,' said Sheepshanks. No-one minded that the driver of the directors' coach kept losing his way in the four days of

the trip. He went to the wrong restaurant for an official lunch with
Inter officials and several times performed U-turns in busy Milan
streets. He even missed his way to the ground for training and had to
ask the courier to ring up her base for directions. The problem was
that both the driver and the courier were from Turin and it wasn't
easy for them to find their way in a strange city.

They eventually found their bearings and on the day of the match
they succeeded in taking the directors and the VIPs to the San Siro.
The place was almost deserted. It was a sign that attendances in Italy
were falling, with European competitive games particularly affected.
Sylvia, the beautifully coiffured courier, ushered the official Ipswich
party to their seats at the top of the second tier and at half-time she
began directing them back down the steps even though the rest of
the officials were making their way up to the steps towards another
exit, leading to the executive rooms – where ample amount of food
and drink had been laid on. 'No, no,' she insisted. 'You must go down,
not up.' An Inter official intervened. 'Please go up, and then down the
other stairs,' he said. Finally she conceded… and the Ipswich directors
made their way to the spacious room to be surprised to see ice cream
being served on a cold, damp evening. 'Some of the finest ice cream
I've ever had,' said one of the wives. Philip Hope-Cobbold said 'Sylvia
is a lovely lady but she got it wrong all the way through the trip!'

According to Mills, one of Ipswich's greatest away performances followed a terrifying ferry trip from Harwich to Ostend. The match was
against Feyenoord, the Dutch club in Rotterdam. It was the first leg
of a first-round UEFA Cup tie on 17 September 1975. 'The chairman
thought it was a good idea to go on a boat,' said Mills. 'He loved going
across the Channel. But this time a storm blew up and the boat rocked
all over the place. All the players got sick and when we eventually
arrived, we jumped straight into bed to recover. We were just able to
go for a light training session, but when the match started it was one of
those occasions when everything worked. We won 1-0 and I thought it
was the best performance I'd seen in Europe. I didn't tell the chairman
at the time because we didn't want to go on another boat trip!'

Bob Wilson recalled an extraordinary incident in Famagusta, when
the Arsenal squad were staying near to the Ipswich hotel on a relaxing

close season tour. 'We were drinking with the Ipswich people and John Cobbold turned up wearing a funny apron,' he said. 'He seemed very proud of it and insisted on telling the story. The apron had three folds and when John lifted the first one it showed a very small penis under a large "HIS". He hoisted the second and it was a woman's vagina marked "HERS". When he lifted the third one there was a huge penis marked "MINE". John couldn't control himself, he was almost wetting himself.

'The next time Arsenal played at Portman Road he had enough aprons made to spread them round our dressing room with plenty to spare. They were neatly laid out for the players. It was known as his favourite apron.'

In these years of success, the directors sometimes arranged end-of-season dinners to thank the players. At one boozy dinner, a senior player rose to toast an inebriated John Cobbold. 'Congratulations Mr Chairman,' he said. 'You've done f—— all again, very well.'

THREE

I'LL START UP A FOOTBALL TEAM

The Cobbold who made Ipswich Town Football Club

A chance meeting between Captain John Murray Cobbold, known as 'Ivan' or sometimes 'Cappy', and Sir Samuel Hill-Wood led to the formation of a professional football club in Ipswich in 1936. One relative said 'he was nicknamed Ivan the Terrible when he was young and the name Ivan stuck.' The Captain hardly played football himself, but was an all-round sportsman and was one of the last of the survivors of the sporting amateurs who preached Corinthian ethics and introduced football into this country. That spirit remains at Portman Road and its reputation for sportsmanship and decency is upheld by the current directors, one of whom is Philip Hope-Cobbold, a grandson of Captain Cobbold, who still lives in his grandfather's old country house, Glemham Hall.

Captain Cobbold was planning to go to a race meeting at Sandown, but it was cancelled and instead he went to his club, White's, for lunch. White's, founded in 1693 and restricted to men only, is the oldest of the thirty-four clubs in London and is situated in St James's Street (which incidentally houses six other clubs). The Captain bumped into Sir Samuel, the chairman of Arsenal and a member of the sporting family which produced several county cricketers, and after a drink was invited to come along and watch a game at Highbury. 'You ought to have your own club,' said Hill-Wood. Cobbold was so enthralled by what he had seen that he did just that. Denis Hill-Wood, the third of the four sons of Sir Samuel, took over as chairman of Arsenal in 1960 and, when he died in 1982, his son Peter was appointed in his place.

Peter, a sixty-nine-year-old former banker, now represents the end of the line of the sporting Hill-Woods. 'Today's chairmen are a different breed,' he said. 'My two sons love football and go to Highbury when they can, but they have successful careers and they can't spare the time. It is rather sad.' Most owners of football clubs, like Mohammed Al Fayed and Robert Maxwell, were more concerned about ego and money than the traditional values. Today's chairmen make most of their money from presiding over a football club. The Cobbolds and the Hill-Woods did it for love.

Sir Sam was born in Glossop and his family started a textile business owned by Wood Brothers. Until 1910 his surname was plain Wood but he used a family Christian name to change it to Hill-Wood. He was a prominent sportsman in the North, captaining Derbyshire between 1899 and 1901, averaging 17.62 with the bat, while his bowling figures were a modest 0-50. He also owned a pack of hounds and went shooting. Just before the First World War, he took over a small works football club at Glossop called Glossop North End, which qualified for entry to the Football League in 1898/99. Despite a population of only 25,000 inhabitants, Glossop was soon promoted to the First Division, only to drop back into the Second. After the war, they did not apply for re-election to the League.

Sir Sam's fortunes declined abruptly, his cotton business collapsed and Wood Brothers went bankrupt. He was the Conservative Member for the High Peak Division from 1910 to 1929 and was forced to head for London, leaving his four cricketing sons to make odd appearances for Derbyshire, the MCC, Oxford University, Cambridge University and the Viceroy's XI in India. They all went to Eton, like himself and his father, and as eventually did his grandson, Peter Hill-Wood (who played as a middle-order batsman for the Free Foresters, scored 30 runs in his only first-class innings). Denis John Charles Hill-Wood, to give his full name, was an outstanding sportsman. He gained Blues in association football, as he called it, and cricket at Oxford University in 1928 and made 5 appearances for Derbyshire, scoring 435 runs with an average of 22.65 and a highest score of 85.

Who's Who of Cricketers (a complete record of all cricketers who played first-class cricket in England with full career records and which weighs a hefty four pounds) described him as 'a steady open batsman and a change bowler.' 'I wasn't all that good,' he once said. 'But I loved soccer.' In his day, batsmen used to walk (give themselves out) when they knew they were out, before the umpire raised his finger.

Sir Sam's greatest claim to cricketing fame was that he scored ten runs off a single ball, playing for Derbyshire against the MCC at Lord's in May 1910. The records show this was the highest total from one delivery in the history of first-class cricket and it must have come from an all-run four and six overthrows! Whether he obtained the runs legally has never been explained.

Later, Sir Sam suddenly inherited a lot of money: enough to buy shares and join the Board of Arsenal Football Club in 1919. He also bought a five-storey house in Eaton Square. The Arsenal of that era was far removed from the present one in terms of probity and its chairman, Sir Henry Norris, a self-made millionaire with large, bull-terrier features and a white, walrus moustache, bought himself into the club while he still controlled Fulham. That would be impossible these days.

In 1919 Sir Henry ploughed £125,000 into Arsenal after engineering the move from Woolwich to Highbury and he wanted his money back. It depended on persuading the League committee members to vote for Arsenal to be allowed into the First Division, although they hadn't gained enough points on the field. They were sixth in the Second Division when the First World War started and professional football was suspended for five years. As the only MP with a voice in football, he proffered a lot of favours to his footballing friends and most of his associates were forced to pay their dues. So many inducements were paid out that he was charged by the FA and found guilty of making illegal payments. After trying unsuccessfully to sue the FA for libel, Sir Henry was eventually banned from the game *sine die*.

There has always been corruption in professional football and the authorities still have not stamped it out. Before the maximum wage was lifted in 1961, hardly a single transfer took place without 'readies' being passed on to the incoming player. It was a nomadic life and a player could move a dozen or more times in his career. He needed money to buy a new house and furnish it and that still applied when the restrictions were lifted and clubs were able to pay the market rate of pay. When the Premiership was launched in 1992, wages rocketed and a weekly wage exceeded the yearly salary of average players in the previous generation. Agents moved in and the more unscrupulous ones asked for 'considerations' for arranging deals – and got them. Managers wanted a cut too and many of them received these illegal payments as well. The game has made ineffective efforts to clean it up over the years and corruption is still rampant.

Leslie Knighton, the Arsenal manager who was harshly sacked by Norris, wrote of Sir Henry in his autobiography 'his influence was enormous. If he had not been such a rebel against petty authority he would have risen to the greatest position in the game. A financial genius, football was his hobby and delight, even though a bagatelle compared with some of his business deals. The game was immensely the poorer for his passing out of it and it was a tragedy indeed that such a man should have gone under a cloud.' Norris lived to see the FA Cup and the League won by Arsenal before he died, an outcast from the game, on 30 July 1934.

Sir Sam, the new chairman, was a different type of man. He was an old-type Corinthian, an Old Etonian and sportsman. Like the Cobbolds, he enjoyed himself and let the professionals run the club. The professional at Highbury was Herbert Chapman and this great innovator led the club to a hat-trick of League titles, following his three League Championships with his previous club, Huddersfield.

Arguably, Chapman was the greatest manager in the history of English football, ahead of Sir Alex Ferguson. Manchester United was the richest club in the world when Ferguson won trophies; Chapman turned a struggling club into the biggest and most successful in the land. Born in Kniveton in the West Riding in 1875, he had an undistinguished playing career with Grimsby, Swindon, Northampton, Sheffield United, Notts County and Tottenham and was banned for a year after being implicated in the burning of the books of Leeds City, another of his clubs. Leeds was expelled from the League in 1919 and Arsenal duly voted in. Six months before Norris died in 1934, Chapman caught a cold watching a third-team game in Guildford and the next morning he was found dead. He was fifty-nine.

Sir Sam had loved Chapman, and insisted that a statue of him was commissioned and positioned in a prime spot in the marble halls in the main entrance of Highbury. Flowers were placed at the foot of the column on the day of matches. However, the custom of laying flowers was abandoned after he died in 1949. Sir Sam was chairman for twenty-two years and his son, Denis, was chairman from 1960 to 1982 – exactly the same time in office. Denis, much loved throughout the game, lived in Hartley Wintney in his latter years and a house across the road was owned by the late Field Marshal Lord Alanbrooke, the friend of Captain Cobbold who played such a big part in the defeat of Germany in the Second World War as Chief of the Imperial General Staff.

Ipswich Town Football Club had been founded in 1878 by public schoolboys, most of them in their teens, at a meeting at Ipswich Town Hall. It was an amateur club, imbued with the principles of fair play. The players were dribblers and scrimmagers in the manner of Lord Kinnaird, who founded the Old Etonians Football Club, reaching the

FA Cup final six times between 1875 and 1883. Lord Kinnaird was renowned as a 'hacker' – a Nobby Stiles-type tackler – who invented the leather shin pad. It was said of him 'he was a mixture of fun and steely resolution, with contagious warmth and buoyant spirit and a full auburn beard.' He was also President of the FA for thirty-three years up to the opening of Wembley in 1923. He once said 'I believe that all right-minded people have good reason to thank God for the great progress of this popular national game.'

The pupils of Ipswich School chose a similar person to be president of their fledging club – Thomas Clement Cobbold, the Conservative MP for Ipswich between 1876 and 1883. He was a pupil at both Ipswich School and Charterhouse and it was said of him 'they were fortunate to have Mr Cobbold because Charterhouse, like Westminster, fostered the association game and Old Carthusians helped to spread the game throughout the land.' Mr Cobbold presented the ball for the inaugural game at Broom Hill, Ipswich, on Saturday 26 October and played in a 2-2 draw, a creditable result according to the official report which said his side had only seven men against the opposition's twelve.

Fred Ellis, the original club's longest-surviving player (who died in 1988 at the age of ninety-four) served in the First World War and, whiling his time away in trenches, he wrote to the Ipswich secretary, Frank Mills, asking for a ball to be played by the troops behind the lines. The ball was duly sent and games were arranged against the background of the sound of guns going off. Fred Ellis used to tell everyone that no Germans took part in the games but if they did, 'we'd give them a hiding!'

Captain Cobbold financed the club in 1936 and his loan of £11,000 enabled the club to turn professional. They played on a council-owned ground at Portman Road, which boasted a small, single-storey grandstand. Ipswich is one of the few clubs which does not own its ground. They signed a sixty-year lease at a nominal amount and that was extended to another one-hundred-and-twenty-five-year lease. When there was discussion about the club buying the ground from the local council in the late 1970s, John and Patrick Cobbold both agreed that the status quo should remain. 'It's the town club, not a club owned by some greedy millionaire who might want to sell up and pocket the proceeds,' said John Cobbold. When the club went into administration in the first half of 2003, that decision proved to be something of a liability as major investors were reluctant to put money up without having collateral.

Portman Road may have been a primitive ground, but it was one of the first in the country to have a clock. Richard Cobbold, the son of Alistair Cobbold who was later chairman, said 'Ivan, as he was called, loved football but I think there was a commercial interest. The brewery supplied their beer to 90 of the 110 pubs in Ipswich and the area and he wanted them to pop in and have a drink! If Ipswich won there was plenty of beer consumed. If they lost, they'd go home!'

A seated season ticket cost two guineas and a standing season ticket cost one guinea. At a lunch prior to the kick-off before the inaugural game there was just one toast, 'Football' proposed by Stanley Rous, Captain Cobbold's great friend. The band of the Scots Guard, recruited by the Captain's regiment, played and 14,211 supporters saw the Town beat Tunbridge Wells Rangers 4-1. In the programme there was a name 'Cobbold' which we assume to be Captain Cobbold. The directors were the Rt Hon. Lord Cranworth from Grundisburgh, the Hon. Douglas Alfred Tollemache, Sir Charles Henry Napier Bunbury from Rendlesham, Sir Francis John Childs Ganzoni MP (who later became Lord Belstead), Robert Nevill Cobbold, Lt-Col. Harold Ridley Hooper, Robert Jackson and Nathan Shaw – an amusement owner who always reversed the charges when he rang the club. Except for Mr Shaw, there was a surfeit of blue blood.

The club's first paid manager was Mick O'Brien. This forty-three-year-old Ireland centre half international from Co. Down had to leave after an adulterous affair with the wife of a Tolly Cobbold publican. The Captain called him in and sacked him on the spot. An adventurous and charismatic man, O'Brien once played for Brooklyn Wanderers in 1926, and in his first season with Ipswich he led the club to the Southern League championship. Captain Cobbold, however, would not countenance cheating off the field and O'Brien was told to go. O'Brien's wife died shortly afterwards and he died himself in 1940.

It was a very sad business. Many football managers in the past have been adulterers (no doubt some still are) and if Cobbold's example was followed, not many would have survived. Football management would have been an even more precarious job than it is now.

The search was on for a happily married manager who had no affairs in the background and Cobbold was keen on Major Franklin Buckley, the manager of Wolverhampton Wanderers. Buckley was known as 'The Major' after reaching that rank commanding the 17th Battalion Regiment (Footballers Battalion) of the Middlesex Regiment and served in both the Boer War and the Great War. A six-footer with a commanding demeanour, he was well educated and had a distinct military bearing. He wore plus fours and, as a non-smoker and a non-drinker, Captain Cobbold was instantly attracted towards him. In his fifty years as a manager, including a brief spell in charge at Norwich, he brought many innovations, including the use of psychologists, while before the 1939 FA Cup final he made headlines with his monkey gland injections for his players. The injections didn't work and First Division Wolves lost 4-1 to Portsmouth in the match.

Cobbold's bid to lure him away was rather cheeky because Ipswich was in the Third Division. His offer was duly rejected. On 10 November 1937, the Captain and his directors astonished the football world by signing a replacement in Adam Scott Matthewson Duncan, aged forty-nine – a man of short stature who was manager of Manchester United. Scott Duncan, one of the outstanding personalities of his time, still had three years left on his contract at Old Trafford.

The Captain sent his car to collect him and when he arrived at Portman Road he told him 'you're not leaving until you sign.' As the Captain was offering an annual salary of £2,000 and a bonus of £1,000 for gaining League status, plus further baits of £2,000 for promotion to the Second Division and £3,000 for reaching the First, there was little debate. 'I'll take it,' he said. He was always money orientated. When the negotiations were done, Cobbold sent a crate of vintage port to the stunned United directors. 'It was a cheap deal,' he said.

Duncan dressed like a City banker and always wore a dark suit, a homburg hat, a white collar and a dark tie. Don Read, the assistant secretary, said 'You should have seen the shine on his shoes. He was an immaculate dresser.' On 30 May 1938, the Captain led a small detachment, including Robert Cobbold, Herbert Foster, Nat Shaw and Duncan, to a Football League meeting in a London hotel to campaign for election to the League. Walsall and Gillingham were the other contenders and, unknown to them, Duncan had driven his Wolseley 16 car to almost every League club to persuade their directors to back Ipswich. The mileage expenses were colossal, even by those standards. 'We'll win,' he said confidently. Captain Cobbold said 'I'm not so sure.' 'I'll put a guinea of it, that we'll top the poll,' said Duncan. Ipswich won the vote, receiving 36 votes to the 34 for Walsall and 28 for Gillingham and the Captain was overjoyed to hand over his guinea.

Back in Ipswich, thousands of cheering supporters lauded Cobbold and his group as they were paraded through the streets in an open-top coach. Ipswich spent thousands of pounds on a glossy brochure and the promotional costs were high. They did it with style. The Captain gave a Churchillian speech saying 'Another page in the history of Ipswich Town is about to open. What the story will be no-one can tell. Of one thing I am certain, that my directors and I will do all within our power for the honour and success of Ipswich Town Football Club.'

Duncan pioneered a trend of dominant managers and on one occasion he received a telegram from the Captain, who was abroad on business, saying 'Buy Rimmer of Sheffield Wednesday.' Duncan sent a telegram back on the same day, saying 'Will not buy Rimmer.' Cobbold responded 'I insist you buy Rimmer.' Duncan replied 'I insist I won't buy Rimmer.' Cobbold cabled back 'Consider yourself sacked.' The correspondence ended when Duncan replied 'Will not accept the sack.'

One of the oldest players still surviving from the pre-War days, Jackie Little (born at Blaydon in 1912), recalled the generosity of 'Cappy'. 'I was an amateur when I started and they fixed me up with a job, a bit of gardening,' he said. 'One day I was in the dressing room when a smart-looking man came in speaking with a posh voice. "Hello Jackie!" he said cheerily. I realised it was the Captain. Later I got engaged and he called me in and said "I've got something for you." He said he was going to pay for me to have a three-piece suite as a present. "Make sure you take your fiancée to help choose it," he said. "If you get older, you need something comfortable to come home to." It was a lovely settee. He was a smashing man, a real smashing man.'

Jackie earned £8 a week and, when he retired in 1950 to become manager of Stowmarket Town FC, they went round with a blanket for a collection for him. 'I got £500 from my benefit,' he said. Another player, James McLuckie, a Scot, born in 1908, was the club's first captain and he usually spoke to Duncan about financial matters. 'After a good win in front of a crowd of 34,000, Jim went to see him about giving us a bonus,' he said. 'Duncan, who was a qualified accountant, said "you're trying to get me sacked." Mr Duncan was pretty tight about money. We only had two pairs of boots, one for playing and the other one to train in and they had to last a year or two.'

The team struggled and in the second season the River Orwell burst its banks and flooded the ground. The offices were flooded and, with no wages, the club borrowed from the police station to pay the players. The club owed £14,195 and the options were to wind it up or seek more money from the directors. Captain Cobbold put up most of the money and as war was about to break out he announced that the club was suspending its activities until the end of the conflict. He rejoined his regiment and never saw his team play again. He died eleven days after D-Day in 1944, blown up by a German flying bomb, while one of his nephews, Robert, was killed at the same time in Italy.

FOUR

BLOWN UP BY A DOODLEBUG

The blue blood of Ipswich Town

Captain John (Ivan) Cobbold married Lady Blanche Katherine Cavendish in the Guards Chapel in Wellington Barracks, close to Buckingham Palace, on 30 April 1919 and, sadly, he was killed on 18 June 1944 at the same place. The Captain was blown up by that most awful weapon of war, the doodlebug – the flying pilot-less bomb that rained over London for a few weeks near the end of the Second World War. Born at Holywells, Ipswich on 27 January 1897, he went to Eton and joined the Scots Guards in 1915, continuing his family's military links. He served in France and was injured, but not seriously. In 1917 he was promoted to the rank of Captain and left at the end of the war to take over as chairman of Cobbold & Company, the brewers.

His sons, John and Patrick, also went to Eton and worked at the brewery and John joined the Welsh Guards at the age of twenty-one in 1947. Why John joined the Welsh Guards and not the Scots Guards, his father's regiment, was uncertain. 'Maybe the Scots Guards was oversubscribed at the time,' said one of his military friends. Maybe it was one of his jokes. Patrick was called up for National Service and joined the Scots Guards in 1952 before he was invalided out.

Captain Cobbold's wedding to Lady Blanche, the second daughter of the 9th Duke of Devonshire, was one of the society matches of the year. It was an almost a double header. On the same day a daughter of Prime Minister Herbert Asquith married Prince Bibesco and the reception was held at the Asquith mansion in Cavendish Square. The Cobbold reception was held nearby at Lansdowne House at the invitation of Lord and Lady Lansdowne, parents of Lady Blanche's mother, Evelyn, the Duchess of Devonshire.

The Cavendish dynasty started in the early sixteenth-century from Suffolk blood when Sir William Cavendish, son of Thomas Cavendish of Suffolk, married Bess of Hardwick, later Countess of Shrewsbury, and began building Chatsworth House in 1552. Sir William was treasurer of the Chamber to King Henry VIII and King Edward VI, and one of his ancestors was reputed to be the man who killed the rebel leader Wat Tyler. Almost four hundred years later a man from Suffolk, Captain Cobbold, would marry Blanche, whose sister-in-law, Deborah Mitford (of the renowned literary Mitford sisters), married Andrew Cavendish, the 11th Duke of Devonshire, who was a football fan and a former president of his local club.

The 2nd Baron Redesdale had six daughters and a son, Tom, who was killed in Burma in 1945. This was one of the most remarkable families

in history. Diana Mitford, the most beautiful of the sisters, married Sir
Oswald Mosley, who founded the British Union of Fascists, in the home
of Dr Josef Goebbels and his wife Magna in 1936. Adolf Hitler attended
the dinner that night and after a row the newly-married couple retired
to their room. 'We went to bed in high dudgeon,' she wrote. Lady
Diana died at the age of ninety-three on 11 August 2003. Another sister,
Unity, was obsessed with Hitler and met him on many occasions. She
shot herself in the head at the start of the Second World War and died
in 1948. Jessica, known as Decca, became a Communist and fought
on the side of the Republicans against General Franco's Fascists in the
Spanish Civil War, and the oldest daughter, Nancy, immortalised the
family in her best-known novel *The Pursuit of Love in a Cold Climate*.
The other sister, Pamela, was less known and loved horses. Deborah,
who still runs Chatsworth House, was known as 'Debo'.

Blanche's father was Victor Christian William Cavendish, the 9th
Duke, who was elected as an MP at the age of twenty-three. He married Lady Evelyn Fitzmaurice, older daughter of the 5th Marquess of
Lansdowne – an unsmiling aristocratic woman who had a fearsome
reputation. She was the Mistress of the Robes to Queen Mary at the
Coronation of King George VI in 1937 and she abhorred gambling,
racing and the lax morals of Edwardian high society, whereas her
husband loved shooting, cricket, golf and owning shire horses. In short,
they were opposites.

The present Duchess said of her in her book *The House, a Portrait
of Chatsworth* 'Evie was careful to the point of meanness over small
things and she could not bear waste of any kind. There is a story, told
me by one of the aunts, of her sticking a three-halfpenny stamp on
an envelope with the wrong address on it. She rang a footman and
he appeared after two or three minutes and she asked him for a kettle
of boiling water. In due course he came back with the kettle and she
solemnly supervised steaming the stamp to remove it for re-use.

'Sharp of feature, small of eye, preferring inanimate objects to humans,
she saw mistakes everywhere and was ever critical of her family and
her servants. I never heard her praise anyone. She was not in the least
interested in human comfort.' The Duchess used the same phrase about

Blanche when I went to Chatsworth to interview her in the summer of 2003. 'Human comforts' for her meant the absence of heating, among other deprivations. Was Blanche similar to 'Granny Evie'? 'She appeared to be on occasions,' she said. 'As a child she didn't speak for a long time. I heard that story but I don't know whether it was true. But I loved her and she adored Ipswich Town Football Club.'

We were sitting in one of the Chatsworth House's huge state apartments, one of the 175 rooms at the gigantic mansion which could accommodate 369 normal-sized houses. An old fashioned telephone rang with the noise of Elvis Presley's 'Jailhouse Rock'. She explained its origins to a group of people who were being shown round and it brought a laugh. You couldn't imagine Lady Evelyn joining in the laughter. 'I was on my own one day and happened to turn the television on and Elvis was performing,' she said. 'I was captivated. I've been to Graceland twice. It's really wonderful really. Very moving. You ought to go.'

A few minutes later two footmen brought in a table laden for afternoon tea. Alas, there was no invitation for me and she asked me to accompany her to one of her private rooms, a long way down a corridor and up and down stairs. 'I remember one occasion which will be of interest to you,' she said as she sat down. 'I was invited to Glemham Hall for a party for Pamela, the elder daughter of the Cobbolds. I loved her, she was such a gregarious young lady. It was in April 1938 and it was so cold. I felt I was going to die. Later, we went to a dinner dance in Piccadilly. I think it was at the Ritz, or perhaps it was Brown's. I sat next to Andrew Cavendish and we were both eighteen. That was our first meeting. Three years later we were married.'

In her book she wrote: 'we were married in London in April. The windows of my father's house in Rutland Gate were blown out by a bomb which fell two nights before the wedding. The glass was swept up and my mother hung rolls of wallpaper as mocked up curtains. Red camellias came from Chatsworth and the reception went on as if nothing had happened.' The Luftwaffe seemed to have a down on these people.

The Duchess also wrote that 'the busiest time at Chatsworth was at Christmas, when all the daughters and sons-in-law and their children came to stay, as well as my parents-in-law and their children, Billy, Andrew, Elizabeth and Anne.' Billy, Andrew's brother, the Marquess of Hartington, was killed in Belgium on 9 September 1944, three months after the death of Ivan Cobbold. His wife, Kathleen Kennedy (the sister of President John Kennedy and who was known as 'Kick'), died in an air crash in 1948 and in 1963, just before he was assassinated, the President visited Harold Macmillan at Chatsworth to see the graves.

Describing the seating arrangements at Christmas dinners, the Duchess said 'like everything else in the house the nursery was arranged in order of precedence. The Hartingtons' children came first, and they had the best rooms and were served first at meals. Next were Captain Evan and Lady Maud Baillie's family of four, Captain Ivan and Lady Blanche Cobbold's four, Mr Harold and Lady Dorothy Macmillan's four, Captain James and Lady Rachel Stuart's three and Mr Henry and Lady Anne Hunloke's three. Each family brought a nanny and a nursery maid, a lady's maid, a valet and sometimes a chauffeur and a groom as well.' The Cobbolds initially batted at three at table – a high position – but over the years their wealth disappeared and they dropped down the order. Patrick Cobbold once said 'we used to kick a ball up and down those huge corridors.' It may have caused offence.

A gossip columnist in 1919 wrote of Blanche's wedding to Captain Cobbold 'Though Miss Asquith's three-act ceremony somewhat eclipsed the Cavendish-Cobbold wedding, the marriage of the daughter of the Duke and Duchess of Devonshire at the Guards' Chapel was a distinctive and distinguished affair. Lady Blanche, a demurely simple bride in ivory satin, defied superstition by wearing chains of pearls and diamonds, which served a useful as well as a decorative purpose, since they helped to keep the train in its proper place. The event was in keeping with the simplicity associated with the Devonshire family, who regard publicity concerning their private affairs with something approaching positive horror.' If Lady Blanche noticed his description of 'simple', the mistress of Glemham Hall might have responded with a withering response.

She was in an irksome mood in the days leading up to the wedding because her father, who was the Governor General of Canada, was on business over there and couldn't attend. The Marquess of Hartington gave her away instead and she was attended by two pages, Lord Calne and the Master of Elphinstone. Leading the six bridesmaids was her sister, Lady Dorothy (who was later to marry the Conservative Prime Minister Harold Macmillan), while the other bridesmaids were Miss Pamela Cobbold (sister of Captain Ivan Cobbold), Miss Jean Follett, the Hon. Elizabeth Elphinstone, Miss Margaret Mercer-Nairne and Miss Felicity Cobbold. Lady Blanche defied the normal custom, carrying a prayer book instead of a bouquet. She was a very independent lady.

Captain Cobbold wore his captain's uniform, with a sword on his left side and his trousers tucked into his puttees, Indian style. His best man was a military hero friend, Captain Patrick Bradshaw, DSO, of the Scots Guards. The list of guests stretched to eight inches of small print in *The Times* and it included some of the leading Lords, Counts, Earls, Viscounts, Honourables and their Ladies of the day. A society magazine writer said 'It was a dignified and delightful wedding and the reception at Lansdowne House was perfectly carried out. Lansdowne House, the scene of many a stately entertainment in days before war came to disturb the peace of the whole world, opened its hospitable doors again in honour of the granddaughter of its occupants.' The honeymoon took place in Scotland and one of the hundreds of presents was a set of coffee cups from the Princess Mary.

The Cobbolds had a happy marriage. The marriage of Harold Macmillan to Dorothy Cavendish, Lady Blanche's sister, was just as happy in its slightly unorthodox way, although it lasted much longer. Harold Macmillan went to Eton and to Oxford University and was destined to work for his family firm of publishers but for the outbreak of the First World War. He was wounded and at the end of the war he accepted an invitation to be an ADC for the Duke of Devonshire, the Governor-General of Canada, and while there he met and courted the Duke's daughter. In the first volume of his memoirs he said 'These ten months were in many ways the happiest in my life. I suppose every young man when he falls in love, is unconscious that anyone else is aware of what is going on. At any rate, when Dorothy accepted me as her future husband, the fact seemed to cause little surprise either to her parents or to the rest of the staff.'

They were married on 21 April 1920 in St Margaret's Church, Westminister, almost a year after Lady Blanche married Captain Cobbold. Bishop Temple, a cousin of the Cavendishes, and John Macmillan, a cousin, later Bishop of Guildford, performed the ceremony. 'In those days it was the fashion to have large congregations, including every conceivable relation, young and old,' said the future Prime Minister.

His grandson, the Earl of Stockton, recalled 'When my grandfather approached the Duke of Devonshire to ask for my grandmother Dorothy's hand in marriage, Blanche having already married into the Cobbold family, the Duke said "God, trade again – but I suppose books are better than beer!"'

The Cobbolds enjoyed the same interests, shooting, fishing, eating and drinking, and they had many friends. Though Blanche bore a severe look on her face most days, she was respected and well liked. She demanded high standards and there were frequent changes in staff, although some lasted for years. Her four children were happy and well behaved. They loved family parties and plenty were held at Glemham Hall, while Christmas was often celebrated at Chatsworth House. They owned dogs of various breeds, mainly large ones.

In the first of the five volumes of his memoirs, Harold Macmillan wrote of these Christmas gatherings 'One of the traditions was to line up the children for photographs. Each section of the vast family averaged four children.' Blanche and the Captain met the norm and Jean, Pammy, John and Patrick were prominently featured. According to Macmillan, there was only one bathroom in Chatsworth House in 1909 and others had to be built because in the 1930s the number of members of family and guests, and staff, swelled to 150. He wrote 'It was a formidable array. The children, of course, delighted in this strange and exciting world. They were spoilt and pampered by the servants and they had many long friendships with them. It was always a new pleasure to be conducted through the great kitchens, the huge pantries, the larders with their stone floors and vaulted roofs; above all, the great building, larger than many butchers' shops, where hung rows of carcasses of oxen and sheep, and game of every kind. Many of the families, including my own, arrived with their ponies.

'The ritual did not differ from year to year. All assembled the day before. As each family arrived, 'Granny Evie', the Duchess, received them at the top of the stairs where the Outer Hall led into the passage to the great Painted Hall. On Christmas Day we had go across the park in the darkness to the church. Then breakfast and the enjoyment of minor presents; balloons to be inflated, trumpets to be blown and roller-skates to be tried. No house is better suited for roller-skating. The whole course is good, with particularly fast going on the stone floor of the Statue Gallery and the Orangery.

'After Christmas lunch, to which the children over a certain age were allowed – the rules were strictly enforced – came the photograph. In those days the ingenious methods by which these can be taken indoors had not been invented. We all trooped out to a particularly cold and draughty part of the garden – by Flora's Temple, outside the Orangery. A walk in the garden followed, which was supposed to be healthy. After tea, came the ceremony of presents given and received. This took place in the Statue Gallery, in which stood the huge tree. First, all the presents to the servants, taken round by the children; then presents from children to grown ups; then, at last, the childrens' own presents from all their different relations. They were perhaps not so expensive or so elaborate as they are today, but with the enormous family interchange, they were very numerous. This patriarchal scale of Christmas is necessarily a thing of the past and so perhaps worth recalling. It lasted until after the Duke's death in 1938.'

A few months after one of these parties, celebrating their silver wedding, the Captain was back on duty in London, attending the Morning Service at the Guards Chapel on Sunday 18 June 1944. He had played an important part in liaising with the American generals in the months before the D-Day Normandy landings and the operations had gone well. The end of the war was in sight and it was a time of cautious optimism and relief.

He invited Stanley Rous to join in the service but Rous, later to become Sir Stanley Rous, President of FIFA, was pre-booked. 'I was the president of Paddington and Marylebone Rotary Club,' said Rous. 'The local padre had called to remind me that I had promised to read the lesson at another service for Rotary Club members. Another friend, Colonel Bertram Sergison-Brooke, known as "Bertie" was also invited to the Guards Chapel and he decided not to go. We were very lucky men.'

There were around 250 officers and men in the chapel just before midday when they heard the frightening sound of a German pilotless plane approaching. Everyone must have said a quick prayer 'Please God, don't land it here.' An observer said later that the missile clipped a building in the Home Office three hundred metres away, changed direction to the east and spiralled downwards onto the centre of the chapel. As it crashed into the roof and exploded, the noise was deafening and smoke and fumes filled the air as the building collapsed, killing Captain Cobbold and 120 of his colleagues. 'It was a horrific scene,' said one survivor. 'I was surprised so many people were able to get out alive. Most of the members of the Coldstream Guards Band and the choir were killed and it was very fortunate that King George VI wasn't there. He often attended services at the Chapel.'

The sirens of the fire engines and ambulances screeched down Birdcage Walk towards the chapel, which was equidistant between Buckingham Palace and the War Cabinet Bunker (where Cobbold sometimes visited the then General Sir Alan Brooke, who shot regularly at Glemham and later became Field Marshal Lord Alanbrooke). The chapel was entirely destroyed except for the apse, which survived almost intact. Incredibly, the altar cross remained in position and the altar candles were still burning. A Nissan construction was quickly put up on the site. The colours of the Guards brigades, which were burned and scorched, were preserved and are still hanging up around the walls of the present building, which was rebuilt to a modern design. The original apse was also retained and the rebuilt building was dedicated by the Archbishop of Canterbury in 1963.

The name 'doodlebug' was coined from an insect in New Zealand and was known as the 'V for Vengeance' weapon (V1 for short). It was designed to terrify the populace and change the course of the war. Fired from concrete bunkers in Northern France, these evil machines carried 1,000lbs of explosive and were launched towards London, travelling around 300mph – almost at the speed of Spitfires and Hurricanes. A regular tactic was for Royal Air Force pilots to fly as close as possible to them, using a wing to tip the doodlebugs' flight controls. It was a highly dangerous exercise but it often worked and these diverted doodlebugs usually crashed harmlessly in fields or the sea. A total of 1,979 were destroyed by these methods by RAF aircraft out of an overall total of 4,261; AA gunners shot down 1,971 and a further 278 were brought down by flying balloons.

The doodlebugs made a frightening, droning noise and when the engines cut out, no-one knew where they would land. It was estimated that they would blow up between five and fifteen seconds after the jet engines had faded, but often they would glide along for a considerable distance before finally dropping to earth. The device could land anywhere up to a radius of half a mile after propulsion had ceased, and in the final seconds there was no noise. The Nazis targeted the Houses of Parliament, Buckingham Palace and Downing Street. Buckingham Palace was bombed on nine occasions without any serious damage. Parliament was also hit but Downing Street escaped. To avoid knocking out the nerve centre of the British war effort, Professor R.V. Jones, MI5's scientific expert, devised a way to save London's key area from damage. Captured German spies who had been brainwashed and talked into defecting were ordered to send false information to their Nazi controllers about the locations where the bombs were landing. By then the boffins at Bletchley Park, the codebreakers' HQ, had come up with the answer to the Enigma code.

The Germans were forced to cut the amount of fuel, which was scarce, and the bulk of the flying bombs fell short of the real targets. Most of them fell in South London, not the heart of the city. Jones lived in Dulwich and Mavis Batey, a former Bletchley Park administrator, said 'He wasn't trying to save his family. It was just that Central London was the seat of government and the densest area of population.'

The terror bombing campaign lasted three months from 12 June 1944 until General Montgomery's forces destroyed the final underground launching pads in Northern France in March 1945. Londoners treated the doodlebugs with contempt, almost amusement. In some quarters it was looked on as a 'fun' weapon and a source of jokes. The real terror weapon was the V2, a rocket packed with explosives which hurtled towards the ground at a speed of more than 1,000mph. Those who were killed often didn't hear it until it was too late. Air raid warnings were pointless, whereas with the V1 you had a chance to take shelter.

The number of deaths in the incident at Wellington Barracks was one of the highest in the doodlebug campaign. In the final weeks of the war, 6,725 doodlebugs were aimed from the Pas de Calais and its environs, killing 5,475 people and injuring 16,000. There were 200,000 cases of damage to property. The government had a policy of not publicising any V1 incidents, forbidding the release of details on the number landing or shot down and also on casualty figures. It was a forlorn attempt to quell possible panic.

The day Captain Cobbold died, Patrick was just two days short of his tenth birthday. Elder brother John was seventeen years old and, as it turned out, he was the last John Cobbold in the line.

Sir Stanley Rous was born in Mutford, Suffolk and played in a local side as a goalkeeper. He became a top class referee, taking charge of an FA Cup final. He was a teacher at Watford Grammar School in his younger days and secretary of the FA between 1934 and 1962, before becoming President of FIFA for more than twenty years. John Waine, the Bishop of St Edmundsbury and Ipswich (who gave the addresses at the funerals of the Cobbold brothers, their mother Lady Blanche and her daughters Pammy and Jean, as well as baptising a number of other relatives), told a classic story about the present Queen. Said the Bishop 'Sir Stanley was at a cup final and it was a particularly dour and unexciting match. Afterwards Stanley said to the Queen "Do you think there were any good performances from anyone, Ma'am?" The Queen replied: "Only from the band!"'

Lord Alanbrooke wrote in his handwritten diary on that fateful day in June 'Arrived up early to find that a pilotless plane had struck the Guards Chapel, Wellington Barracks. Amongst them to my great grief Ivan Cobbold! And on my writing table there was a letter from him written the day before, sending me on a wire from the Duke de Luna who is fishing at Cairnton and asking me to lunch this week! It all gave me a very nasty turn, and I cannot get him and poor Blanche out of my mind. Hungerford Bridge had also been hit and most of the windows of the War Office were blown in again.'

Later, Lord Alanbrooke added 'The death of Ivan Cobbold was a ghastly blow to me. I had grown to know him very well in those weeks along with him at Cairnton and I had grown very fond of him. Both he and Blanche had been kindness itself to me. The blow was, I think, made all the worse by the fact that when Brian Boyle was telling me of his death, I was actually picking up Ivan's letter off my blotting pad. His invitation to lunch was with him that week and it made a very large lump in my throat.'

The Germans seemed to have the Cobbolds on their death list because, in an amazing coincidence, a flying bomb landed on a 300-year-old tree in the grounds of Glemham Hall a few weeks after Captain Cobbold was blown to bits. Almost all of the 400 windows were shattered by the blast, but fortunately no-one was hurt. Lady Blanche was in residence at the time, mourning her husband's death, along with four members of staff and about twenty evacuees from the Dagenham area and she said 'When the windows were blown out, the glass cascaded down the stairs and it sounded like an avalanche.' The evacuees helped in sweeping up the glass. (There was no evidence that any of them were relatives of Sir Alf Ramsey who was born in Dagenham.)

The latest owner, Philip Hope-Cobbold, formerly Hope-Johnstone, does the cleaning of the windows himself, but only at ground level. 'The rest are self cleaning,' he said; 'When it rains God takes over.' One of the oldest trees in the garden, a cedar lebanon dating back to the early eighteenth century, has had drastic surgery on a number of occasions and is still standing.

Built around 1560 onwards, the red brick mansion was designed by the de Glemham family. Their name was taken from Great (Magna) and Little (Parva) Glemham and they lived in the Hall for more than

150 years. Originally the house was built in Elizabethan style, but between 1712 and 1723 considerable changes were made, giving it an overall Georgian façade. It doesn't give the impression of being elegant, like some of the country houses in East Anglia. The windows are deep and rectangular, resembling a portcullis. The building is 'E' shaped and is situated a third of a mile off the A12 between Ipswich and Lowestoft. It can be seen from the road on both sides and makes good viewing. Most landowners hide their country houses, protecting their privacy. The Cobbolds were always open and approachable. When the brothers were in charge, they would welcome visitors and show them round, often giving them a glass of wine. In the spring, hundreds of daffodils light up the drive and that happens now.

The house is open to the public for several days in the year and there are more visitors these days. The only snag of letting in strangers is that it gives potential burglars a chance to look around and plan a raid. Alarms were fitted and many windows were sealed after a particularly costly burglary. The gardens are the best feature. To the south the beautiful rose garden is enclosed within sheltered walls, and includes a summer house, a lily pond and classical urns. The wide lawns and garden are framed by yew hedges, a topiary and an avenue of Irish yews.

Spreading cedars and beeches complete a very traditional setting in the 300 acre park. At the back there was a magnificent grass tennis court which wasn't fenced in. The players and their friends had to find the balls among the flower beds and in the trees and hedges. John Cobbold took great pride in it. He was not a good player but he loved playing in his young days.

The Glemham family sold the house to members of the North family in the 1700s and the Norths lived there until 1923 when Captain Cobbold bought it from Lord Guilford. Before that the Cobbolds used to live at Holywells, another country mansion in the Ipswich area which was eventually demolished in 1962.

Captain Cobbold and Lady Blanche ran Glemham Hall with a staff of more than twenty servants and gave frequent, well attended parties for them and their families every year. Lady Blanche was cast in the role of Commander of Chief and one of her nephews David Paul, a regular visitor when he was a boy, said 'she never messed with anyone, her word was the one that counted.' Guests were entertained with candle lit dinners and the men wore black ties and the ladies were dressed in formal, long dresses. The children were sent to their rooms to amuse themselves. There were plenty of things to occupy their time, including train sets, hundreds and hundreds of soldiers, toys of all sizes and shapes from the Victorian era including a giant rocking horse, various prams and bicycles and three wheelers. There were thousands of books, often hidden away in corridors and cellars.

Twelve large volumes of *British Sports and Sportsmen* were untouched for decades and in the library there is a slim volume entitled *No Love for Johnnie* by one-time Labour MP Wilfred Fienburgh, published in 1959 which the author signed. John Cobbold had just lost his third parliamentary election and it may have been a personal lament. Another book, in a prominent place, was *Ouch − all the insults you need*. He obviously learned a few and practised them in the Ipswich boardroom.

Many of the rooms were fifteen yards by fifteen, dwarfing modern bedrooms. They were almost impossible to heat. In one room a giant stuffed turtle has survived. There were few lavatories and most of the forty-odd bedrooms still have potties under the beds. The staff collected them after breakfast. The brothers Cobbold lived in different parts of the house, sometimes switching to other quarters. John liked the Green Room which featured a library. There was a boar skin on the floor of his bedroom and his lavatory was early Victorian, with wooden seat and huge pipes. A sign still hangs over it saying 'Our drainage system is antiquated and very sensitive! The Master of the House.' A very large water heater gurgles away and an old set of skis are propped up near the huge wrought iron bath, which is more than three feet deep and big enough to drown yourself. Water meters are still frowned on for obvious reasons.

For years after the end of the Second World War some of the bedrooms were still illuminated by 'blackout' bulbs, used to restrict the light after dark and minimise the risk of bombing raids by German aircraft. There are many portraits hanging on the walls of the Cobbold

ancestors, showing stern expressions and wearing starched collars,
beards and moustaches. There are also countless pictures of groups of
Eton boys through the generations. Most of the rooms had carpets but
the steps down to the servants' quarters had no carpets or any covers.
'We used to go down there and we thought it was spooky,' said David
Paul. 'Lots of noises. There must have been a ghost there.'

Glemham Hall is situated in Little Glemham, a hamlet of around 140
inhabitants. Great Glemham, two miles to the North, has 170 inhabitants. Blanche's four children grew up at Glemham Hall and they all
agreed it was a good way to start life. They loved their nanny, known as
Nanny Moore. She had a Christian name, Alice, but was often known
as 'Blossom.' When she was passed retirement, in her eighties, she was
allowed to remain and died there. There were frequent birthday parties, featuring entertainers, fireworks, pony rides, hunting and fishing,
dogs of all sizes, tennis and cricket. There was even a cricket ground
at the back until it fell into disuse. The pitch was under prepared and
the standard of play was indifferent. John Cobbold hated cricket but
Patrick played a few games.

   While a governess taught the girls, Pammy and Jean, John and
Patrick were despatched to Wellesley House in Broadstairs. They found
it windswept and desolate in the winter and they missed their shooting
and hunt meetings. They were both sent to Eton, their father's school.
Eton featured in the life of Cobbolds back to the early 1800s.

   When he returned from his military service in Palestine, John
Cobbold found the regime at Glemham Hall too restrictive and
moved out to another Cobbold-owned property, Capel Hall a few
miles away at Trimley, near Felixstowe. It was secluded, situated on a
peninsula between the Orwell and Deben estuaries and it was much
more attractive in looks and situation to Glemham Hall. Its construction began in 1464 and the first owner was Sir William Amberville.
Thomas Cobbold bought it in 1735 and it was retained in the family
for 266 years until it was sold to a haulier in 2001. There were some
twenty-eight bedrooms and John Cobbold took a delight in showing
his guests the *trompe l'oeil* mural in the reception hall by Lincoln Taber,
a pupil of Annigone. Charles Hope-Johnstone, one of his nephews,

inherited it in 1983 after his uncle died. Hope-Johnstone, a bachelor who gave exotic parties, only survived another eleven years before he died of AIDS.

John Cobbold was extremely lucky to escape a bombing incident at the Hilton Hotel in Park Lane in 1965, twenty-one years after his father was blown up. A device weighing between 5 and 10lbs was planted on the ground floor by two members of the IRA, and it went off, wrecking the front of the lobby. The building was shaken and some people were knocked down in the road outside. A man and a woman were killed and sixty-two others were injured. An Arab man shouted 'I've lost my leg!' The limb had been ripped off. A warning was telephoned to the *Evening News* off Fleet Street and eight other calls were made on the same day. This one turned out to be authentic but the police had no time to clear the front of the hotel. That call proved to be a life saver. A police officer said 'If we had evacuated the hotel the casualties could have been far worse. Hundreds of people would have come down through the lifts and out into the lobby. It would have been carnage.'

John Cobbold left ten minutes earlier and was unhurt. It was reported that he had been drinking coffee at the time. 'I don't think it was coffee,' said a club official. The hotel was almost full with 750 guests, including the US singing group the Supremes. Later, Cobbold was reluctant to speak about the incident again. It brought back too many memories of his father's tragic death.

His brother Patrick dined regularly at the Guards Club and frequently visited the chapel. When he died in December, 1994, his memorial service was held in the chapel and was attended by coach-loads of current and ex players, staff from the various estates and friends. Prince Michael of Kent, a long time friend of the brothers Cobbold, arrived on his own and left on his own. He was clearly moved. 'Patrick loved the Scots Guards,' said one guest. 'As the service ended a lone Scots piper marched out across the parade ground playing the Last Post. Patrick would have loved that.' Two of his nephews, Ivan Paul and Philip Hope-Cobbold, read a lesson each and Bishop Waine gave the Address.

FIVE

SLIDING DOWN THE
BANNISTERS IN HIS PYJAMAS

There were regular parties at Glemham Hall, whether Ipswich Town were promoted or relegated or stuck in the middle of the table. And that still happens. The pre-season party was staged in mid-summer, with a marquee on the lawn at the back and, if the club won something, there was an excuse for another one. John Cobbold was the star. When he signalled it was time to bring the festivities to an end, he often slid down the bannisters in his pyjamas wearing his slippers with the initials JC, shouting 'You buggers can stay but I'm going to bed.' One day one of his favourite players, Paul Mariner, arranged for him to be carried down the stairs, clad in his pyjamas, and shouted to the assembled guests 'you don't want a splinter on your backside!'

Sometimes he gave dinner parties for the parents of the apprentices who were signed by the club and one evening he told the startled proud mothers and fathers 'You've done a great job to produce your little Johnny but now it is time to go to bed to get cracking upstairs and do your damnedest to produce another one!'

Mr John was twice banned for driving while drunk, once while at the wheel in his pyjamas, and he had to recruit a full-time chauffeur. The first time, in 1965, he was accused of having the equivalent of thirteen whiskies and was fined a nominal £65. A year later, he was fined £150 and banned for three years. Said Mariner 'We never knew how he managed to get his licence back. He was frequently stopped by the cops and let off with a warning.'

His friend Mike Hollingsworth said 'years later his ban ended but he decided not to drive again. He had a chauffeur by then and loved getting drunk. If the day ended with him not drunk he was most disgruntled. He was a lonely man at times. He would ring me and invite me round with a few friends to bring out a bottle of champagne. He loved Buck's Fizz and squeezed the oranges himself. A lot of people took advantage of his generosity but he didn't mind.

'He had some pretty lively parties at Capel Hall but it's best not to talk about them publicly. He treated everyone the same, from a king to a pauper. Once I was round I noticed this distinguished looking man getting out of a car with a lady and I thought they looked like the Macmillans. I was wearing my working clothes and looked pretty scruffy and I was about to leave. "Stay," said Johnny. "Come and meet them. Have a drink." So I sat down with the Prime Minister and Lady Dorothy for a chat.'

During an industrial dispute at the Cobbold brewery, the pickets once tried to stop him going in but a shop steward waved him through. 'It's all right,' said the shop steward. 'He doesn't do anything anyway.' John Cobbold's middle name, Cavendish, came from the family name of the Devonshires. When Lady Blanche married 'Ivan' Cobbold, one of the members of the Devonshire family said 'At last you've married into money.' However, the fortunes of the family soon changed after the 10th Duke died in 1950.

Andrew Cavendish, the next son in line, took over as the 11th Duke of Devonshire and was a heavy drinker and gambler. He admitted that he had become an alcoholic, but in the last twenty years of his life he was a teetotaller. 'Thanks to my family, and perhaps from assistance from Above, I held on,' he said 'The days of fast women and slow horses were thankfully behind me.' He died on 3 May 2004, a month before his autobiography was published. It took him twenty-four years to pay off £7 million death duties and at eighty-three he was named as the tenth richest man in Britain with a fortune estimated at £1.48 billion. His art collections contained works by Rembrandt, Titian, a Leonardo da Vinci (valued at £20 million) and also works by his friend Lucien Freud. The total is worth around £1.275 billion.

Chatsworth House and its art collection is now managed by Chatsworth House Trust, a registered charity. The Trust looks after land and property worth £210 million, including farmland around Chatsworth, Lismore Castle in Waterford, Ireland and Bolton Abbey in Yorkshire. The restaurant, named 'The Burlington' at The Devonshire Country House Hotel at Bolton Abbey, is renowned as one of the finest in the country. The hotel, which originated from a coaching

inn from 1753, was the venue for one of the oddest marriages of
recent times in Yorkshire, involving the children of Fred Trueman,
'The Greatest Living Yorkshireman' and the American actress Rachel
Welch. It turned out to be a tempestuous wedding and the marriage
did not last long.

The 11th Duke always wore yellow socks that matched his racing
colours and had a home in Mayfair and also owned the prestigious
London club Pratt's. He promised to continue hunting on his land
even if the law prohibited it. He and his wife had three children and
eight grandchildren, including the model Stella Tennant. In the Spring
of 2003 the Duke had letters published in both *The Times* and the *Daily
Telegraph* about the Iraq War – with opposite views. And after his wife
published *The Chatsworth Cookery Book* he said 'My wife has done for
chickens what Eisenhower did for golf and Kennedy for sex.' They
were married more than sixty years and he summed up the secret of
their long partnership saying 'tolerance.' He said 'I was very lucky. I
owed it to nepotism.'

Barry Taylor, a former vice chairman of Barnsley and a senior member
of the FA Council, recalled an occasion when Patrick arrived at the
boardroom at the Oakwell Stadium, announcing that he had just come
from Chatsworth House. Taylor said 'it was in the middle of winter
and I said to him "Patrick, you can't be visiting Chatsworth House,
it's closed to tourists." Patrick replied "you f——ing idiot, I stayed the
night because I am a member of the family."

'He swore with this posh voice and no-one was offended. I first met
him in 1980/81 when the Football League published a directory with
details of directors and one section of the questionnaire was "interests."
Patrick wrote "shooting a line, passing the buck and fishing for compli-
ments." John wrote "always out, indoors only infrequently, watching
other people mow my grass and like a snifter." Under "clubs" John
wrote "White's, Keyhole Club until it was closed by the police."

'Everyone loved them and I knew that it would take two days of my
life when I went to Ipswich's boardroom. They stuffed us with food
and drink and we used to stagger back to our cars afterwards. Patrick
wore these threadbare jackets with holes in them and I once asked him

what he did with them afterwards. He said "What do you think, I wear them you f——ing idiot!" Once in the Barnsley boardroom one of our elderly directors was recovering from a stroke and was sitting in a chair. Patrick said to him "now you old c——, are you still alive?" Anyone else would have caused a rumpus but no-one was upset, especially the man concerned. Another time I was at Ipswich after having been filled up with booze and Patrick came up to me with a huge, greasy bacon sandwich. "Here, eat that in the corner over there and die!"

'After one of Ipswich Town's relegations, I asked him what it was like being in the Second Division. "I meet a better quality of f——ing director," he replied. He's right. Patrick and John were wonderful men. Great personalities and wits. There are none left in football now, sadly. They were great at deflating egos. One director, an MP, turned up at Hull and was introduced to John. "Which part of the Labour Party are you f——ing up?" he asked him. He was nonplussed.'

John Cobbold never changed his approach to drink and drank almost up to his death in 1983. He contracted cancer of the spine and died at the age of fifty-six. 'Everyone thought it was liver, but it wasn't – although his liver wasn't too clever,' said a friend. There was plenty of speculation about his last words. Patrick was with him when he died and according to a friend of David Sheepshanks the story went like this 'Johnny said to Patrick "give me that paper" pointing to a copy of the *Daily Telegraph*. Johnny looked at it and said "C——face, it's the wrong date!" He then expired!'

He left only £2.5 million in his will and most of his last remaining wealth and property were given to friends and relatives. Patrick had already taken over as chairman and the policy of entertaining non-stop continued, with liberal measures of wine and spirits, accompanied with laughs and jokes.

In fact, several members of the Cobbold family died from the ravages of alcoholism and one of the directors talked about 'the curse of the Cavendishs.' He said that alcoholism passes through the male strain and one of the sufferers was Ivan Paul, who grew up with the present chairman David Sheepshanks, both Old Etonians. Paul, a member of the Cobbold family, tried to have the Board removed at an extraordinary general meeting in 1994 when John Lyall was about to leave as manager and Patrick was very upset about his damaging campaign. A week before the meeting, when the directors won the vote, Patrick died in his bath from a heart attack at Glemham Hall on 16 December 1994, listening to classical music. He hadn't been ill. The only reason anyone could give was the upheaval in the boardroom. That constituted the first crisis in the club and there hadn't been a crisis before in his reign, or in his brother's reign either.

'It was an awful time,' said Sheepshanks. 'John Lyall was hard to control and was a very forceful personality. He was very opinionated and was from the old school. His view was "if you weren't a former player, then you didn't understand the game and your opinion did not count." The club was going downhill fast and it was almost bust. He promoted Mick McGiven as team manager and Mick is a very good, honest man but it proved too difficult for him.

'Then he wanted John Wark and Paul Goddard as his assistants, which we only accepted on the basis that John Lyall retook the reins "as a hands-on" manager. Regrettably, that never happened and he became increasingly ostrich-like and almost rude to the point of maligning the Press. All in all, it was a sorry state of affairs as the club plummeted to the bottom of the League, leaving little semblance of the style for which we had been renowned.

'We met at Glemham Hall and the Board members were split over whether to sack him. In November we had another meeting at Glemham and we took the decision to dismiss him. Lyall, one of the outstanding coaches in the Greenwood school, now has little interest in football and spends a lot of time fishing. He seemed bitter about events when I met him some years later but I can't think why.'

Paul, a farmer who owned a wine shop in Paris and a business in High Street Kensington, died at the age of forty-eight while playing tennis. He was also a good golfer. John Kerr, a well respected farmer and businessman who lives at Blaxhall Hall, Little Glemham, was appointed chairman before Patrick died. 'I was given the short straw,' he said. His father Willie, a Scots farmer, was a long-serving director of the club.

'Johnny and Patrick gave their lives to football,' he said. 'They took everything personally and drink helped them to cope with the pressure.' Before he died, Patrick transferred his 4,000 shares of the 32,000 shares in the company, to John Kerr, who was the chairman. Later these were transferred to the next chairman David Sheepshanks.

Kerr employed an accountant and new directors were appointed, including Lord Ryder, who was Chief Whip in the government headed by Margaret Thatcher. 'If I was in London, Richard would invite me round to Downing Street for a nightcap,' said Kerr. Up until recently, Lord Ryder was deputy chairman of the BBC and had to make the demeaning announcement after the Andrew Gilligan affair, apologising on behalf of the corporation. Ryder has an enviable reputation for facts and figures and the histories of football and cricket.

Sheepshanks grew up with Ivan Paul and attended the children's parties at Glemham Hall. They went to Eton in the mid-1960s and remained close friends there until they started to drift apart. They came from land owning families and, while Paul went to Paris, Sheepshanks ran a successful local business, Suffolk Foods. In 1987 Sheepshanks was invited to join the football club and in 1995 he took over as chairman. He introduced modern business methods but retained the courtesy and approachability of the Cobbolds. After Robson left, the club found itself in a state of turmoil and it took some years to sort it out.

The appointment of George Burley in succession to Lyall was a formative time in the club's history. Sheepshanks and Kerr wanted Burley but some of the other directors wanted a more experienced man. Burley had recently been appointed as manager of Colchester at the age of thirty-eight after playing 500 games for Ipswich. He desperately wanted the job and impressed the directors with his vision about how to improve the club. The names on the list included Howard Kendall, Martin O'Neill, David Pleat, Peter Reid, Mike Walker, Russell Osman and Mick Mills. It was reduced to two, Burley and the former Everton manager Howard Kendall. The younger man won, although it was a messy affair. Colchester refused to release Burley and Ipswich had to pay compensation of around £130,000.

★

Burley is a very upright, conscientious, and somewhat serious young man. Bill Nicholson, the great manager of the greatest Tottenham side in the 1960s once recounted a typical story about John Cobbold. Nicholson said 'Bobby Robson asked me to speak for George Burley in a FA Disciplinary Committee. George was booked by Clive Thomas and it was a ridiculous decision but I decided not to take part. I met John Cobbold at the hearing and he mentioned that another player was appealing as well. The player's offence was kicking the ball away. "Can't you speak for him, too?" he said. "I can't do that," I answered. "I saw him kick the ball away. He was guilty." "Ah," said Cobbold, "but he didn't kick it very far, did he!"'

SIX

ALF TURNS THE CLUB INTO A CHAMPIONSHIP WINNING TEAM

Scott Duncan was sixty-seven when he retired as manager and died at the age of eighty-seven in 1976. Not knowing the managerial capabilities of the candidates to succeed him, the directors took advice and settled on Ramsey, the thirty-five-year-old Tottenham, Southampton and England right-back who played in England's most humiliating defeat, the 1-0 defeat by the USA in the 1950 World Cup. Ramsey had no coaching qualifications and his creed was 'treat the ball like a prized piece of jewellery, never let it go.'

He learnt not to give the ball away when he used to walk four miles to and from his school, Becontree Heath School in bleakest Essex. His parents had no transport and there were no convenient buses or trains. Most experts believe that the players of his era incurred fewer injuries than today's players because they walked so much in their earlier years that their legs were strong and resilient. Football was rougher then and referees were more lenient. And in those days their chief pastime

was a walking sport, golf. With having the afternoons off it was a
pleasurable way to occupy their spare time and they always carried
their own bag of clubs. They couldn't afford a caddy and the electric
trolley was unheard of.

Ramsey's only book entitled *Talking Football* was published in 1952
and had just 110 pages, making it one of the shortest autobiographies
ever published. Later, when he became more famous, he was offered
fortunes by the leading publishers to collaborate with a more substantial book but rejected every offer. After the 1966 World Cup success,
a Fleet Street football correspondent wrote to him suggesting that he
should meet to talk about a book. He had a good relationship with
him and Alf was always courteous and helpful – unlike the relationships
he had with many other writers. Alf wrote back on 12 September
1966, and his letter, dictated to his secretary, read 'Thank you for your
letter of the 5th September. I am not considering the possibility of
writing a book in the foreseeable future as my commitments during
the months ahead are particularly heavy. Many thanks for your kind
congratulations which are greatly appreciated. Yours sincerely. Signed
A.E. Ramsey.'

Alf was a reserved, almost shy man, and he resented his privacy
being invaded. There were many myths about him. In his ghost-writ-
ten book, written in stilted prose, and full of clichés (featuring the
adjective 'grand' on almost every page), the writer claimed that Alf was
born at 6, Parrish Cottages, Dagenham in 1922 but the official book
of the records of every Football League player gave his birth date as 22
January 1920. He had two years lopped off his age – or did he?

When Ipswich FC commissioned a statue of him, positioned close
to the corner of the Cobbold Stand and the North Stand, his date of
birth was given as 22 January 1920. The sculptor provided a remarkable likeness. The statue has never been defaced by graffiti. Most
footballing statues, including those of Billy Wright outside Molineux,
Wolverhampton, Billy Shankly at Liverpool's Anfield, Brian Clough's
at Nottingham Forest and Herbert Chapman at Highbury are similarly
untouched. Those who go to football, even the hooligans, revere their
heroes and are reluctant to demean the memory of such men.

On 16 July 2002, another statue of a footballing hero was unveiled at Portman Road. Sir Bobby Robson's statue was situated sixty yards from Ramsey's, which was surprising because there was plenty of space on the corner to house both. A council official explained that it was more appropriate to put Sir Bobby's halfway up the road. But the probable reason was that the two heroes lived separate lives and had little or no contact so it wouldn't be right to put the statues next to each other.

Sir Alf's statue has his left hand in his pocket and his face bears a serious demeanour. The inscription reads 'Sir Alf Ramsey 1920-1999, Ipswich Town manager 1955-63, Division One Champions 1961-2, England team manager 1963-74, World Cup winners 1966. Erected by ITFC Supporters Club in recognition of a great man, August 2000.'

It was noticeable that Sir Alf was less decorated than Robson who was awarded the CBE before he was knighted and has an honorary MA degree. The council commandeered a corner from a car park to erect Sir Alf's statue. As you face the Ramsey statue, you can turn sharp left to see the Robson statue away up the road. The Robson statue says 'Sir Bobby Robson, CBE, MA. Ipswich manager 1969-82, FA Cup winners 1978, UEFA Cup winners 1981, England team manager 1982-1990, World Cup semi finalists 1990. Donated by TXU and Ipswich Borough Council in association with ITFC Supporters Club in recognition of a great man, July 2002.'

Robson's statue is much more animated and the vast majority of the 2,500-strong crowd who attended the ceremony thoroughly approved it. The sculptor, Sean Hedges-Quinn, a local man, depicted him in a typical pose, smiling and pointing to the Cobbold Stand where the brothers Cobbold might well have been holding glasses of wine in the restaurant named Centre Spot. His wife Hayley was expecting their second child and he said 'If Hayley goes into labour tonight I don't think I will ever have a day to match it. It will be the proudest day of my professional life and the proudest day of my personal life.' Unfortunately, Hayley did not give birth on the same day but still, it was a great day for his family.

Robson was portrayed wearing his suit for the 1978 FA Cup final and he said 'Just one problem, the kipper tie. They were all wearing these kipper ties in those days. "Coach" (the nickname for Hedges-Quinn) was so methodical, taking measurements, like my fingers and even my fingernails, that the job was remarkable. I am delighted with it.

'You know the most wonderful thing about this? That I am still alive to see it. Most people honoured in this way never actually see the statue, so this really is quite rare. It was a very strange feeling to see myself in statue form. Hard to put it into words. Obviously I had never seen anything remotely like it before.'

One of the few footballing heroes to see his own statue in this country was Denis Law, the former Manchester United and Manchester City forward. Like Robson, he suffered from cancer. Clearly emotional, Robson said 'I feel very privileged and honoured to know that the town has this sort of warmth towards me. I have always had a strong affiliation with Ipswich, not just the football club but the town itself. My home is still there. I spent almost fourteen years at Portman Road, which is a long time in management by any standards.

'Who knows, maybe I would still have been. It was only the lure of managing my country that eventually pulled me away. Mr Patrick was the chairman and he wanted me to stay. It came down to me deciding whether I went or stayed, and the pull of England won. I always said that would be the only job to end my time with Ipswich. I lost count of the number of jobs I was offered and rejected. After we won the UEFA Cup in 1981 I was offered the Manchester United job among others.

'You know, it is really something that Ipswich supplied England with two managers, and their best two if you go by what we achieved in the job. It is not a giant of a club but they can't take that away from them. It is a unique achievement, something that sets it apart and nobody else can match. The club, the town, they must be proud of that.'

As he attempted to pull the cord to remove the cover, the cloth stuck on the finger of the statue's raised arm. The audience laughed and cheered. 'That was John Cobbold's doing,' said one friend. Said Sir Bobby 'Tell them to take a handkerchief down now and again, so they can give me a polish. We should try to keep the bird mess off!'

Robson, who was twice struck by cancer in the 1990s, launched an additional appeal for money to pay for a second cancer scan machine at Ipswich Hospital. He signed the bonnet of a car which was later auctioned. Already he had his Bobby Robson Jubilee Appeal which yielded £70,000 for cancer treatment equipment at the hospital. He was treated there and he said 'I will never stop giving my support for the people who saved my life.'

Robson has been closely involved with five books about his life – a testimony to his popularity. Sir Alex Ferguson had one and Arsene Wenger has yet to start his first. Ramsey's slimline one, published by Stanley Paul in the year of the Queen's Coronation, was soon remaindered at 3s 6d in old money. Ramsey explained in his book why he put such a premium on accurate passing. He said 'My three brothers, Albert, Len, Cyril and myself walked four miles a day to school and to break the monotony of our plod, we always took with us a small ball, often a tennis ball. On either side of the long, country lane was a ditch. In winter, after the rains, it was often two or three feet deep, so you will appreciate it was to our advantage that the ball should not find its way into the ditch. It was agreed that the fellow who kicked the ball into the water should go in after it. Rather foolishly, I made this mistake on one occasion, took off my shoes and socks, waded in and got out of my depth and for a week afterwards was confined to bed with a severe cold, having been told by my mother what a foolish lad I had been to go in after a ball which was not worth so much. It taught me a lesson.'

The Ramsey brothers were forced to keep playing with battered and decrepit balls. New ones were difficult to obtain. They had little money to spend and Alf was twelve before he visited a cinema. 'I was football mad,' he wrote. Years later a journalist wrote to him to ask him what was his most prized possession when he was a boy. The journalist wanted to compile a feature on famous sportsmen and their favourite possession. Alf wrote back just two words 'A football.'

He left school at fourteen and, instead of opting to play football professionally, he went to work as a grocer's boy. He explained 'The grocery trade interested me for some unknown reason and I started as an errand boy working for the Co-Operative at twelve shillings a week. Of that sum I handed over ten shillings to my mother, put a shilling in a box for savings and kept a shilling for myself.'

When he was called up into the Army in 1940 he said it was 'one of the greatest things which happened to me.' He soon rose in the ranks and was promoted to sergeant. He started to overcome his shyness, and grew accustomed to talking with junior ranks. Most of the great managers of that era, like Bill Nicholson, Bob Paisley, Bill Shankly, Stan Cullis, Ron Greenwood and Sir Walter Winterbottom, served in the armed forces and later became adept at addressing footballers.

Ramsey claimed he never drank more than a single drink after matches and soon gave up smoking in the Army 'because it affected my wind'. That was not strictly true. Some of the Ipswich players spotted him smoking earlier in his managerial career. Each time he had to try and hide the offending Woodbine. He was a gambler, sometimes backing on dogs and when he was at Tottenham one of his team mates, Eddie Baily, asked him how much he had won after one of his selections came up. 'Mind your own business,' he told Baily.

Ramsey was turned down by his nearest club, Portsmouth FC, just before the outbreak of the Second World War and found himself serving at Barton Stacey at an anti-aircraft unit in 1940. After playing for a battalion side against a Southampton team – Ramsey's side lost 10-0 – he was invited to play for Southampton as an amateur. Bill Dodgin Senior, who later became Southampton manager, recommended him to Tom Parker, the Saints manager. Dodgin was a centre half and, at the time, Ramsey filled a more attacking role at inside forward (also playing at centre forward on occasion).

In his first game at Southampton, against Luton, he gave away a penalty: not a good start to his career. Despite his lack of height, he played as a centre half for a while. Dodgin finally decided his best position was right-back. Realising he was too slow, Ramsey spent hours each day working on sprinting and kicking the ball with precision. Eventually he was picked for England and played 32 times between 1949 and 1954. He was a stylish, classical defender never a fast mover.

When he first joined Southampton he was asked how much he needed to cover the cost of his travel to the Dell to discuss his signing, and he replied 'Tuppence ha'penny.' The club chairman said 'Are you sure? What about a taxi fare?' 'No,' said Alf. 'That's what I spent.' Later, the club treasurer conveniently forgot to pay him his £10 signing-on fee. Dodgin offered him £4 a week in the summer and £6 during the season and an additional £7 when he was picked in the first team. Ramsey turned the offer down. He finally settled on £6, £7 and £8. Alf was renowned as a man who was scrupulous about money, once saying 'I earn the maximum of £1,000 a year and I think I'm very well paid.'

While he was in digs in Southampton, he met a startlingly vivacious young lady named Victoria. Unfortunately she was still married, to a Southampton businessman. The marriage broke down, ending in divorce. The new relationship with the prominent footballer soon blossomed and eventually they married on 15 May 1949, after Alf joined Tottenham Hotspur. They had a daughter, Tanya, who is married and lives in the USA. The transfer fee was £21,000 – a lot of money for a thirty-one-year-old defender. A Tottenham player named Ernie Jones went to Southampton in part exchange. At first Ramsey lived with his parents in East London but bought his own house just before he married Victoria. He played for Spurs between 1949 and 1954 and gained successive championship medals as Spurs won the Second and First Division titles.

On one international trip he shared a room with Jackie Milburn, who was the man who succeeded him as Ipswich manager in 1963. They spoke about football into the early hours and Milburn said later 'Alf was never a great one for small talk when he was with England. Football was his one subject of conversation. He was always a pepper and salt man, working out moves and analysing formations with the cruets on the table.'

He was still bereft of coaching experience, unlike some of his colleagues who were converted by England manager Walter Winterbottom, founder of the FA coaching scheme. He had great respect for Winterbottom, a former teacher and lecturer, and at thirty-three he was ready to use the experience he gained as a teacher in the Army. Ramsey learned a lot from Arthur Rowe, the Tottenham manager who preached the 'push and run' style of football. Rowe was a Cockney who had an enviable sense of humour and in 1955 Ramsey found himself out of the first team. He was ready to move on.

★

One of the Ipswich directors heard that he was about to retire from playing and told John Cobbold that Alf was a possible candidate for manager. Cobbold asked the club secretary to sound out Tottenham about Ramsey. 'We got permission from Tottenham,' said Cobbold, 'and after a bit of humming and hawing he decided to accept our offer.' The day Ramsey arrived to take up his post he was invited into the boardroom and Cobbold poured two glasses of whisky and handed one to the new manager. 'This will be the first and last time I ever offer you a drink in this boardroom,' he said. He then tossed the key to the drinks cabinet in the direction of Ramsey and said 'from now on, Alf, feel free to come in and help yourself.' Ramsey rarely came to the boardroom and never poured his own drink.

Ramsey was on a modest salary without perks when he took over as manager at Ipswich in 1955. He was relatively poorly paid then and that never changed in his managerial career. He should have had an agent – they were abhorred in those days – but never had one. On arrival at Ipswich he issued a polite message to the supporters 'May I begin by saying I am very pleased to meet you. And I sincerely hope that our association will be a happy and successful one. In the past you have supported the club 100 per cent and I would like to feel that in this, my first year as manager, you will do the same. May our slogan, as Mr Scott Duncan has said in previous years, still be "Up the Town." A. Ramsey.'

Conditions at Portman Road were primitive. The offices were built by the Army as a part of a barracks before the First World War. Ramsey's cramped office sprung a leak and buckets were used to catch the water. The dressing rooms were often dirty and unkempt. The wooden floors were not planed down and anyone foolish enough to walk barefooted on them risked collecting a hefty sliver in his foot. There was just one communal bath, with the players sitting shoulder to shoulder in the water, most of them smoking cigarettes. The water was heated by an dilapidated, coke-fired boiler outside.

But few of the players complained and the imperturbable Ramsey sat with them to explain what he wanted. Some were given lectures, although not in a carping way, and he hardly spoke to others because they followed his instructions implicitly. There was just one window in his office and it looked on to a concrete wall. The coke was piled up to the window. One of the wives kept ringing up with her complaints and one occasion when he heard she was on her way to see him, he jumped out the window to escape, sliding down the coke to rush off.

Ramsey rarely encouraged long discussions at his flat, antique desk which was empty except for a couple of sheets of paper. There was no telephone on the desk itself but an old fashioned black instrument was perched on a small ledge on the wall behind him and when it rang, he had to swivel round on his chair to pick it up. Later he graduated to using Scott Duncan's antique rolltop desk in the next office. He wasn't a chatty person. David Rose, the long-serving secretary, recalled 'I sat near his office and met him most days but he was always fairly curt. I would say something like "I thought so and so had a good game" to get the conversation going and he would say "Oh, do you think so? I didn't think so." He did that to cut me off.'

Ramsey set a dubious record at the start of his managerial career, becoming the first manager of the club to lose on his debut. In his second season, however, Ramsey took the side from the twenty-fourth position in the Third Division to take the title in 1956/57 with 101 goals. Asked how he felt, he replied 'I am very pleased.' Ted Phillips, the unheralded twenty-year-old centre forward from Leiston, scored 41 League goals in as many matches.

Ramsey soon struck a good relationship with John Cobbold, despite their different backgrounds. He came from a rough area in Dagenham yet he held his ground in any discussions with Cobbold. 'You silly bugger Alf,' Cobbold would say, walking off to play cards with his cronies. Ramsey made most of the decisions at the club. The directors invariably approved his decisions, subject to the club's financial restrictions.

Ramsey had two love affairs, football and his wife Victoria. His marriage to Lady Vicky was sublimely happily and she is a much admired and much liked lady in the town of Ipswich. Outside her close circle, there is little known about her and the ebullient Cobbold never talked about their private lives or his own, except for making jokes. As a confirmed bachelor, Cobbold was asked at one of his drinking parties what he did for sex. 'I suppose there is always the dogs,' he said with a titter. He had a couple of Great Danes, 'Thumper' and 'Bosie', and they were very boisterous, often making off with steaks and chicken from the frequent barbecues.

There were suspicions that he was a homosexual, but no-one would admit it in public, or even privately. Those closest to him refused to confirm it. 'There are some things you can't talk about' said one of his former employees. In September, 2001 Sir Elton John (who has never hidden his homosexuality), said in an interview in a newspaper that there were two homosexual football club chairmen – himself and John Cobbold. A few days later, publicising his new album *Songs from the West Coast* on the *Michael Parkinson Show*, the former Watford chairman backtracked and didn't name Cobbold. Someone close to the club said 'I knew John to be a homosexual but so what? There are plenty of homosexuals who are proud of it. But in those days it wasn't something to broadcast. There were rumours about riotous parties. What he did in his private was up to him.'

Bobby Robson said 'I was closer than most people to the situation and in the fourteen years I worked with him there was never any suggestion that he was homosexual. I was sure of that. I looked on him as someone who wasn't interested in either sex. His passion was the football club. He loved it and did everything he could to make it a successful and happy club. He was a great motivator. He was so enthusiastic and wanted us to do well while at the same time ensuring that it was done the right way. I'd knock those rumours down. They weren't true.'

There was a story earlier in Cobbold's spell as chairman when he upset a player who had been invited to sign for the club. The player was George Ley, a left-back from Portsmouth and he turned up at Capel Hall with his wife. After a fee was agreed with Portsmouth, John Cobbold showed them round Capel Hall and pointing to one of the donkeys, he said: 'Have you ever f——ed a donkey?' Ley's wife was shocked and the couple left abruptly. The transfer didn't go through, not surprisingly.

One of John Cobbold's nephews, Charles Hope-Johnstone, the son of Pamela Cobbold and William Hope-Johnstone, was well known to be homosexual and, after John died, he inherited Capel Hall. He used to host flamboyant parties and at his funeral a lot of exotically dressed men of all ages turned up. Mr Patrick was on a fishing trip to Scotland and had to return for the funeral in Little Glemham. When he arrived, he said to one of his relatives 'I'm not staying too long. I'm petrified!'

Patrick once came close to marriage, announcing his engagement to a popular young lady from Hampshire. A friend described her as 'very nice and eminently suitable.' The marriage never took place. 'He was far too young,' said John. 'He was only twenty.' According to friends, he had several other romances, one with an air hostess whom he met in the Bahamas when he was the ADC for the Governor. A year later, John organised a holiday for Patrick and a friend in the Bahamas and the girl turned up. The affair was over by then and Johnny said to his brother 'You made the right decision.'

SEVEN

MR PATRICK IS SHOT IN THE LEG

In April 1954 the Ipswich daily newspaper filed a brief, and startling report. It said Lt Patrick Cobbold of the Scots Guards, aged twenty, was accidentally shot in his right leg during an Army exercise at Pickering in Yorkshire and was on the danger list. Patrick was commanding the Scots Guard Demonstration Platoon at the Detachment of the Guards Training Battalion on the Yorkshire Moors when it happened.

His friend Major Andrew Napier, who was the Training Officer, said 'It was a very intense and tough fourteen days with night courses. The recruits underwent their final field training with live firing exercises at the end of their six month training before posting to their Battalion. Patrick was supervising section attacks with live ammunition when one recruit stumbled and fell to the ground with his rifle going off accidentally. The .303 bullet hit Patrick in the right leg and left thigh.

'It was a very bad moment. I was about two hundred yards away when the firing stopped and I saw that he had been wounded. He was losing blood which we stopped and then carried him on a stretcher to an ambulance some six hundred yards away. It was a forty mile drive to the York Military Hospital, and the doctor took one look at Patrick and said he couldn't deal with gunshot wounds. That was rather surprising as it was a Military Hospital.

'We were told to take him to the City & General Hospital and then gave him a morphine injection to ease the pain. Unfortunately the first doctor had not recorded that Patrick had been given morphine and the first thing they did at the City and General Hospital was to give him another one, and that nearly killed him. A quick antidote was administered which saved his life. I can still remember the name of the second doctor, Dr Willie Dryburgh. He did a magnificent job and I knew that Patrick was extremely grateful to Willie and kept in contact for many years.

'Patrick stayed in hospital for almost six months before he returned to the barracks at Pickering. He kept his dog there and one of the guardsmen looked after it. The accident left him with a hole in his leg and he wasn't fit to play any sport again. There is no doubt that his wound caused him much discomfort, especially in cold weather, and he always had to be very careful about what he was able to do. He loved stalking and fishing. His great love was fishing, standing up to his waist in rivers, fishing for salmon in Scotland. He had to be cautious about wading in and avoiding rocks. Eventually he had to give up fishing at the Findhorn river because the water was too treacherous. He loved solitude and just being on the river surrounded by such glorious scenery.'

Telephoned by a correspondent of the *Daily Telegraph*, brother John said of the shooting 'He's rather poorly. It was entirely bad luck. No-one was to blame.' The incident became a matter of State when the Foreign Secretary, the Rt Hon. Harold Macmillan, his uncle, told a meeting in his Bromley constituency 'I think what was happening was that the boy was out on Army manoeuvres with other National Service boys when a rifle went off. He was very seriously injured indeed. He has lost a lot of blood.

'I apologise that my wife (Lady Dorothy) is unable to be present tonight. She thought it right to be with her sister at this time, but she hopes to be back next week when we begin the real work.' By this he meant the next General Election. Mr John was the Conservative candidate in Ipswich, hoping to have his uncle on the same platform. When Mr Macmillan became Prime Minister he brought in a new style of table at the Cabinet Room in 10 Downing Street (boat shaped), so that the Premier had eye contact with everyone around it.

A War Office spokesman promised that a court of inquiry into the accident would be held. If there was a report, however, nothing was published. A handwritten telegram was despatched to Lady Blanche Cobbold from Cambridge at 9.40 p.m. on 17 April 1955 marked 'Priority'. It said 'Cobbold, Glemham Hall, Woodbridge, Suffolk. Regret to inform you that your son Lt Patrick Cobbold, 433517, Grenadier Guards (actually it was the Scots Guards) dangerously ill at City Hospital York, the result of gunshot wounds. If in order to visit him you desire [*sic*], obtain free military warrant providing third class return to York for not more than two persons one of which must be a relative application. Should be made to the nearest police station.' It was unsigned. Lady Blanche left early the next morning... travelling by first class without a warrant.

Her sister Dorothy arrived later and the sisters kept a vigil for several nights before the patient began improving. After a few days, she journeyed home to attend to her other duties. Another call was put through to Glemham Hall and brother John was told his brother's condition had worsened. This time Lady Blanche left immediately along with John, catching a late night express from King's Cross. It was a worrying time for everyone.

When Patrick eventually recovered, he donned his uniform to pose for pictures sitting in a wheelchair, with his leg sticking up. Under his peaked cap, he wore a broad smile. 'It was a bit of a laugh,' he said. As he convalesced, Johnny rang him from home on a daily basis. 'Your twenty-first birthday is coming up soon,' he said. 'What about a party to celebrate your recovery?' Patrick was hesitant. But he was talked into it and Johnny hired The Forest and the Vale, a hotel and restaurant in Pickering. 'Johnny invited the whole platoon, and a few more,' said a friend. 'It was a very boozy night and Johnny picked up the bill. He was a very gregarious man. Patrick came to the pub in an ambulance and went home the same way.'

Patrick's Army career had started when he was called up for National Service at eighteen, after an undistinguished school career at Eton. He enjoyed it so much that he signed up for a two year regular engagement, after serving with the 1st Battalion Scots Guards in the canal zone in Egypt. There had been some firing but none directed at him. He had plenty of leave to join his brother, relatives and friends at shoots in Suffolk and at the family's 25,000 acre estate, Camusericht in Perthshire. He made frequent visits to the family home at Glemham Hall. The central heating, installed in 1913, never functioned properly and one of the guests, the former Arsenal captain and renowned manager Joe Mercer, brought his own water bottle. 'This bloody place is freezing,' he said. 'Icicles are hanging from my nose and ears.'

On another occasion, some friends were being entertained in the dining room when Lady Blanche placed a gas heater next to the dining table in an abortive attempt to warm the room. There was no help to serve the meal and Patrick did the serving. After they sat through a chilly dinner, everyone got up to move into a small, cosy room next door which was heated by a roaring, open fire. Lady Blanche didn't believe in having fires in the dining room.

The Cobbold brothers insisted on dressing properly for dinner, with ties and jackets. Although Mr John kept his favourite rooms, including a bedroom filled with Victorian toys, prams, bikes and games at Glemham, he usually lived at Capel Hall, near Felixstowe. The first floor room is still intact, preserved as a Victorian nursery. In 1979 Glemham Hall, which was open to the public at the time, was burgled and two John Constable paintings were stolen along with several silver antiques. The value of the haul was £2.5 million and the property was never recovered. Lady Blanche and Patrick were in the Hall at the time and heard nothing. Security was almost non existent. Lady Blanche stuck up a notice in the space where the paintings were hung, saying 'Stolen!' Patrick referred to the robbers as 'You bastards.'

John Constable, one of England's greatest artists, had visited a home of the Cobbold family (named Honlywells) on many occasions, often sketching in the gardens. He was a longstanding friend of the Cobbold family. Six years later there was another burglary. 'I think it was an inside job,' said Philip Hope-Cobbold. 'One of the thieves was picked up by the police and I don't think much was found. Since then we've had alarms installed.'

The two millionaire brothers, one extrovert and the other much more introvert, often hosted parties to showbiz stars and football people. Tommy Trinder, the comedian who was the chairman of Fulham, was an occasional guest when he spent the summer seasons in Felixstowe. Before dinner one day, John Cobbold, Trinder and Ken Brightwell the veteran director, were sitting on a large sofa when Thumper, the dog, jumped behind it, tipping it over and spilling the occupants.

Trinder usually attended Fulham's games at Portman Road and always wore an Astrakhan coat. He told one of his players 'If you score a hat-trick, this is yours.' That was a dangerous boast because one of his players, Scotsman Graham Leggatt, had scored several hat-tricks during his career. Leggatt duly scored three goals and asked for Trinder's coat. 'That doesn't count,' said Trinder. 'One of the goals was from a penalty.'

Brightwell, who watched his first Ipswich game when he was aged four, recalled an occasion when the directors arranged a dinner at the Orwell Hotel in Felixstowe to celebrate promotion to the First Division. 'The wives looked very elegant in their expensive evening dresses and Johnny's sister asked us "Do you like my dress?"' he said. 'My wife said "Yes, it's very nice." Pamela, Johnny's sister, said "I bought it for £1 in a second-hand shop in Saxmundham!"'

Mr John didn't like ostentation. Brightwell said 'Eldon Griffiths, the local Tory MP who was Minister of Sport, used to come to our matches and once put his Dispatch Box in the middle of the board-room floor. Johnny took one look at it and kicked it out of the way, under a table. He would welcome a dustman to the Board if he thought he was a genuine man but he hated snobs.'

Brightwell also recalled the way he used to perform grace at meals. He'd say 'for what you are about to receive, the chef should be shot!'

Brightwell, who died in 2003 at the age of eighty-three, was an interesting character. He made his wealth from fitting television aerials in and around Ipswich and the material used for the aerials came from scaffolding once used to renovate Westminster Abbey. He was a rally driver, a builder and finally, an estate agent. One close season he went on a club tour abroad and part of the journey was spent on a liner. The weather deteriorated sharply and he was so ill he had to stay in his cabin. The Cobbolds arranged a surprise visit by two players, David Johnson and Colin Viljoen, who were attired with large sheets. In the half light they looked like ghosts, wailing and screaming.

Whatever the occasion, Mr John wore scruffy clothes and bore a Chaplinesque appearance. One day he noticed his brother, who dressed more like a city financier, was wearing a check shirt with a piece of bone sticking out from a frayed collar, and recognising it, he screamed 'You s——! Take that off, it was Papa's!'

Johnson, who played almost five years with Ipswich, recalled a similar story about Patrick. 'On a flight to a game Patrick noticed that the belt on his trousers had fallen,' he said. 'He said to one of the stewardesses "I wonder if you have a piece of string, I need to make some repairs." The stewardess returned with some string and Patrick tied it around his waist to keep his trousers up. Coming back from the trip I realised he was still using the string. He hadn't bothered to buy a proper belt.

'We were staying at the Atlantic Hotel in Liverpool before a game against Everton and Patrick told his brother that his shirt was stained and he should wear another one. Next day John came down to go on the coach and he was wearing the top of his pyjamas. "I f——ing well forgot to bring a clean shirt," he said. They were a weird pair, absolutely mad – unbelievable, eccentric, but lovely people. One day Mr John told me that he wrote the words for the song *Spanish Eyes*. I found it difficult to believe it but he swore it was true. He liked music and he did play the piano. He also had a bottle of whisky in his car and when the doctor told him it was bad for him be switched to champagne. "Easier to drink," he said.'

The tall, upright Patrick had a more restrained sense of humour and many of his interests were involved with the Scots Guards from which he was invalided out of the Army. He was about to take a job with the brewery when a much more desirable opportunity came up, ADC to the Governor of the Bahamas, Sir Raynor Arthur, KCMG, CVO and Commander in Chief, between 1957 and 1960. Promoted to Captain, Patrick found it a wonderful wheeze in the colony. Apart from resting on the beach and drinking in various bars, he had little to do except perform perfunctory duties attending the Governor. The highlight was the visit of Prince Philip on the weekend of 25–26 April 1959, when he sat four up from the Prince at a Parliamentary dinner at the Fort Montagu Beach Hotel.

He recalled that the Prince was able to remember everyone's name. As a local writer named Richardson approached, the Prince said 'Ah, you're Richardson.' It was Patrick's job to brief the Prince's Equerry. The menu was 'filet de Yellowtail, sauce verte, conch chowder, Supreme de Volaille Bahamien, endives braises, tomatoes farcies, pommes de terres Parisiennes, Salade de Saison; Sabayon Mousse aux Ananas, and café.'

Patrick returned to a rather spartan England (where rationing was about to be phased out) and started working at the company's brewery at Walthamstow, sharing a flat with Major Andrew Napier in Eccleston Square. The Major recalled 'I did the cooking. Patrick didn't fancy it. He loved good food but he used to pick at it rather.' The future Premier's nephew was signed up as a Special Constable and loved his unpaid, part time job. 'One day he was on duty at Downing Street and rang the flat saying that he had left his whistle behind and the Specials were about to be inspected,' said Napier. 'Guardsman Myers had to take it round. "Here you are sir" he said. "Here's your whistle. You may need your whistle!"'

'Patrick was a public spirited man and was very generous. He was our best man when we married in 1960. He was a great chap and I miss him very much.' He had become a heavy smoker and John also smoked excessively. They risked catching fire, frequently singeing their clothes with cigarettes butts and unextinguished matches. John's long-serving chauffeur Roger Nightingale, who sat near him in the directors' boxes of football grounds, said 'He'd smoke as many cigarettes as there were minutes in a game, ninety, and frequently lit up when he was already smoking the same cigarette. He was a nervous wreck during games.'

★

Mr John owned a twenty-four-foot boat, which he took across the English Channel to Holland, Belgium and France, journeying up and down canals. 'One day, after a few drinks he found himself in a bar and suddenly announced he couldn't remember where the bloody boat was,' said Nightingale. 'They had search parties all over the place before someone found it.

'Another time he was sitting at the quay at Harwich, having a drink, when he fell over and dropped ten feet into his boat. Luckily it was high tide otherwise he might have been seriously injured. He claimed that he still had his drink in his hand and he hadn't dropped any of it. Then there was the matter of the German speedboat which suddenly arrived at the Felixstowe Ferry. The two occupants looked exhausted and John started chatting with them and invited them for a drink. Not too long later, he said "you look whacked, why don't you stay at the Orwell Hotel?" They agreed and John picked up the bill.

'A few hours later police arrived in strength and surrounded the hotel. They burst into the hotel and dragged out the Germans. Apparently they were drug runners and the police inspector in charge gave John a big bollocking. One day a monkey turned up on his boat and he took it back to Capel Hall. The monkey started picking the cherries and that amused him. But it wouldn't come down and he said "I'll have to get rid of this f——ing monkey, I don't like it and he doesn't like me." I had to call the RSPCA and two men turned up and caught it and took it away.

'On one of his frequent trips to Scotland he was driving his Land Rover when he lost control, the vehicle overturned and ended up in a ditch. He wasn't hurt but one of the old Ipswich players, Tommy Parker, lost part of his ear. John was very upset and kept apologising.'

In the late 1960s, Ipswich had one of the best youth sides in the country and the captain was Mick Mills, who later became the record holder for appearances in the first team, with 741 matches. 'The chairman loved being in the company of youngsters and he spent a lot of time watching our games, encouraging us and congratulating us,' he said. 'Then he'd offer a drink and a few more. Dutch football was in its infancy and the clubs were starting up their youth set ups and we were often invited to take part in tournaments in Holland. I will always remember one trip. He insisted on taking his boat across from Harwich to Amsterdam and a couple of players who accepted his invitation found it was a bit upsetting. They were sick for most of the trip.

'There was only one member of the crew, a character called "Soapy" – so called because he never washed. The chairman had crates of bottles under the floor and when he tied the boat up in a canal in Amsterdam, right next to the main railway station, he started on the wine and hardly stopped. There were parties daily and he took the players round the Red Light to see what it was like.

'Reg Tyrell, the chief scout, arranged the matches in an under-18 competition and he signed his son Clive on, although he was over age. He also registered Trevor Whymark in the name of Lynch, Reg's wife's maiden name. The chairman used to call me "Mickey" although no-one else did. He called most of the others "you f——ing c——!" so I suppose he had more respect for me. No-one was upset about his swearing. He spoke in this public school accent and it was his normal way of behaving.'

Cobbold needed a chauffeur in the 1960s, after being banned from driving and his first employee had to be sacked for forging cheques. Typically, he declined to press charges. 'I was too bloody soft,' he said. One night Nightingale, who was nineteen at the time, was working behind the bar at the Great White Horse Hotel when Cobbold told some of his friends about his dilemma in finding a suitable replacement. Cobbold said 'Do you drive?' Nightingale said 'Yes.' 'You'll do,' said Cobbold. 'When can you start? What about now?'

'I can't go right now,' said Nightingale. But he started the next day. 'He was a wonderful friend,' said Nightingale. 'That was the most exciting, the funniest and the most frantic twenty or so years I ever experienced. He had a great sense of humour and he could pick up little comments and turn them into big jokes and have everyone rolling around with laughter. He was an exceptionally kind person. After a time he gave me a deposit to buy a house and when he died, he left the house to me. It could be a twenty-four-hour-a-day job and was very difficult to fit a life like that around a marriage. In the end it cost me two marriages but I never regretted it.

'Sometimes he used to invite people back to Capel Hall when there was no-one left to serve dinner. He was involved with the Felixstowe tennis tournament and a lot of famous people were invited. One time Prince Michael and Princess Michael came. I had to cook some beef and dumplings and afterwards he said "those f——ing dumplings were burnt! You're fired!"'

EIGHT

MR JOHN BECOMES THE YOUNGEST DIRECTOR

Early in John Cobbold's reign at Portman Road he was elected President of the South East Counties League, a competition for developing young footballers, and was invited to speak at a dinner in a London hotel. Lawrie McMenemy, the former Southampton and Sunderland manager who was also manager of Northern Ireland, sat next to him and he said 'He was knocking back the wine and as he stood up, rather unsteadily, he looked round and slowly collapsed head first into the table, knocking glasses and cutlery everywhere. He was greeted by uproarious laughter followed by prolonged clapping. His speech never started and he was carried out to a car owned by Sidney Wale, the then chairman of Tottenham. A couple of people helped him into the car and he was driven to Liverpool Street, put on a train while he slept all the way back to Ipswich. God knows what happened when he arrived.'

To make sure he could be identified in these circumstances, Mr John started the habit of writing his name 'J. Cobbold' on the cuffs of his shirt. On 1 November 1948, he was elected a director of the Board of Ipswich Town FC at the age of twenty-one years and four months. He was one of the youngest directors in the history of the Football League (which was founded in 1888). He never played football, other than taking part in a kick about, and preferred playing tennis. He did not play tennis at a high standard, but was enthusiastic. One of his habits was to decline to shake hands with his opponents after matches were concluded. 'That's etiquette,' he explained. 'You should never shake hands on private grounds.'

Asked about his likes and dislikes, he said 'My real likes are as follows, in this order. One, girls – they are the best inventions ever invented. Two, good company, which always improves with a glass in one's hand. Three, living in the country, fishing and shooting. And finally, four, football, for the good fun and companionship it gives me.'

Mr John first aired his likes and dislikes at his coming of age, held at Glemham Hall on 13 August 1948, attended by 1,400 relatives, friends and workers. Marquees were installed around the grounds to cope with the large number. As the *Suffolk Chronicle & Mercury* reported, he had just relinquished his commission in the Welsh Guards and was about to undertake a course in brewing in Cheltenham, ready to start work at The Cliff. The Ipswich brewery was closed for the day to enable the staff and their families to play a part.

The newspaper recorded 'Tenants and employees of the Cobbold estates at Glemham, Falkenham and Trimley were there as well as tenants of licensed houses in the two counties, Suffolk and Norfolk. Continuous rain, although interfering with some of the programme, failed to detract from the cordial spirit of the event. Sports were carried out, but open air dancing and fireworks had to be cancelled. Presentations followed tea. On behalf of the private tenants of Lady Blanche Cobbold, Mr Roland Everitt made a speech of congratulation. As the oldest farmer on the Glemham estate he appreciated the honour of being selected to speak on behalf of the tenants. He said "It was a great pleasure to propose the health of Mr John and I thank Lady Cobbold for the invitation and respectfully point out that the tenants realised the responsibilities to be undertaken by Mr Cobbold. They recognise in the son much that they had admired in the father. Between us and him there is a tradition, a regard and esteem which has come down from our ancestors, and which is a characteristic of our national life." Mr C. Packard and Mr C. Davis then presented Mr Cobbold with two paintings.

'One of them, a Constable, was later stolen. The tenants of Capel Hall had collected for a cigarette box, and it was handed over by Mr A.J. Reynolds. An antique lacquered bracket clock, together with an illuminated address, was also presented by the Cliff Brewery and Lower Brook Street employees. On behalf of the licensed tenants, Mr R.W. Borrett made a presentation of an antique mahogany writing bureau and bookcase, together with an album with subscribers, and a travelling clock and tea service.'

At the time there were literally hundreds of people employed by the Cobbold family and the wage bill was high. But not many of them were paid a lot of money. Most of them lived in rented houses and hardly anyone owned a car. They used to walk, or ride a bicycle. Mrs Mollie Gibson, daughter of the head gamekeeper at Glemham from 1928 to 1941, still has vivid memories of the annual Christmas parties for the school children in the village. 'We dressed in our Sunday best and on entering would be taken to the big hall where a massive Christmas tree stood in the corner with a lovely blazing log fire,' she said. 'After the party games and the Christmas tea and crackers we would go back to the big hall where Lady Blanche would hand every child a present from under the tree. When it was time to go home, she would stand at the door and give each child a bag of sweets and an orange.

'On Christmas Day, Captain and Lady Cobbold would invite the head of the different departments on the estate to dinner and tea at the Hall. We used to enter the servants' hall where a very long table would be laid out with wines and ales and crackers. The servants would wait on us all and then sit down with us for a lovely Christmas dinner. After, the men would chat and drink, while the ladies sat beside the fire and chatted. Teatime came and a large Christmas cake would be brought in by the cook. We would all sit down and enjoy the goodies and homemade cakes. They were lovely times, sadly now in the past.'

One relative said 'Mr John was loved by everyone. He remembered everyone's name, however humble they may be.' Later, Mr John had two white donkeys, a mother named 'Alka' and male compatriot 'Seltzer'

– who came from an illicit encounter with a stray male donkey. They were the butt of many jokes at Glemham Hall, particularly about the naming of the baby donkey. 'Can't think of a bloody name,' said Mr John. One day the directors were gathering before a game in the boardroom and Don Howe, the former England coach and football club manager, said 'I've got a good one.' 'A bottle of champers to the man who comes up with the best one,' said John. 'Burp,' said Don Howe. 'Fantastic,' said John. 'Barman, fetch another bottle!'

John Cobbold always had dogs, mainly shooting dogs, although he rarely shot personally (unlike his brother Patrick who was a good shot). When a shoot was arranged, eighteen beaters were employed, earning £10 a day – good money at that time. Jack Bayfield, the former head gamekeeper, was still working part time in his eighties. He was born in 1918 and comes from a long line of gamekeepers. 'My father lived until he was ninety-two,' he said. 'It's the healthy life. We used to get up at 5.00 a.m. and didn't take much time off. Mr John loved to come along but he didn't shoot too much. He left it to Mr Patrick and his friends. He used to crawl along on his stomach to retrieve the birds. He wore knickerbockers and got mud all over them. On a good day we killed between 150 and 200 partridges, duck, woodcock and pheasant. Mr John preferred a woodcock. He used to like eating the head. Mr Patrick liked partridge.

'Mr John had a dog named Cindy and I remember Cindy popped out of a hedge with something hanging from his mouth. Mr John grabbed hold of it and held it up to some of the ladies. "Look at that," he said. "It's a condom!" He was always playing jokes with condoms. After it was over, the whisky bottles came out. We loved a nip of whisky. Then it was back to the Hall and the staff cooked the birds. It was real tasty!'

Mike Hollingsworth, one of the tenant farmers whose family lived close to Capel Hall, described Mr John as 'a true gentleman who had a soft heart.' He said 'He told me he'd given up shooting. It was around the mid-1970s and he said "I shot a partridge and went to pick it up. The bird was still alive and it looked so mournful that I decided not to shoot another bird and I stuck to it."'

★

After being demobbed, Jack Bayfield worked at Sandringham up to 1955. 'I met King George the Sixth many times after I left the Army' he said. 'I was called up at the start of the Second World War and was in the British Expeditionary Force in France before it had to be evacuated back to England. I walked eighty miles to Cherbourg and managed to get away on a small boat. We were lucky. The Germans stopped advancing on the orders of Hitler. I don't know why he did it. If they had carried on, we'd be in trouble. We might have lost the war.

'Then I served in Burma under General Orde Wingate. He was a rum 'un. One day our CO said "Bad news Bayfield, you're on your way to the jungle." I said "that's good news, sir. I don't mind being in the jungle. I used to spend enough time in them on the shoots."'

When he was demobbed, he worked for the Royal Family. 'The King was a nice, reserved man,' he said. 'I remember he wore a kind of metal jacket with a battery fitted to warm him up. He always wore special heated gloves as well. He had something wrong with him. He always stuttered. The Queen Mother was a lovely lady. She always used to ask how I was going on. She sent the staff a Christmas card every Christmas without fail. I used to meet the Princesses, the present Queen and the late Princess Margaret. The Queen was a very friendly person. These lords and ladies used to come along, including Lord Stanhope, the First Lord of the Admiralty and Mr Churchill. "Winny" was a very nice man and he was a good shot.'

Captain Cobbold often joined King George VI on shoots around Sandringham. The King died on 6 February 1952 after 'a good day's shooting at Sandringham' in the words of Sir Edward Ford, his assistant private secretary. Sir Edward, who has survived into his nineties, recalled 'he loved shooting and nor was he put off by the freezing Norfolk winds. The Queen Mother told me how the King had greatly enjoyed his day and had then spent the evening quietly with her and Princess Margaret. All things considered, and if one takes into account the King's tragically young age of fifty-six, it was a very good way to go.'

Today, the news of a death of a King or a Queen would be flashed around the world within seconds. Sir Edward and the courtiers had a code word to pass the news on and it was 'Hyde Park Gardens'.

Unfortunately the code word wasn't passed on to the present Queen, who was at a safari lodge in Kenya. Eventually, she was told by Prince Philip after one of his equerries heard it on the BBC. Sir Edward went to see Sir Winston Churchill and found him in his pyjamas lying in his bed, although it was 9.15 in the morning. There was a candle lit by his bedside which he used to re-light his cigars. Sir Edward also had to go round to Marlborough House to break the news to Queen Mary, the King's mother. Sir Edward coined the phrase '*annus horribilis*' which Queen Elizabeth used in that memorable Christmas broadcast in 1992 after two royal marriages broke up and Windsor Castle caught fire.

By coincidence, Patrick Cobbold also died in the night after a day's shooting. 'It was a shock,' said Jack. 'He was as fit as a fiddle. A lovely man.' Jack used to be invited to special dinners at Glemham and Capel Hall and some of them were in honour of Harold Macmillan. 'I remember when we went to his eightieth birthday and we had to carry him from his car and put him in a wheelchair. When he rose to speak, he spoke beautifully. He brought a lot of suits and it wasn't easy to pack them in. Mr and Lady Dorothy Macmillan used to stay in the Green Room but it didn't have a lot of privacy. People could walk in. It was a cold place. The warmest place was in the cellar.'

Lady Blanche and the late Queen Mother were both widowed at a comparatively young age. Their marriages were love matches and neither of them wanted to remarry. Lady Blanche lived at Glemham for another forty-three years after her husband died. The Queen Mother was widowed for fifty years. Both of them were very stoical and courageous ladies.

Captain Cobbold and Lady Blanche remained regular visitors to Chatsworth House. The Duke, born in 1920, won the Military Cross in the Italian campaign in 1944 serving with the Coldstream Guards. His wife, the Hon. Deborah Vivien Freeman, hosted the parties and took them out hunting. She once said 'I just love all the people involved in hunting. They are some of the best people in England.' In the television coverage of the countryside protests at Westminster in September 2004, one suspected that she might be in the heaving throng, dodging the flying batons.

One of the guests at Glemham Hall was the Superintendent of the Norfolk Prison. 'He asked Mr John if he had been inside the prison,' said Jack. 'Mr John replied "damn close, I've been banned from driving a few times." He used to tell us "if Ipswich win, I have to celebrate and if they lose, I have to drown my sorrows!"'

Jack said there was a lot of poaching going on at Glemham. 'We used to scare them away,' he said. 'One US Serviceman was caught by a special policeman and he got six months. They were tough on poachers who didn't have a licence.' Jack, a jolly man with a deep laugh, came from a large family and they gathered at holiday times for celebrations. They still do. 'We used to tell stories,' he said. 'We didn't have televisions in those days. One of my sons Stephen is a story teller. He is always entertaining the family and he speaks at weddings and parties.

'He tells stories about Suffolk country folk and one of them he often repeats is about a mean father on the eve of Christmas. It was getting late and the old Dad went out the door and not long after there was a loud noise. He came back and one of the children said "What's that noise, Dad?" The Dad replied "I've got bad news for you kids. Father Christmas has been shot dead. There'll be no presents for you lot this Christmas!"

'Stephen goes to watch the Town and when he went to Milan he went to see the Inter *v.* Town game and visited the cathedral. He said to David Sheepshanks "I've never seen so many lights on top of that. Who has to replace those bulbs?"'

Jack lives in a cottage in an isolated spot off the main Woodbridge-Lowestoft road, half a mile from Glemham. He walks to the Hall most days. 'Mr Patrick left the cottage to me to live in it until I go,' he said. 'He was a very generous man. Mr John was the same.'

Professional football had resumed in 1945, but the Cobbold family was still grieving over the death of Lt-Col. Ivan Cobbold and his successor as chairman of the club, Philip Wyndham Cobbold, who died three days after Christmas Day 1945. Captain Peter Temple Chevallier, managing director of Fisons, took over until 1949. Captain Chevallier had a distinguished service record in the First World War and was awarded the DSO and the MC.

Another Cobbold, Alistair, was chairman between 1949 and 1957. An Old Etonian, he went into the Stock Exchange before joining the Royal Navy as a midshipman, rising to become a Lieutenant Commander. He was mentioned in despatches in the landings in Madagascar in 1942 and later became the High Sheriff of Suffolk. He was also chairman of the Cobbold brewery. He was a keen sportsman and insisted on walking over the centre circle to the directors' box from the other side of the ground, accompanied with his wife and her friends. Some of the ladies wore high heels. His son Richard recalled 'I remember seeing Lady Bunbury, Lady Cranworth and Lady Blanche sitting in the stand knitting furiously and complaining bitterly about the referee. But they were never allowed to sit in the directors' box.'

One of his relatives, Mrs Cicely Augusta Cobbold, attended a home game at Portman Road and died three days later at the age of eighty-six. She was twice elected as Mayoress of Ipswich, in 1910/11 and 1933/34, and was a noted shot. She helped John Cobbold's election campaigns in the mid-1950s. Richard said 'I joined the Supporters Club once and my father was very upset when he was told I had been featured in the local newspaper with a headline saying "Richard Cobbold joins the Supporters". He thought it wasn't the done thing for a Cobbold. I loved watching Tommy Lawton and some of the Ipswich fans started a campaign to sign him. A few of them asked my father "why don't you buy him?" He answered "Yes, if you give me the £25,000." He went to Notts County instead.'

Obviously nepotism played a part in Mr John's rapid promotion to chairman of the club when he took over on 6 May 1957. He used to call in at Portman Road and opened letters occasionally, chatted with members of the staff and then went off for a long lunch. He never even had his own desk. When his brother succeeded him as chairman he had no desk either.

Midweek football was banned by the government at that time and with so much work needed to rebuild the country there were restrictions on workers being allowed off on most Saturday afternoons. But attendances were still high and the tickets were cheap. The audience was almost all male. Women rarely stood on the terraces; it was unladylike.

John Cobbold was at his best when the East Coast Floods hit Ipswich. The River Gipping overflowed and the Portman Road pitch was covered with a three-foot deep lake. 'I asked for water for my whisky but this is ridiculous,' he said.

In the club's early days Scott Duncan had a club rule, banning players driving cars. He considered them too dangerous. Scott Duncan poured out the drinks in his office after matches and one day Cobbold noticed that his manager was about to add a lot of water to one glass. 'What's the hell going on?' he said. 'That's for the ref,' said Scott Duncan. 'Oh, that's all right,' said Cobbold.

John Cobbold rarely drove himself. While his rich friends drove Bentleys and Rolls Royces, he owned Rovers (3.5 coupes and 2000s) and during a time of petrol rationing he bought a Hillman Imp to save fuel. Most days he presided over a lunch at a local hotel followed by gambling on his favourite card game, pontoon. Half a dozen of his friends usually turned up and it turned into a long day.

Freddie Gales, the hotel owner, owned a six-seat aircraft which flew him and his friends to away matches. Often there were scary trips and on returning from a flight in a severe storm, the plane was tossed around like a leaf in a gale. Cobbold said later 'It was terrifying. I thought that was it.' The pilot needed great skill and courage to head the aircraft down towards the grass field. As the wheels touched the ground, the machine aquaplaned on the water lying on the surface, tipped over and finished up with its tail high in the air and its nose poking into the ground. The public school accent of Cobbold, shaken but uninjured, was heard to say 'Where is my f——ing drink?'

Ipswich won promotion to the Second Division in 1953/54 and Cobbold held a boozy celebration party. He attributed the club's success to a seven-leaf clover which Duncan mounted on the wall of his office. The clover was presented by a US pilot who was serving in England. Duncan, continually ribbed by Mr John, was presented with a twenty-one-year service medal by the Football League Management Committee, only to learn that they asked for it back because they realised he hadn't been working in football during the Second World War.

The harassed manager was upset to discover that he had bought a
new Austin car the day before a price reduction was announced. 'That
cost me a fortune,' he lamented. Cobbold recounted a story about his
first, and last, scouting mission. 'I was on holiday in Scotland when our
manager rang me to ask if I could check on a Stirling Albion player,'
he said. 'I didn't know where the f——ing place was and he explained.
So I went to the ground, told the directors of the home club that I
was a director of Ipswich and I was given tremendous hospitality. They
had a marvellous system where the boardroom table was covered with
dozens of glasses filled with whisky. I consumed quite a few and then
arrived back to my shooting lodge and wrote what I thought was a
long and thorough report on the player and it sent to Mr Duncan.
Four days later he rang me and said "the player I asked you to watch
wasn't even playing. You're fired." I never went scouting again.'

In 1955 Duncan quit as manager but stayed on to become secretary for the next three years before retiring to Helensburgh near
Loch Lomond. One of his final acts was to sign the ex-Chelsea inside
forward or left-winger Jimmy Leadbetter from Brighton. Thin and
spindly, Leadbetter didn't look like a footballer and he was continually
chided by the Cobbold brothers and his fellow directors. But he turned
out to be a key player in taking the club to the title. *Guardian* sports
writer Frank Keating said of him 'He was an ageing, spindle-legged
Scottish winger who looked like a cross between Sir Alec Douglas-
Home, Hughie Gallagher and the elder Steptoe.'

James Hunter Leadbetter was born in Edinburgh in 1928 and was
twenty-seven when Scott Duncan signed him from Brighton. He
looked in his forties, with his drawn, thin cheeks and receding hair.
When he attended the re-union dinner to celebrate the fortieth anniversary of the championship win, in April 2002, he appeared to be no
older than in his playing days – although he was seventy-four. 'Aye,' he
said. 'My cheeks have filled out and my hair has gone but I'm keeping pretty fit back in Edinburgh. I used to play in a local league in
Edinburgh until I retired at fifty-three and now I do a lot of walking.
I lost my teeth when I was whacked by an elbow in a game. That was
the only injury I really had. I saw a dentist and he said there wasn't
much they could do about it and told me I ought to have them out.

So I had the whole lot out. I had dentures up and down and they're fine. Makes me look handsome.'

What finally decided Duncan to give up was an incident on the morning of a cup tie when one of his players, Jack Parry, was seen working on a roof, pointing a chimney. 'Get down you clot,' he shouted. In the New Year's Honours List in 1958 Stanley Rous, the great friend of Captain Cobbold, was knighted for his services to football. 'I'll have to call you Sir Stan,' said John Cobbold. The fledgling chairman was probably the nicest of the Cobbold family and also the wittiest, but he wasn't a great success in his working career. He had too much fun and not enough will to succeed in business. He preferred the life of a playboy. The following season after his arrival at the boardroom, Ipswich experienced their worst season since the club was founded. The club just avoided re election from the Third Division (South) otherwise it might well have ended in one of the minor leagues.

Readers of a local newspaper were asked in a quiz 'Who was Tom Brown?' They meant Tom Brown of *Tom Brown's Schooldays*, the book which was compulsory reading in the post-war years. This particular reader, however, wrote 'Tom Brown is the goalkeeper of Ipswich Football Club...' The Ipswich goalkeeper Tom Brown played in every match that season and let in 86 goals. He hailed from Troon and lived and worked in Ipswich after he retired.

At around that time John Elsworthy was signed as an amateur. He too worked his remaining years in Ipswich, running a post office. Once signed, these Ipswich players rarely move out of the area. Born at Nantyderry, South Wales, Elsworthy was an eighteen-year-old RAF National Serviceman and he wore size twelve boots when he arrived. 'We were only given a couple of pairs of boots and they were supposed to last until they fell apart,' he said. 'I had to buy my own laces.' When he turned up at his digs, he found himself being invited by the new director to have a drink. 'John Cobbold wasn't the normal kind of director,' he said.

'I was serving in Brighton and Scott Duncan heard about me and he offered me £7 a week in the season and £5 a week in the close season. I soon accepted, especially as I was offered a part-time job.

Scott Duncan was a wily old bird. He told me "if you see any good young players, let me know and I'll make it worth while for you." I don't think he did!' Elsworthy learned his footballing craft playing on the coal dust pitches of South Wales and Cardiff tried to sign him. He was tall, powerful and determined – in the same mould as that of Ron Burgess, the wing half from the oddly named Cwm. Burgess made his name at Tottenham Hotspur and his colleague and later manager Bill Nicholson once said of him 'he was the finest player I ever played alongside.'

The loyal Elsworthy represented Ipswich between 1949 and 1965 and is the only player to win two Third Division (South) medals, one Second Division medal and a First Division medal. 'I played in 41 of the 42 games when we won the First Division title and I qualified for a bonus of £12.50 a game,' he said. 'I paid £30 tax on it and I went out to buy my wife a washing machine for £88.

'Alf Ramsey was an unbelievable manager. In his first season we hardly got a corner and that upset him. He spent hours practising corners and he'd go berserk, sounding off about players not being in the right place. By the next season we averaged twelve or more each game. He was so knowledgeable about the game, and so single minded. Unfortunately, he never wrote a book. What a tale he would have had to tell! He loved Ipswich and he was still living there when he died.'

Ken Bean, a former nightclub and bingo hall owner, first met John Cobbold in the early 1960s. He used to hire out the Manor Ballroom, which he owned, and the Ipswich Supporters Association sometimes used it for testimonial dinners for Ipswich players. 'He used to say to me "hello old Bean!"' recalls Ken. 'One day Patrick Cobbold was making a speech at one of these dinners and as he finished, with everyone clapping, he was about to sit in his seat when he fell flying backwards to the ground. John had taken his chair away. Both of them thought that was a big joke. Everyone liked them but they were oddballs.

'On another occasion I was in Norwich and the local Anglian TV station wanted John to appear on one of their programmes. He was willing to be interviewed and when the programme, which was live, was underway the presenter asked John "Can you tell me what you do at Ipswich Football Club?" John said "F—— all!" There was a stunned silence. No-one had heard that word uttered on television before. I think it was around the time that Kenneth Tynan used it but I think John got his in first.'

Ipswich reached new peaks in the 1950s when Ramsey coaxed his side to a memorable performance in front of 53,550 fans at Old Trafford, eventually losing to two Bobby Charlton goals. Two weeks later five of the players who played for Manchester United died in the Munich air crash. In the next Ipswich game there was a two-minute silence.

When Scott Duncan finally retired at the age of seventy, Ramsey became secretary and manager with Wally Gray, former assistant secretary, becoming financial secretary. The owlish Gray was renowned for his parsimony. When Ron Gray, the chief scout, asked for 1s 3d for a hacksaw he bought to use at the club, he replied 'Where's the receipt?' During a train journey he dropped 5d and spent a long time crawling under the seats to find it. Eventually he found it but one of the directors said "That'll cost you 2s 6d to pay for your suit!"'

On another occasion he found a 10s note and immediately claimed it. Harold Smith said of him 'He was notoriously tight with money. One Friday night he phoned me to say that the hot water cylinder was leaking and he needed someone to come out on Saturday morning to mend it. The company I contacted didn't work at weekends but Scott Duncan said it would be worth their while. After the work was finished Scott Duncan thanked the workman and gave him two tickets for Ipswich Reserves *v*. Reading Reserves.'

The staff consisted of five people: Scott Duncan, Wally Gray, groundsman Freddy Blake, David Rose (the office boy who became club secretary), his secretary Pat Goldbold and an office boy. In the 2000/01 season the total number of full-time staff had passed the 140 mark. Rose started work as a junior office boy in August 1958 at the age of fifteen and, by 2000, he was the longest serving secretary in League football – outlasting even Arsenal's Ken Friar.

Ramsey was in charge and under him was the secretary Walter Gray who was an amateur goalkeeper at the club. According to John Cobbold's posthumous reminiscences in *The People* he claimed 'Alf asked me to give him a chance to prove himself as secretary and he quickly passed at least two of the chartered accountants' examinations, which are not easy. It was a remarkable achievement for someone whose entire career had been spent as a professional footballer. In Alf's first year, while Scott Duncan was still there, there was obviously a lot of friction between the two and I can't remember how many times Alf offered his resignation. But it was never accepted and the future proved just how right the board was.'

Rose soon became an institution at the club. He worked twelve hours a day over a six (sometimes seven) day week. He said 'My father worked in engineering and I was probably going to follow him. But one day the Chief Education Officer of Ipswich turned up at assembly at my school and asked if anyone wanted to work at the football club. I put my hand up and was invited to start the next week. They told me I was on trial for a month and I'm still on trial! When Wally retired in 1975, I took over from him and became secretary at the age of thirty-two.

'Alistair Cobbold, chairman at the time, was uncle of Johnny and Patrick. He was an austere type of man, much different to his nephews. Johnny was a marvellous man, a true gentleman. He had this air of being born into gentry and acted like it. He used to pull plenty of practical jokes. One day he shoved a big firework into a little bin, put a match to it and the lid blew high into the air, almost a hundred feet high.' Rose finally retired at the end of the 2002/03 season to complete forty-five years. The club arranged a testimonial dinner for him and David Sheepshanks made it into a *This is Your Life* evening with scores of his secretarial contemporaries turning up to make contributions.

Rose's final year was a trying one, with the club being caught up in the ITV Digital collapse and demotion to the First Division. Typically, he is still at the club, working part time. The modernised ground was totally changed from what it had been when he started. The former Army barracks, which was once used as the offices, was totally lacking in comforts and hadn't been improved. There were still holes in the wired windows, caused by stray bullets from the Second World War.

The veteran trainer Jimmy Forsyth, a Scotsman, washed the players' socks himself 'because socks shrunk when they did it themselves and we couldn't afford to keep buying new ones!' Rose recalled that Forsyth often hid the balls to protect them from too much usage. 'I always used to complain about the lack of balls,' said Ted Phillips. The players travelled by train or bus, or by bike. One of the first of the players to drive to the ground was the South African born goalkeeper Roy Bailey, signed from Crystal Palace. Bailey once recalled 'One day we arrived at Liverpool by train and I was astonished to find that Alf Ramsey got us to troop across the station yard to a bus. We got on and went to Anfield by bus. Alf paid the fares and sat back at the top of the bus with Jimmy Forsyth. The players always called him "Alf" but when he left in 1963 the practice ended. The players started to call the manager "Boss" or "The Gaffer" or something else.'

Phillips had a good relationship with Alf, but he rarely found that his manager would confide in him. Phillips took his season's goal total to 46 in 1955/56, partnering Ray Crawford (known as 'The Jungle Boy' after serving his National Service in Malaysia). Crawford, the son of a professional boxer, was as almost a prolific scorer as Phillips. In 1959 Ipswich reached the fifth round of the FA Cup, losing to eventual final losers Luton. Mr John was on holiday in Switzerland before the fourth round, played at Stoke, and sent a terse telegram to Ramsey saying 'I insist on a win.' He must have been drinking again. It was rather cheeky. However, the team duly won.

In the 1959/60 season, Ipswich was one of two of the ninety-two Football League clubs who went through the season without having a player cautioned or sent off. 'You couldn't say the same for the directors,' Phillips recalls. On a particularly cold night at Portman Road, hunching his shoulders and pulling up the collar of his fur-lined overcoat, Mr John said in the direction of Ramsey 'this is a bloody bad game. Wake up Ramsey!' Nottingham Forest were the opponents and they suddenly conceded an own goal. The Ipswich crowd cheered, some of the directors joined in but Alf sat in the front row without a murmur. 'Jump to attention Alf,' said the chairman, 'We've scored.' Ramsey eventually responded. 'Bloody cold isn't it?' he said. Later, the elder Cobbold was to recall 'That was the only time I think my brother Patrick gave anybody a rocket. He said "Alf, concentrate more on the game and less on the weather."'

NINE

MR JOHN LOSES THREE ELECTIONS DESPITE HAVING HAROLD MACMILLAN IN HIS CORNER

The name of John Cobbold is often found in the records at the House of Commons. There have been five Cobbolds serving as the Member of Parliament for Ipswich, stretching back to the mid-eighteenth century: three of them were named John, one Thomas Clement and the other Felix Thornley. One represented the Liberal party and they were all winners. Unfortunately the latest John Cobbold, the last of the line, was a three time loser in the 1950s. He admitted he had only played one game of football in his life and an ambition, namely scoring a hat-trick, was never fulfilled. 'I was picked for my platoon in Palestine, didn't do very well and wasn't picked again,' he said. His brief, political career recorded a different kind of hat-trick – three successive defeats at the hustings.

But it had all started so well. He soon struck up a rapport with the average voters and quickly won their esteem with his repartee and wit. Major Andrew Napier recalled 'At an election meeting at the Corn Exchange a large and irate man rushed from the back of the hall brandishing a chain above his head and yelling "You f——ing capitalist, I would like to punch your bloody brains in!" There was a shocked silence and Johnny responded "You'd have an awful job. I haven't got any brains." There were roars of laughter and the irate man disappeared. That one remark was thought to have earned him 2,000 votes, but alas Johnny failed to be elected, which was a great sadness. He would have been an excellent MP for Ipswich.'

John Cobbold started his abortive political career in 1950, when he became honorary treasurer of the Eye Division of Suffolk Conservative Association. Two years later he stood unsuccessfully as a Conservative candidate for the West Ward of the Ipswich municipal elections. Interviewed by an *East Anglian Daily Times* reporter he said 'There is no hope for this country under Socialism and everyone should work to his utmost to keep them out of power. It is a great honour to me, as a local man whose family has been in this area since 1723, to be chosen as the representative of the Conservative Party.' One of his main platforms was increasing pensions and, if pensions were not increased, he said, he would resign. He repeated his threat to resign on a number of occasions, and several times the level of pensions remained unchanged.

His chief adversary in his first General Election, in 1955, was a Labour heavyweight named Richard Stokes – a seasoned fifty-eight-year-old campaigner who had won the seat on four previous occasions. A Catholic, an Army Major and a former Minister of Works, Minister of Materials and Lord Privy Seal, Stokes had the advantage of being chairman and managing director of one of the biggest employers in the area, the local engineering company Ransomes and Rapier Ltd. The local newspaper showed a picture of John Cobbold standing behind a trestle table covered by a table cloth and on the table was a black cat, sitting attentively, looking at the audience. It caused a lot of laughs but the cat brought no luck to the smartly dressed, eager Conservative candidate. Stokes polled 32,306 votes to John Cobbold's 28,724 and in his speech Cobbold credited his campaign as a moral win. 'We have forced the Labour vote down by 754 votes compared to the previous General Election,' he said. Lady Blanche stood next to him, clapping enthusiastically.

In the next contest, a by-election in 1957 brought about by the death of Stokes, the great-great-grandson of the first Cobbold elected to the House of Commons put much more effort into his campaign, compiling a large, badly designed sheet entitled 'John Cobbold's News Letter, Ipswich Parliamentary Bye-Election 1957, polling day Thursday, 24th October.' It was distributed to almost every house in the town and its environs. Unfortunately, the word 'by-election' was misspelt 'bye-election.'

On the right was a picture of the candidate, his right hand stretched forward as though he was about to shake hands and his left hand was stuck in his jacket pocket – like the pose which the Duke of Edinburgh often affects. He wore a check, double breasted jacket, fawn trousers and brown brogue shoes. Underneath there was a invitation to 'meet your local candidate John Cobbold. Aged 30 and unmarried. Served as a Lieutenant in Welsh Guards during the War. After training as a brewer, became Managing Director of Cobbold and Co. of Ipswich. He is also Chairman of Ipswich FC. Was adopted for Ipswich in 1952, and contested in the 1955 General Election when he reduced the Socialist majority. Was re-adopted in May, 1956, as prospective Conservative Candidate.

'I have always been prepared to contest a Bye-Election in Ipswich but I very much regret the reason for the present one. Mr Stokes is sadly missed by his many friends of all political creeds, but a Bye-Election must now be fought, and I offer myself as your candidate. I have three main reasons.

'First, my great belief in the progressive Conservative policies which put the nation before any Party advantage. Secondly, my distrust of Socialism. I believe that Socialism is foreign to our British way of life and personal freedom. I also fear that it might be used as a stepping stone towards a Communist State. Thirdly, I believe that a Member of Parliament, whatever his politics, should be a local man, who knows and understands the problems of his Constituency.'

His claim that he 'served as a Lieutenant in the Welsh Guards during the War' was a slight exaggeration. He would have been aged twelve at the start of the Second World War and was just eighteen when the conflict came to an end. The former Liberal MP Dingle Foot, who held the Dundee constituency between 1931 and 1945, was Cobbold's opponent and came from the prominent left wing family in Plymouth. His brother Michael Foot, who was later a leader of the Labour Party and Minister, was renowned for his brilliant oratory and unkempt appearance, while another brother was the distinguished diplomat Sir Hugh Foot. Dingle Foot was the youngest member of Winston Churchill's wartime Coalition Government as Parliamentary Secretary to the Ministry of Economic Warfare and was one of the British delegates at the San Francisco Conference in 1945 which drew up the United Nations Charter. Educated at the now-closed

Bembridge School in the Isle of Wight and Balliol College, Oxford, he was President of the Oxford Union in 1928 and was called to the bar in 1930. He became a QC in 1954. Two years later he swapped parties and joined the Labour Party.

Cobbold's campaign organisers told him to keep bringing up the subject of Foot's change in politics and the avuncular QC showed a sense of humour when he was asked if he should forsake the Liberals and vote Labour. 'Yes,' he said. 'Follow my example.' Cobbold's key slogans were 'Keep the Outsiders Out!' and 'It's Cobbold of Ipswich – for Ipswich.'

The Times special correspondent said 'Today as he strode around the suburbs with his tireless grin, shaking the hands of everyone in sight, Mr Stephen McAdden, the Tory MP for Southend East, was cheerfully booming over the amplifier "keep the outsiders out…The rejects of other constituencies!" This may not cut much ice with every proud insider of Ipswich, but Mr Foot, via his publicity agent, has at least been driven to the expedient of compiling and issuing a statement about his wife's connexions with East Anglia, beginning in 1748 with a niece of the historian Thomas Gibbon. Then there is the undeniable fact that Mr Foot's virtues, great dignity and a devastating lack of guile, do not altogether, alas, make for an ideal parliamentary candidate, Labour or otherwise.' In those days the national newspapers devoted a lot of space to key by-elections and their best writers were sent to the front line to pen graphic accounts.

Cobbold said of his opponent 'As a voter I would be wary about someone who had changed his party recently. I am a local man with the interests of the town at heart and am not very keen on people who charge around the countryside seeking a seat. It's going to be a fight, without kid gloves and I'll win!' A report in the *Daily Telegraph* said 'The Tory candidate has flair for slogans. His Land Rover was heavily bespattered with blue and white pamphlets and posters and two enormous vote catching photographs of himself. He used a short burst over a loudspeaker saying "Beware of the Socialists, they'll nationalise your homes and for Heaven's sake don't vote Liberal. What a waste!" Every few yards he dismounted to knock at a door. He certainly had a gift with kissing babies!

'He usually majored on food saying things like "Have you forgotten that miserable piece of cow we were grudgingly given by the Socialists with their controls? Remember how you eked out your rations with a little bit of snoek or whalemeat, or off-the-ration offal?" Snoek is a fish from African waters which was imported at low cost from the poorer countries. "I never ate it," said the candidate.' Ronald Camp of the *Daily Mail* reported 'Mr Cobbold has sensibly cut out factory meetings and instead, concentrating on a full coverage of residential areas.'

The Liberal candidate Manuela Sykes, a lecturer, was nicknamed 'Little Audrey' by the Cobbold camp and when she posed for pictures showing the three candidates, she stood on a step while Cobbold and Foot stood on the pavement. She bore an amazing resemblance to Cherie Blair, QC. She had little support, financial or otherwise, but worked prodigiously hard, canvassing in the streets and addressing countless meetings at night. She said 'we were aiming for 8,000 votes but now I expect 10,000.' As it turned out, she polled 12,857.

Cobbold invited Miss Sykes and Dingle Foot to attend a home game against Grimsby at Portman Road on 20 October 1957 in an obvious attempt to win the vote of the football fans. It was probably the first and last time three opposing political candidates sat on the front bench of a football club's directors' box. The ploy didn't really work for Cobbold. Miss Sykes was attractive and perky and there were plenty of wolf whistles around the terraces. At half-time Grimsby led 1-0 and Cobbold said 'if we lose at home the consumption of Cobbold beer in the town drops dramatically. If this score doesn't change my vote will drop even more.' Fortunately for him, his team finished up winning 3-2.

Earlier in the day, two vicars had invited the candidates to speak for ten minutes each at a church hall, and again Miss Sykes outscored her rivals. *The Times* correspondent reported 'she earned so much applause that she warned that her ten minutes would be reduced if that continued. The audience found that very endearing, as they did at another interruption when with a smile she ended a particularly long verbal ramble by Foot saying "I've forgotten how that sentence started!" Later she described another Foot claim, this time about the cost of living, as "piffle!" If Mr Cobbold spoke with charm and Miss

Sykes with passion, Mr Dingle Foot did so with the authority to be expected from his years and experience.'

Dingle Foot concentrated on foreign affairs, continually lambasting what he called 'The Wicked Men of Suez' – the Tory leaders headed by the former Prime Minister Anthony Eden. Clarissa, Sir Anthony's wife, described the failed invasion of Egypt in 1956 by the Anglo-French forces as 'like the Suez Canal flowing through our front room.' Michael Foot spoke passionately and at length at one of his brother's meetings and Hugh Dalton, the former Chancellor of the Exchequer, also spoke – albeit less passionately.

Cobbold should have been a short favourite to win the seat because he was a local man who was chairman of a thriving and popular football club. He was also given overwhelming support from the Tory leadership. The Prime Minister of the day, Harold Macmillan (his uncle), wasn't available to speak – he was with President Eisenhower in a summit meeting in Washington – but his wife, Lady Dorothy, arrived to whip up support and the Rt Hon. Iain Macleod, the Minister of Labour at the time, the Rt Hon. Viscount Hailsham, QC, chairman of the Conservative Party and Derek Walker-Smith, QC, all addressed packed meetings.

Lady Dorothy and her sister, Lady Blanche (the candidate's mother), drove to the local Tory headquarters and photographers snapped them having a cup of tea with the candidate and two hundred supporters. The cups and saucers were made of bone china. Did Lady Dorothy bring a message from the Prime Minister? 'Certainly not,' she said. 'I have come here as Mr Cobbold's aunt. I have plenty of election experience, you know.'

That night the Corn Exchange in the centre of Ipswich was packed for the visit of Lord Hailsham. Ronald Camp reported: 'The Hailsham bell rang out long and loud here tonight at the most crowded, excited meeting of this by-election campaign. Socialist hecklers began to ring a bell almost as soon as Viscount Hailsham began to speak for the Tory candidate, Mr John Cobbold.

'Immediately the new Tory Party chairman responded – using the bell with which he roused the Party Conference at Brighton. Gripping it with both hands he swung it up and down until the noise of the hecklers' bell was drowned. He told them "Anything you can do, we can do better. We can ring louder and longer than you." Then he said "Now we have had our little game, let us put our toys away." A voice from the floor shouted "Shut up Hailsham, you are talking rubbish!" Hailsham shouted back "Do you have a double first at Oxford, my man?" "No I haven't," said the man. "Well I have," said Hailsham. "Shut up and sit down".

'Lord Hailsham said he had resolved to speak at every by-election for the first few months of his new position. His general is going to fight in the front line. If there are any bloody noses or cauliflower ears to be got, let them be mine. If we win this by-election, as we mean to do, we shall take no credit except for the excellence of our cause. If we lose, let there be no backbiting, no blaming of the candidate, the organisation, or the agent. If there is any blame let the party chairman take it.' Three days later, perhaps Hailsham should have been there to take the blame because the Conservative candidate lost.

Cobbold had had a bad day the previous week, as William Barkley, the eminent *Daily Express* sketch writer wrote 'Mr Cobbold nearly upset his morning cup of tea today when he read the newspaper headlines. They were all about the Government changing its attitude to the inclusion of agriculture in the European free trade area. When he saw that he said "oh dear". When he read deeper he convinced himself that Mr Reginald Maudling did not really mean anything. Mr Cobbold refuses to believe that the Tory Government will go back on its pledges to agriculture, especially as East Anglia is a farming county. "If it did," I asked him, "would you resign?"

'This is a rather tender point. Mr Cobbold has already announced before he is elected that he will certainly resign within six months if the Government does not do something about old age pensions. So he burst into laughter and said "I cannot keep resigning all the time otherwise I would never be there at all." He is an endearing fellow. Following Dick Stokes, who, I gather, was increasingly popular with the Tories and less popular with the Socialists, it is difficult to fill the blank in representing this old city. There is some criticism of Mr Cobbold because he is not as old and established as Mr Stokes, who was sixty. Mr Cobbold is just of that age to be no longer a Young

Conservative and therefore to be pensioned off as an old boy. He is thirty-one. I must say if I had a vote in Ipswich it would go for Mr Cobbold, who is alert, intelligent and has deep, three-hundred-year-old roots in the city. [Actually the 'city' wasn't a city and never will be.] That is pretty decent of me because, as I indicated formerly, if I had a vote in Gloucester [the previous by-election] it would have gone to Mr Lort-Phillips, the Liberal. It happens that Mr Lort-Phillips is coming here tonight to support Little Audrey, Miss Manuela Sykes.'

Just before midnight of 24 October the result of the by-election was declared by the Mayor, Mr Robert Ratcliffe, from the balcony of the Town Hall in front of 2,000 people. As the noise abated he read out from a sheaf of papers in a stentorian voice 'John Cavendish Cobbold, Conservative, 19,161.' There were cheers, but not uproarious cheers. Half a dozen women in the front of the row in the main square, dressed in fur coats and hats, clutching their handbags, forced a smile or two. The Mayor continued 'Dingle Michael Foot, Labour, 26,898 votes.' The bulk of the audience threw their arms into the air and yelled like football fans. They knew that Dingle Foot couldn't be caught by Little Audrey. As the bedlam finally subsided, the Mayor intoned 'Manuela Sykes, Liberal, 12,587 votes.' Loud cheers and shrieks. He had to shout to say 'I declare Dingle Foot member for Parliament of the constituency of Ipswich.' A roar erupted from all sides and the festivities, dancing and singing and hugging, went on for more than an hour. The pubs were closed and no-one could have a drink. The losing candidate would no doubt have loved one – and a stiff one at that.

Dingle Foot was the first to shake the hand of Miss Sykes, a graduate of London University who had increased the Liberal vote by 50 per cent. A picture, taken by an *East Anglian Daily Times* photographer, showed Miss Sykes, wrapped up in a white fur coat, standing alongside Cobbold, who wore a somewhat fixed smile, clad in a check jacket, a woollen waistcoat and a blue tie. Foot, aged fifty-two, his dark hair combed back in the style of the 1950s, stood next to his wife Dorothy, who surprisingly wore a rather serious expression. 'We have got the decisive victory we expected,' he said. Cobbold said 'The Liberal intervention obviously affected the election more than I would have thought.' The Conservative vote had fallen by 9,563 – a crippling blow for Cobbold and his party. Hugh Gaitskell, the Leader of the Socialist Party, said 'It was a most satisfactory result. It seems to be a case of Dingle bells, Dingle bells, Dingle all the way.' The next day Cobbold told the local *Daily Star* 'I will stand again.' And he did.

Within a few weeks he faced opposition from some factions of the local party. A group called the Ipswich Conservative Action Group called for his removal and pamphlets were sent through letter boxes saying that Cobbold was 'an unsuitable candidate.' His opponents claimed 'that wealth and privilege rather than professional ability and qualities of leadership led to his adoption and the procedure was undemocratic.' Privately, he told his associates 'they can f—— themselves.' A *Daily Telegraph* correspondent rang his home at Glemham Hall and he responded more restrainedly, saying 'It is up to the people of Ipswich. If they do not want me as a candidate I am willing to stand down. But this is the first intimation I have had of any lack of support. My leadership wasn't inspiring during the last General Election when I polled 19,191.' The dissidents circulated 4,000 members of the local Party and claimed 2,276 were in favour of his resignation with 509 against and 2,317 in favour of Lt-Col. Walter Hardy, a local builder, with 389 against.

During the summer the pro-Cobbold lobby built up and enough votes were pledged at another meeting of the local party to adopt him as the candidate for the 1959 General Election. This time there were few famous Tory politicians speaking on his behalf. Lord Chesham was one of the few at a lively meeting at the Corn Exchange. Cobbold enlivened the proceedings with a cheeky verbal onslaught on the US President Dwight D. Eisenhower, Harold Macmillan's old friend and leader of the free world, over foreign policy. There was so much heckling that he had difficulty in speaking over the babble and finally shouted out 'Do you want to listen to the facts, or are you frightened?' He showed plenty of courage to keep going against such determined opposition. There were even boos when he said 'The Conservative Government has done a great job and Mr Macmillan is one of the greatest Prime Ministers of all time. It would be a tragedy if the Tories lose. Never before have such a large number of people enjoyed the present prosperity. There is more money to spend and more to save.' A voice shouted 'You've never had it so bad, you git! Sit down.' The *Evening Star* reported 'Mr Cobbold, sporting a moustache, battled with countless interruptions but stuck to his guns.'

When the 1959 General Election was declared, in front of only 500 noisy, sometimes rowdy people at the Corn Exchange, Dingle Foot retained the seat but his majority was reduced from 7,737 to 3,215 – the lowest since Ipswich became a Labour seat in 1938. An electorate of 77,633, polled 81 per cent of the votes with Foot taking 41 per cent, Cobbold 36 per cent and Sykes 23 per cent. Cobbold's percentage had risen and he was picked up by a couple of younger, male Tory party members and chaired into the Conservative Club for a celebration party. But he knew it was all over. A month later he announced that he wasn't going to stand again. 'Three times is enough,' he said. 'I'm not going to try again because I get impatient with pessimists. I like to do things with more oomph.' He mentioned playing the Eton game in one of his St James's clubs and throwing lumps of Stilton at his foot-ball lunches. His political career was over. He had showed pluck and enthusiasm, but his opponents were probably right. His accent counted against him in a town which had 25,000 paid up trade unionists. He was still only thirty-two. His friend Mike Hollingsworth claimed later that he switched parties and voted Labour. 'He got very disillusioned with the Conservatives and he finished up voting for Labour,' he said.

The first MP from the Cobbold dynasty had been John Chevallier Cobbold, of Holywells, born at Ipswich on 24 August 1797, and edu-cated at the Grammar School at Bury St Edmunds and Eton. He rose to be the Lord of the Manor of Wix Bishop, High Steward of the Borough of Ipswich, a JP and MP for Ipswich between 1847 and 1868. His wife was Lucy, third daughter of the Revd Henry Patteson, Rector of Drinkstone and Wortham, Suffolk, and sister of the Rt Hon. Sir John Patteson, Judge of the Queen's Bench. He was a banker and also chairman of both the Eastern Union Railways and the Ipswich & Bury St Edmund's Railways. Both lines kept better time than the present lines in that part of the world: leaves often fell on them in the autumn, but the trains seemed to run more efficiently than modern

ones. In his twenty-one years in Parliament he was opposed to conces-
sions to the Roman Catholics and in favour of 'a judicious extension
of the franchise.'

The custom of the Cobbolds was to take the maiden name of
the mother to hand it on to the son, so the next John Cobbold to
become MP was John Patteson Cobbold of The Cliff, Ipswich – the
home of the Cobbold brewery on the banks of the Orwell. Educated
at Eton, J.P. Cobbold was a Captain-Commandant in the 1st Suffolk
Rifle Corps, the Mayor of Ipswich for a short time and MP for the
constituency in 1874 and 1875, until his death in the latter year at the
age of forty-four. He was the elder son of John Chevallier Cobbold
and was a banker and a brewer.

John Chevallier Cobbold's portrait is hanging at Glemham Hall,
along with a few more of the family portraits, all unsmiling and stern.
The portrait of John Cavendish Cobbold, the best known Ipswich
Football Club chairman, was the first of the line to be portrayed with
a grin on his face. John Cobbold (1746-1835) had fourteen children
and his wife Harriet was the daughter of the Revd Temple Chevallier
of Aspall, near Debenham, whose brother John was the local squire. A
lot of members of the Cobbold married into the clergy and the last
John Cobbold of the line once said 'they had to do it to keep them
on the straight and narrow'.

Harriet's first cousin was the mother of Earl Kitchener of Khartoum,
the First World War Field Marshal who drowned when his ship went
down in a storm in the North Sea. Kitchener was elected High Steward
of Ipswich in 1909, a hundred years after Admiral Nelson was given
the post. Nelson was fêted at a dinner at the Assembly Hall in Ipswich
attended by 300 dignitaries, including Mr and Mrs John Cobbold.
Nelson had bought a cottage called Round Wood, near Woodbridge
in 1789, but was rarely there before going off to defeat the French
and Spanish navies.

Another Cobbold who became an MP, in this instance between
1875 and 1883, was Thomas Clement Cobbold, who lived in King's
Street, St James's, London. He was the third son of John Chevallier
Cobbold (who broke ranks by being educated at Charterhouse, not
Eton – the Hill-Wood family tended to be taught at Charterhouse).

T.C. Cobbold entered the diplomatic service in Constantinople in 1854 and moved up the ranks in Lisbon, Oporto, Turin, Stuttgart and Baden Baden, finally becoming Secretary of the Legation at Rio de Janeiro.

Ipswich was the first town in England to build a prison which had separate sections for men and women and for ordinary criminals and debtors. Those who became drunk and disorderly in Cobbold public houses ended up in the new accommodation. Cockfighting attracted large crowds at the Cock & Pye in Upper Brook Street, which later became a Tollemache & Cobbold house. In 1835, after the Great Reform Bill three years earlier, a young reporter from *Morning Chronicle* named Charles Dickens was sent to Ipswich to observe the scene. While he was staying at the Great White Horse Hotel, which still survives, he started writing his book *Pickwick Papers* which was published a year later.

John Chevallier Cobbold also built railways, connecting Ipswich to Colchester, Bury St Edmunds and Norwich. The port of Ipswich expanded rapidly as the Cobbolds' interest spread into banking. Four of them were partners in Bacon, Cobbold & Co., another bank known as Cox, Cobbold and Co. and a third, Bacon, Cobbold, Tollemache. The banks eventually became Capital & Counties Bank (now part of Lloyds Bank). The head of another branch of the Cobbolds was the Lord Cobbold who was the Governor of the Bank of the England between 1949 and 1961.

The family was already full of brewers, soldiers, solicitors and vicars when a new name appeared. Henry Chevallier Cobbold was followed by John Dupuis Cobbold, educated at Eton and Cambridge University, who was High Sheriff of Suffolk and Mayor at the start of the First World War. One of his relatives was Lt Robert Henry Wanklyn Cobbold, educated at Marlborough and Cambridge University, who was killed while serving for the 2nd Battalion of the Rifle Brigade in 1916 and also that year 2nd Lt Bevill Tollemache, a close friend of the family, was shot and killed at Givency. As Lt Tollemache lay dying, he said to his men 'Please leave me, you will be captured.' They tried to save him, however, but some of them were slaughtered, too. The

Tollemache family were brewers and the company merged to become Tolly Cobbold in 1957. The Hon. Douglas Alfred Tollemache was one of the first directors to be appointed at the founding of Ipswich FC as a professional club in 1936.

There were literary figures among the Cobbold family, including the celebrated Elizabeth Cobbold (1765-1824), a writer, painter, botanist, musician, public speaker and philanthropist who was a friend of Sir Joshua Reynolds, Thomas Gainsborough and John Constable. Her daughters were tutored by Gainsborough before he left to make his name in Bath. Constable, born in East Bergholt, became a friend for thirty years and he often painted in the grounds of the Cliff Brewery. Its views of Ipswich across the river and its rushing stream turning the brewery's great water wheel was reminiscent of his beloved Flatford Mill. Often Mrs Cobbold sketched by his side.

In a letter to his wife about Elizabeth Cobbold, Constable wrote on 6 September 1807 'I have put off wrighting (sic) several days on Mrs Cobbold's account, most likely you have heard by your own family that she got a dreadful fall down a cellar at a milliner's shop. Her head is very much hurt, indeed so much so that for some days it was a doubtful matter. We think her now she is past danger. I should have been sincerely sorry had she made her exit, with all her faults I like her, there are many better, but there are but few like her, she is an original.'

Again in 1819, Constable wrote to his wife 'I was at Ipswich yesterday. Passed the morning with Mrs Cobbold and found her very kind in her enquiries after you and our darlings and very pleasant. She has a good deal of gout and was wishing for more. She says it has done her good.' Constable painted many portraits of the Cobbolds and their nine daughters and several are still on show, including ones at the Louvre and in the British Museum.

Elizabeth's husband John Cobbold, born in 1746, took over the brewery business in 1777, when his father Thomas Cobbold (1708-1777) died and he ran the business until 1835. The first Tomas Cobbold (1680-1752), who was a maltster, had founded the business in 1723 at King's Quay Street, adjoining the churchyard behind the Cups Hotel in Harwich. It was an exposed part of the coastline, with winds whipping in from the North Sea, but he soon profited from his decision to make beer for the soldiers at the Landguard Fort, opposite Harwich, and the sailors when their ships docked for supplies.

In a souvenir album published by Cobbold & Co. in 1923 to celebrate its bicentenary, Felix Walton, one of the directors, wrote in the foreword 'To do justice to the capacity and energy, and to record the history of the Cobbold Family, would require a substantial book. For two centuries and through eight generations in direct male line, they have built up a business which has contributed largely to the commercial prosperity of Ipswich. This souvenir published on the occasion of a Fete at Holy Wells to celebrate the bicentenary of the Cliff Brewery July 30th, 1923, is a simple record of some facts which may be of interest. It may be taken too as an acknowledgement and appreciation on behalf of the townspeople of Ipswich of the many services, generous gifts, and noble requests, for which they are indebted to various members of the Cobbold family.'

The first page contained 'The Pedigree of the Cobbold family' starting from Richard Cobbold of Tostock, who died in 1603. There are copious handwritten notes, in pencil, throughout the album. The author confessed that 'there was no likeness existed of Thomas Cobbold, the founder' and the first of the line to be pictured was John Cobbold, of the third generation. John Cobbold was a round faced podgy man. The next John Cobbold, of the fourth generation, was born in 1774 and died in 1860 and he had white hair and beard, with a touch of a smile. The next, John Chevallier Cobbold, MP, also had white hair and a beard with bright eyes and someone had written next to his picture 'J.C.C. admitted Attorney of the King's Bench, 25th June, 1822'. John Patteson Cobbold, MP, sixth in the line, lived from 1831 to 1875. Batting seventh in the Cobbold team was John Dupuis Cobbold, born in 1861, died 1929 at Trimley St Martin. He smoked through a cigarette holder and had dark brushed black hair and a bushy moustache. He was High Sheriff of Suffolk and Hon. Colonel of the 4th Suffolk Territorial Regiment and was also a Major in the First World War. Coming in at eight was John Murray Cobbold, also a High Sheriff of Suffolk who had a distinguished record in the First World War. Lt-Col. Cobbold must have been very frustrated that neither of his sons, John and Patrick, had children because that ended the direct male line. He was a handsome man in his peaked Scots Guards cap and uniform and a pukka gentleman.

TEN

DRINK AND BE MERRY!

None of the Cobbolds, right back to 1723, were big beer drinkers. They preferred wine, whisky and the odd brandy. The brothers John and Patrick stuck to wine, whisky and occasionally champagne. If anyone invited them to have a beer, they always insisted on a half, not a pint. Bob Wilson, the former Arsenal and Scotland goalkeeper and former TV presenter, knew them well and liked them and said 'they could drink for England'.

Writer Felix Walton recorded that 'Ale in some form was recorded to be in use when the Romans appeared in England 55 BC. Three drinks are mentioned, mead, cider and ale. This latter seems to have been a product of the Southern Counties where agriculture was to a certain extent already practised.' The other great brewing family in Suffolk was the Tollemaches, whose ancestors have been traced back to 1080. The Cobbolds and the Tollemaches first met in the mid-nineteenth century when John Chevallier Cobbold was introduced to John Tollemache through politics when they were MPs. John Tollemache was created Baron Tollemache of Helmingham for services to agriculture. The Baron wasn't a drinker (he must have been one of the few in either family). The Tollemache family, formerly living in Bentley, near a previous home of Bobby Robson, moved to Helmingham Hall, near Debenham, in 1490 and still live there. It was restored after the First World War and has a moat and the drawbridge is still raised and lowered. The first Lord Tollemache was reputed to be able to drive his coach-and-four into the courtyard of Ipswich's most famous hostelry, the Great White Horse, the hotel which was patronised by Nelson and Charles Dickens.

Three of his sons, the Hons Douglas, Stanhope and Mortimer Tollemache, ran the business and achieved a major coup by introducing their product to the students of Cambridge University; generations of Cambridge students were to be confirmed Tolly drinkers. Meanwhile, John Dupuis Cobbold extended his interests to other parts of East Anglia, branching out to Colchester and Eye. By 1896 it was clear that the Cliff Brewery was too small and too inefficient to meet the demand and the buildings were totally rebuilt.

The Cobbolds were sympathetic and helpful employers to their staff. Around the turn of the century they put up notice boards which recorded the names of their wives and children. One wife was listed as 'invalid'. The workers were encouraged to take up their grievances and they always received a reply. Sometimes they were sent cheques to settle pressing debts. They arbitrated on disputes, including one case when an irate employee complained that a neighbour had damaged his fence. But they could be strict if a pub tenant failed to meet his payments. One letter in 1878 was addressed to a Mr G.S. Cook, the tenant of the Station Hotel, Wivenhoe, telling him: 'We are persuaded you are doing no good for yourself or us and you ought to take the earliest opportunity to give up the Station Hotel. We have given you a good opportunity to recover yourself this summer, and all the while you have been going backwards instead of forwards.'

They organised parties for everyone on the staff, including a fete in July 1919, 'to celebrate the marriage of Captain John Murray Cobbold of the Scots Guards to Lady Blanche Cavendish, daughter of the Duke of Devonshire, sister of Dorothy, the wife of Mr Harold Macmillan'. The fête was staged by the staff, not the bosses, and the lunch menu failed to take into account any vegetarians because it read 'roast beef, boiled beef, roast mutton, boiled mutton, ham, veal and ham and steak and kidney pie, fruit tarts and custard and cheese'. A marquee was put up in the ground of the Cliff Brewery and 385 people were invited. Smoking was encouraged and the order to Messrs W.A. and A.C. Churchman, the local suppliers, read 300 cigars (to be selected), 4 one-pound boxes of cigarettes and 10 pounds of tobacco.'

When another party took place four years later, the numbers for lunch had swelled to 450 with 1,150 turning up for tea. It was a windy day and the committee noted a minute in the report 'Resolved that £1 extra be paid to Messrs Cowell's man in London whose box kite flying the banner broke from its rope at tea time and was lost.'

Between the two world wars, the Cobbolds ran 270 licensed properties and even the advent of the Depression in the 1930s did not seem to affect their business. After the Second World War broke out, most of the staff was called up. Lady Blanche worked in the brewery and remained as an active director until 1957, when the Cobbold and Tollemache families signed in a merger and the brewery was known as Tolly Cobbold. Another director, Robert Cobbold, a major in the Army, was killed in the fighting around Cassino, in Italy, and the chairman, Lt-Col. John Murray Cobbold met an even worst fate. Philip Wyndham Cobbold took over as chairman and his son Alistair, a Lieutenant Commander in charge of a frigate, also joined the board. When his father died soon after, he succeeded as chairman.

John Cavendish Cobbold was sent to learn the business at a Cheltenham brewery after leaving the Army and for a few weeks was chairman before Sir Thomas Bland, TD, DL, deputy chairman of Barclays Bank and High Sheriff of Suffolk, took over the merged companies. After Sir Thomas died in 1968, the chairmanship passed to the Rt Hon. Sir Allan Noble, KCMG, DSO, DSC, formerly MP for Chelsea and Minister of State for Foreign Affairs. Three years later Lord Tollemache, a great grandson of the first Baron, succeeded him.

Mr John became production director and put an hour or two in making everyone a friend. Richard Cobbold, son of Alistair, said 'He was adored by the staff and he knew the names of everyone, including their wives and children. He took an interest in everyone and was a great humanitarian. But I have to say he wasn't a great businessman.'

John and Patrick spent more time at the club than at the brewery and, in 1977, Tolly Cobbold was sold to the Ellerman Lines shipping company for the lowly sum of £5.7 million. The losses mounted and six years later the twin millionaires David and Frederick Barclay bought the company and all its pubs for just under £50 million (it is worth noting that in 2004 they bought the *Daily Telegraph* for £600 million). In 1989 Tolly Cobbold was sold to Brent Walker's Grand Metropolitan Group in a deal which could only be described as 'pretty messy and horrible'. George Walker, the top man at Grand Met, brother of the former heavyweight boxer Billy, struck a hard bargain. Most observers thought the company should have been sold for much more than the rumoured £2 million. Patrick Cobbold departed, with a heavy heart, and Lord Tollemache also left, ending almost three centuries of local involvement with the firm.

More than a hundred of the pubs were sold and the Walkers wanted to demolish the Cliff Brewery and build a marina and a leisure centre. They were thwarted by two senior executives, Bob Wales, the finance director, and Brian Cowie, the sales and marketing director. They applied to the Ipswich Borough Council to have the brewery listed and within forty-eight hours the council put the eighteenth-century building on the list, scuppering any plans to redevelop the prime site. There was a lot of unpleasantness in the months that followed but, with the support of the work force, Wales and Cowie successfully completed their management buy out from Brent Walker in June 1990.

Tolly Cobbold was still afloat, but it was sinking fast. Cowie, an affable Scot, was found dead at the cottage on the brewery site, having ended his own life. At the end of June 2001, the death knell for Tolly Cobbold was sounded when the company was taken over by T.D. Ridley & Sons Ltd at Hartford End, near Chelmsford. Brewing ceased at Ipswich at the end of the year with the production of Tolly Original transferred across the county boundary. Most of the seventy-strong staff were retained at the company's distribution operation in warehousing near the brewery. The Cliff was to be redeveloped into luxury loft style flats. The Brewery Tap, the pub on the site, closed at the end of the year. Patrick Cobbold and his directors had acquiesced in selling almost all the remaining of the pubs by the Walkers in 1989, leaving the brewery totally vulnerable. At their heyday, Tolly Cobbold owned 270 pubs. After the death of Captain Cobbold it was 110. John Cobbold boasted that he had drunk in all of them. Following the Walker brothers' intervention, there were six. 'We did well to hang on for another thirteen years,' said one of the directors.

You couldn't imagine the Cobbold brothers leading a rebellion, but one of the early Tollemaches, Richard Tollemache, led a revolt against the imposition of heavy taxes in 1381 and also against the excesses of the clergy. Two of his friends, Thomas Sampson (a wealthy yeoman of Harkstead) and John Battisford (a parson at Bucklesham), joined him. Perhaps Richard Tollemache should have taken charge 600 years later.

One of the early residences of the Cobbolds was The Old Manor House on St Margaret's Green, now a British Legion Club. 'It was at this house that Margaret Catchpole first went into service, as cook to the family continuing with them when they removed to Cliff House in 1797,' said a local historian. 'She stole the horse for which at Bury Assizes she was condemned to death, her sentence being commuted to transportation for life. The Old Manor House appeared to be an unattractive ivy clad building facing a road but the family went up market moving to Cliff House which had beautiful gardens, full of trees. The estate of Holy Wells had been in the possession of the family from 1789 and featured a lake, a waterfall, The Rhododendron Valley, the Pine Valley and an Italian garden.' As the *Evening Star* correspondent wrote 'It is a truly wonderful house with grounds which was admired throughout the county.' The public was admitted for one day every year with the proceeds being shared between the Queen's Institute Fund and 'nursing in Suffolk.'

The building, much enlarged over the years, featured oak panelling taken from the Tankard Inn and Neptune Inn and an overmantel from Eldred's House in Fore Street. The billiard room was particularly imposing and the carved panelling was later left to the local Council. By then the family had bought Glemham Hall in 1923 and sold Holy Wells in 1931.

The weaving trade, which had made Suffolk prosperous in the eighteenth century, had given way to industrialisation and the population of Ipswich soon doubled as the villagers moved into the town. In 1746, the year of the Battle of Culloden, Thomas Cobbold moved to a new site, Holy Wells, on the shore of the River Orwell, taking one of the coppers from King's Quay Street with him. (The original was still being used at the Cliff Brewery until the doors were finally shut.) The springs in Harwich were tainted by sea water, so Cobbold turned to the crystal clear springs of the Holy Wells estate at Ipswich, originally owned by Queen Edith, wife of Edward the Confessor. Local people believed in the miraculous curative properties of the water and made pilgrimages to the scene. The name of Ipswich came from two granges, Wicks Episcopi and Wicks Ufford within the mediaeval boundaries of 'Gripes Wic'. Wicks Ufford belonged to Earl Gyrth, who was killed in combat with William the Conqueror at the Battle of Hastings.

The Cobbolds moved into shipping, building twenty vessels which launched a flourishing trade to the Continent, India and China. A 220 ton barque built in 1847 was named *John Cobbold* and it is documented as once coming to the aid of a stricken vessel. But in the same storm, another ship sank with all hands. The Cobbolds had their own wharf by the start of the nineteenth century, although the calm prosperity was shattered when bread riots erupted. Volunteer constables, maybe forbears of Special Constable Patrick Cobbold, used their truncheons to beat back the assailants. A contemporary article described the scenes as the cavalry cleared the rioters from the streets, adding 'it says much for the good name of the company throughout all the disorders, the rioters were careful not to harm the premises of the Cliff Brewery'.

The father of Cardinal Wolsey was born in Ipswich and a school built in the name of the Cardinal still stands near the Cliff Brewery. A Richard Cobbold of Ipswich was said to have been a wine merchant to Elizabeth 1 and, in 1565, the Queen stayed at Christchurch mansion – which later became one of the Cobbold homes until it was presented to the Borough of Ipswich by Felix Cobbold in 1894. The Cobbolds were land owners before they took up brewing and one of their descendants was Reynold Cobbold, who outlived all his sons when he died at the age of 102.

In terms of longevity, the Revd Richard Cobbold, the son of Elizabeth and a friend of famous artists, held the family clerical record.

As well as holding the post of rector at Woolpit, he was incumbent of St Mary-le-Tower, Ipswich, for fifty-two years until he died in 1831. The funerals of most of the Cobbolds and some other notable locals, including Sir Alf Ramsey, were held in St Mary-le-Tower Church. The church still receives £2 a year from a Cobbold public house, the Swan Inn in King Street, as expiation for a murder committed on its premises.

Elizabeth was the forerunner of dating parties, inviting up to a hundred of potential beaux to her annual St Valentine's Day gatherings. She wrote odes and encouraged the guests to write their own. She had seven children from John Cobbold at the Cliff, and her husband previously had fourteen from his first marriage, bringing up the total to twenty-one. The Revd Richard (1797–1877) was her twelfth son and a renowned poet and painter. His best literary work was *The History of Margaret Catchpole* a social history about a young Suffolk girl.

Margaret had a chequered career. In her teens, she saved the life of her mistress by riding to the nearest doctor to summon assistance and later pulled William Cobbold, one of Elizabeth's sons, out of a river. Later she became embroiled with a smuggling gang and was sentenced to death for stealing a horse. After escaping from prison, she was arrested, tried and sentenced to death again only for Elizabeth Cobbold to plead successfully to a judge to commute her sentence. She was deported to Botany Bay at the age of twenty-six and wasn't heard of again.

Another of Elizabeth's sons, Revd Edward Cobbold, died at his own hand in 1860. A local newspaper reported that Edward, a talented writer and poet, became deranged and chopped his own head off with a ceremonial sword at Hatchett's Hotel, in Dover Street, London. There was no evidence of anyone else being involved. Yet another poet in the family was Dorothy Cobbold, who started writing poetry at the age of seventy-two and wrote prolifically until she died at the age of eighty-six.

ELEVEN

LADY EVELYN MURRAY

The first lady Muslim in England

The first reference to the Cobbold family in the Domesday Book was 'Cubold' and in 1223 there were mentions of Robert le Cobeler, Corbould, Corbound, Cubill, Cobell, Cobel and Cubel. Throughout this long history, the wife of John Dupuis Cobbold, Lady Evelyn Cobbold, the seventh daughter of the Earl of Dunmore, was the most remarkable woman in the whole family. She was the Queen Mother figure and lived until she was ninety-seven. The grandmother of Captain John Murray 'Ivan' Cobbold, she was one of the first titled women to become a Muslim and also the first to cross the Libyan desert in 1911. Angus Sladen, one of her great-grandchildren, described her as 'a very strong personality'. Two of her ancestors, Lord Charles Murray, the first Earl of Dunmore, and Lord William, the third Earl, were imprisoned in the Tower of London for 'pro Royalist activities'. William fought at Prestonpans, Falkirk and Culloden. The family motto, very alliterative, needed some interpretation: it was 'Forth Fortune and Fill the Fetters'.

Lady Evelyn inherited her love of travelling and writing from her father, Charles, who was Colonel in Chief of the 4th Battalion of the Queen's Own Cameron Highlanders. He wrote accounts about his time in the Pamirs, Kashmir and Western Tibet, and his books were lavishly illustrated in watercolours. As a child, Lady Evelyn spent the winter months living in a Moorish villa on a hill outside Algiers and learned Arabic. 'My delight was to escape my governess and visit the mosques with my Algerian friends,' she wrote, 'and unconsciously I was a little Moslem at heart.' She also lived in Egypt and became friendly with T.E. Lawrence, whom she sometimes gave money to when he was almost destitute. Alexander Edward, her younger brother, served in India and was awarded the Victoria Cross in the Afghan War in 1898, the MVO in South Africa in 1906 and the DSO in the First World War in 1917.

She wrote several books, was a first-class shot and loved stalking. Her second book, entitled *Wayfarers in the Libyan Desert* was a classic of its time and genre. She wrote expressively and sympathetically about the Arab psyche, explaining that Muslims didn't fear death. 'The warm sunshine, the great silence of the desert, is made for peace,' she wrote. 'The stress of Western life is unknown and these people possess an impregnable faith, joined with the power of concentration, and they find their happiness in dreamy contemplation.'

Her writing attracted fan mail from around the world and a correspondent from Hyderabad gushed 'Your work *Pilgrimage to Mecca* is one which will assuredly turn the hearts of Muslims towards you from every corner of the world, should they but chance to read it once'. Lady Evelyn, a society beauty from the family seat at Dunmore in Stirlingshire, was a regular visitor to the Arab world and first met John Dupuis Cobbold in Cairo. They were married in 1891 and the ceremony was attended by scores of nobility. An anonymous writer from *Gentlewoman: The Illustrated Weekly Journal for Gentlewomen* dated 23 April 1892, wrote 'The Cobbolds have been proverbially lucky, and Dame Fortune assuredly never granted the present head of the family a greater favour than when she led his steps to Cairo the winter before last, while Lord and Lady Dunmore with their daughter Lady Evelyn, were staying there, as has been their habit for several years past in the cold season. As you enter the drawing room and are prettily greeted by Lady Evelyn, you have sufficient proof of Mr Cobbold's taste and critical judgement in his matrimonial choice. In Lady Evelyn's quiet and gentle manner there is evidently a store of reserved force, and her endeavours to make your visit an agreeable one are tempered with regret that Mr Cobbold's business engagements have that day called him away, for as Lady Evelyn kindly remarks, "My husband so much wanted to meet you, while his local knowledge would, doubtless, have interested you."'

Such eloquent writing would certainly improve the writing in the issues of today's *Hello*, or *OK!* The journal was priced sixpence and the article started 'For more than a hundred years past the prosperity of Ipswich has been as much due to the energy and public spirit distinguishing the family of the Cobbolds, as their opulence is attributable to the town itself. Quite a story, diversified with strange incident and charming romance, might be written in connection with the Cobbolds, from John Dupuis Cobbold, the present owner of Holywells, back to his ancestor John Cobbold, the progenitor, up till now, of six generations.

'The name of Cobbold is woven into the history, not only of the town but of the county, for it may be remembered that the John Cobbold aforesaid – was the parent of twenty one children and that succeeding members of the family have continued to be blessed with numerous olive branches.

'Ipswich is a curious old town, evidently once confined within the walls of fortifications, from the winding nature and narrowness of the streets. It was intimately connected with Tudor times, and displayed immense enterprise in shipping operations, while its breweries and granaries have long been associated with the Cobbolds. As Lady Evelyn's pony cart, with a high spirited cob, negotiates the tortuous streets, you note many fine old houses of the Charles II period with picturesque gables and carved brackets. You rapidly pass the Tudor gateway, the sole relic of Sir Thomas Wolsey's college, which supplanted an Augustinian Priory, and was in time demolished by Henry Vlll, when the Cardinal went out of favour. And you recalled the fact that, in the "White Horse Hotel" in Tavern Street, Mr Pickwick intruded on the privacy of the lady with the yellow curl papers. (Charles Dickens was a frequent guest).

'Within hail of the Gas Works, just outside the town, beyond which are the granaries and wharves connected with the old Cliff Breweries of the Cobbolds, the pony cart turns sharp left, through the opened lodge gates of Holywells (the home of Mr John Dupuis Cobbold and Lady Evelyn). Cut partly on the side of the hill, the road twists at acute angles, ascending to the elevated ground on which old John Cobbold built the present house. (Holywells was demolished later and became a park).

'You will not have been five minutes in the house before you will have ample evidence that Mr John Dupuis is an ardent sportsman, that is to say with the gun, for, as Lady Evelyn will presently tell you, the fox is tabooed on the estate, "the cult of the sacred bird". But every

representative of "fur and feather" from home covers and from foreign
jungles, seems to have fallen to his unerring aim. In no house, perhaps,
with the exception of Sir Samuel Baker's, have I come across finer
specimens of the skins of wild beasts and of birds, beautifully preserved
by Rowland Ward, than at Holywells. A huge brown bear on his hind
legs is so well posed that he seems ready to embrace you, and makes
a prominent figure amongst the couches covered with skins innu-
merable, gaudy Indian sleighs, bright rugs, carved screens and quaint
bureaux, whilst the painter's art is represented by many rare walls.

'As I was chatting with her in the drawing room, which opens out
into the conservatory, I noticed amongst the handsome appointments
of the room, a lovely inlaid cabinet panelled with sepia drawings,
quite unique but for the existence of its fellow, the property of the
King of Denmark. A screen inlaid with green jade, silver, mother-
of-pearl, especially took my fancy, and another screen was delightful
to the eye with coloured sketches of Lady Evelyn's favourite views
of Egypt, while a grand armchair of lacquer, a family relic, was very
interesting.

'Faithful to dear old Ipswich, her husband has covered his drawing
room walls with pictures of its quaintly ancient architecture. Some of
these date back quite two hundred years, and seem to form a link, in
point of time, between the jar of the loveliest Christmas roses, and the
antique silken embroideries which cover many a couch. Attachment to
Ipswich gives the works of Gainsborough, who was born in the town,
still greater value in Mr Cobbold's eyes, and he is very proud of his collection; whilst the same love for everything connected with the locality
enhances the beauty of the magnificently carved oak, which has been
transferred from many an ancient panelled room in Ipswich, notably
from the house formerly occupied by Henry VIII, to furnish his private
smoking den. This is a perfectly ideal room in point of colouring. The
dark oak of the panelling has many a curved legend thereon; the grand
overmantel is grouped with carved oak figures over the open grate,
which is adorned with Damascus tiles, and makes a charming contrast
to the deep crimson morocco covering of every chair and lounge.

'Another room, which would prove particularly tempting to a studious mind, is the library, which leads out of the drawing room. It

is lined with hundreds of volumes, and you may rest assured every work treating of Suffolk may be found there. It is well stored with cabinets filled with rare Delft china, and the quaint wallpaper was sent to Japan to be painted, I was told. Crossing the central hall, you enter the dining room through a little cosy antechamber. The portraits of many generations of Cobbolds look down at you and you would gladly make the acquaintance of the newly arrived scion of the house, Miss Winifrid Evelyn, aged three months, but excursions from the nursery are chiefly confined to the beautiful grounds, backed by fine woods and watered by a pretty lake, on which black Australian swans disport themselves.' As the anonymous author ends his interview, he concludes: 'Lady Evelyn very kindly drives you to the station in her victoria with the high stepping roans, and when you take leave of her, you cannot but reflect that the county society has every reason to congratulate itself on the acquisition of such a charming member.'

Some of the Cobbold trophies and furnishings were moved later to Glemham Hall and are still there. Five years after the article was published, Lady Evelyn gave birth to John Murray Cobbold, the founder of the professional football club, in 1897. Guests were sent pink invitations headed 'Festivities at Holywells' and a line at the bottom informed them 'All Amusements free of charge'. Winifred, her first child, was the subject of a detailed, illustrated album which has survived. Winifred was born on 10 January 1892 and there is a poignant sepia photograph of her staring up from her high pram, wrapped up in masses of clean white clothes. There was no semblance of a smile from the hundreds of pictures, nor even from the Hon. Mary Fraser and Lady Evelyn who leant their heads against a stuffed bear in an unusual, stunted, pose. In another picture, taken on an unmade up, tree lined road a melancholy Lady Evelyn with her dachshund (named Jim), the baby Winifred and an apprehensive husband John Dupuis looked as though they were expecting an imminent assault from dissenting peasants.

Lady Evelyn wrote in the weighty album 'On the 15th of January, Father went off to Biskra in Algeria to shoot and Baby and Mamma went to Leckhampton Court for the month of February. We came home again on 5th March and Father came back too. Here is a photo of Baby one Sunday in March when Father and Mamma and Jim were all taking care of her. Here is also a little photo of Mamma and Jim, the dear little dachshund given to Mamma in January which Baby used to tease and worry dreadfully. But Jim was very good and so patient and he grew to love Baby and go for walks with her.' Mamma, of course, was Lady Evelyn. Another daughter, Pamela, was born at Holywells in 1900 and was described as 'a very pretty baby' by her mother. On a fishing trip to Norway she reported 'it was a very bad fishing year'. Except that 'Dada' got one of 27lbs and Mama got one of 26lbs!

In 1911 she went on her greatest adventure, leading the expedition from Egypt and across the Libyan Desert. She wrote 'there were twenty-three white people, twelve baggage camels, two dromedaries, a sand cart and pony, five donkeys, twenty-three Arabs and our drago-man called Fadlallah and his assistant Toulba, known as Toulba The Terrible. Four tents were pitched to sleep all through the day and we travelled at night to see the Pyramids in the dawn. We lived on dates, milk and bread. Women bow their heads alone to Kismet, meeting death undaunted for when it comes they recognise the will of Allah. Old and young, they accept what fate brings, knowing no fear.'

By the end of the Great War, the marriage between Dada and Mamma was breaking up and they separated. Her husband bought the Glencarron Estate for her. As it was more than five hundred miles from Ipswich, the trip might seem to be rather time consuming but in those days it was possible to catch an express train from London to Inverness quicker than the present day. A short ride from Inverness to Glencarron would deposit the traveller in time for lunch. A correspondent of *The Scots Magazine* observed that 'like so many such establishments built for the Victorian sporting gentlemen, Glencarron had its own railway halt'. Lady Evelyn loved being there when the salmon was running and she also loved working on the gardens. The Lodge, used by her grandchildren, was a square, ugly looking four-storey building. But that was the place where she wanted to be buried, 'where the stags can walk over my grave'.

Her husband died in 1929 and that gave her the chance to fulfil her ambition to achieve the Hajj – the journey to Mecca every devout

Muslim yearns for. She had to be persistent. She wrote to King Ibn Sa'ud asking for permission to travel, only for the King to tell her that she was barred from going to Mecca because she was a Westerner. Undaunted, she contacted the King's son, Emir Faisal, and finally she was allowed to proceed. She journeyed in a hired Ford car, lent by a friend who was an associate of a Mr Philby (whose son was the spy Kim Philby). At the age of sixty-six, she arrived in Mecca in 1933 and finally attained the dignity of a 'Hajj'. She wrote in her book 'I was garbed in a straight, white robe, over which I wear a long white coat reaching to my feet. I swathe my hair in soft muslin and a tight turban of the same kind binds my hair, allowing no strand of hair to show. I cover my face with a thin straw mat pierced with holes to allow me to see and breathe from which a long white muslin veil falls halfway to the feet.

'My luggage was small. I had none of the usual impediments of European clothes, no hats, even frocks or rows of shoes. The mosquitoes buzz round and I take refuge under my net, but one of the enemy has entered, and as I may not kill it, I unpack a tube of Flit that I was given on leaving Jeddah, a priceless gift. I smear it on myself, and if the mosquitoes close to commit suicide, I feel no responsibility.' The Ipswich daily newspaper reported 'Lady Evelyn can claim to be the first English woman to make the pilgrimage to Mecca. The territory is forbidden ground to all save those who have professed allegiance to Islam. Lady Evelyn gives a vivid account of her experiences when she made the journey to the Holy City, which for more than 1,300 years has been the centre of Islamic devotion.

'Arrived there, she circumnambulated the Kaaba seven times, kissed the black stone which was the corner stone of the edifice rebuilt by Abraham, drank of the waters of the well of Zem Zem, which saved the lives of Hagar and Ishmael, made supplication, ran seven times along the path traversed by Hagar in her desperation, and afterwards visited the graves of the Prophet's family. Lady Evelyn further describes how she journeyed to Arafat, the mount marking the place when Adam first met Eve, and returned thence armed with seven stones to fling at the rock shadowing the place where the Devil tempted Abraham to disobey the Divine command to sacrifice Isaac.

This graphic article is fully illustrated from photographs, some of them taken by the pilgrim herself.'

When she was ninety-five, Lady Evelyn fell and broke a leg in her London house and asked to be moved to Glencarron, sensing that her end was imminent. On 25 January 1963, in the middle of one of the coldest years for centuries, she died in a nursing home in Inverness. *The Scotsman* had a headline 'Earl's daughter who became a Moslem' and *The Times* reported 'She had all the ingredients of the indomitable British lady traveller. When over the age of sixty, she, who had been a Moslem for many years, undertook the pilgrimage to Mecca.'

It should have been a Highland funeral. There was a piper to lead the way and some of the mourners wore kilts of Murray and Atholl tartan, but the temperature was below freezing and their kilts were hidden by their overcoats. Fierce winds blew hail and sleet into their faces. According to her religion, she had to be buried upright in a grave, facing Mecca. The nearest Imam was based at the Shah Jahan Mosque in Woking, Surrey, and had to be driven to the North of Scotland, a hazardous journey which took three days.

Several dozen freezing mourners stood bracing themselves as the service began. The views were magnificent, commanded by the peaks of Moruisg and Maoile Lunndaidh, but the low cloud and the swirling hail obscured them. The Imam took out a compass to take his bearings. After a long pause, he said suddenly 'It is not facing Mecca, it is 20 degrees out.' The faces of the bearers and the gravediggers blanched. One could be heard to say 'Christ, we're not going to dig another one! It would need a pneumatic drill to get into the frozen ground.' There was a long silence. Finally, the Imam relented and performed the rites. The coffin was lowered and the wreaths were heaped on to the earth. 'The deer will get the flowers,' someone said. Another of the gravediggers said 'I am sure Lady Evelyn would approve!'

There are two rectangular headstones on the slope: a small one of Lady Evelyn's (which has been defaced) and the other, a taller one, commemorating the death of Squadron Leader Algernon 'Toby' Sladen, who was the son of Winifred, Lady Evelyn's elder daughter. He was awarded the DSO in the Second World War and died in 1976.

1 Lady Evelyn Cobbold, daughter
Winifred and son John Murray Cobbold,
the Army officer who was the first
chairman of Ipswich Town FC when they
became professional.

2 King George VI shooting with Captain
'Ivan' Cobbold, August 1939.

3 *Above left:* Patrick at Eton.

4 *Above right:* John at Eton as a seventeen year old.

5 Glemhall Hall, home of the Cobbold family, where John Cobbold played a pretty poor game of tennis.

6 The stairs at Glemhall Hall which John Cobbold slid down in his pyjamas at parties.

7 Capel Hall, John Cobbold's country house, where he hosted some risqué parties.

8 Mr John at a delapidated Portman Road in 1958, after he became the youngest director in the Football League.

9 Patrick on parade in Bermuda.

10 Lt Patrick Cobbold in command of the 1st Battalion Scots Guards demo platoon at Pickering, Yorkshire in 1955. He was shot in the leg (covered up) by one of his soldiers.

11 Alf Ramsey.

12 Alf starts in his spartan office, 1958.

13 Alf, with a rare drink in his hand, JC, with always a glass in his right hand, and the late Roy Bailey, one of the best goalkeepers at Portman Road.

14 A happy Sir Alfred and Lady Victoria.

15 Patrick, Lady Blanche and the Conservative candidate.

16 Lady Blanche and her mother Lady Evelyn, the Duchess of Devonshire, the first Muslim aristocrat to be welcomed at Mecca.

17 Colin Viljoen about to score. Far left is West Ham's Frank Lampard Snr over Geoff Hammond, and Bobby Moore is centre.

18 & 19 Jimmy 'Sticks' Leadbetter in 1962 – and forty years later. Not much difference when his dentures are in place.

20 The celebration dinner at the Savoy Hotel for winning the First Division Championship in 1961/62. Alf Ramsey is left of the trophy (long table at top) and John Cobbold is flanked by Alan Hardaker (right) and Bob Lord (left). Patrick Cobbold sits with the players (in front of the trophy) with Roy Bailey (left) one of the few smiling. Another is author Brian Scovell (leaning back in forefront).

21 Sir Alf Ramsey's statue with golfing colleague Len Barnes.

22 Bobby Robson behind the Iron Curtain with his assistant Bobby Ferguson. Brian Talbot is the man on the left.

23 Mr John (bottom, centre left) with the President of the Ukraine.

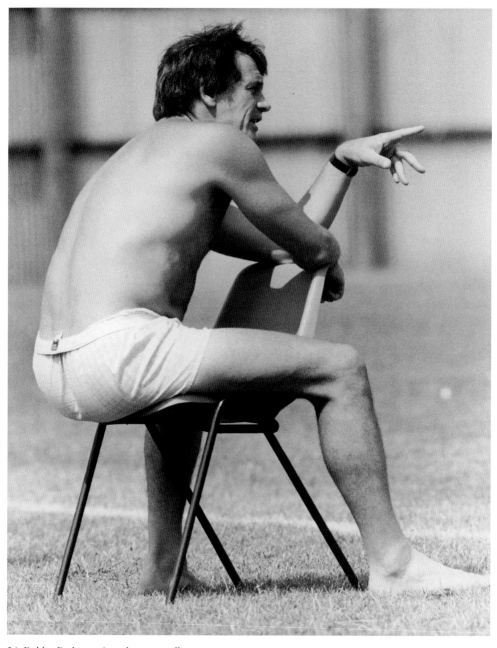

24 Bobby Robson gives the team talk.

25 *Opposite above:* Bobby Robson flanked by the Cobbolds and, going round from the left of Mr John: Bryan Hamilton, Geoff Hammond, Ipswich skipper Mick Mills, Brian Talbot, Kevin Beattie, –?–. George Burley, Les Tibbott, Murray Sangster and Harold Smith (directors).

26 *Opposite below:* Mr Patrick, Bobby Robson, Mr John, Willie Kerr and another man watching a video.

27 Frans Thijssen is congratulated by John Wark (left), Alan Brazil and Russell Osman.

28 Allan Hunter keeps his eye on the ball as John Wark (left) watches Liverpool's Graeme Souness.

29 Mr John in a hurry as he hands over a cheque to one boy, George Burley, and shakes the hand of another. The boy on the left has a quizzical look.

30 *Below left:* Patrick entertaining Italian sponsors and one of his more docile animals.

31 *Below right:* FIFA president Sir Stanley Rous cuts the tape with Patrick as the Pioneer Stand is opened.

32 A dinner for Ken Brightwell and Harold Smith (front) on retiring as directors. From left to right, back row: David Rose (secretary), John Kerr (former chairman, current director), David Sheepshanks (chairman), the late John Kerridge (former director), Richard Moore (director), Philip Hope-Cobbold (director), George Burley (former manager).

33 The day John Lyall arrives as the new manager and Patrick shows some anxiety already.

Lady Evelyn's granite slab carries a translation of the opening verse of the 23rd Chapter of the Koran, beginning 'Allah has made the heavens and all the earth'.

Lady Evelyn had four grandchildren: Pamela (1920-1994), Jean (1921-2002), John (1927-1983) and Patrick (1934-1994). The girls had governesses and were educated at Glemham Hall in their early years. Jean and Pamela were in the ATS and Pamela married twice, with both marriages ending in divorces. Neither of her brothers married and perhaps they were deterred by her marital experiences. Her first marriage was to William Vernon Hope-Johnstone, ending in 1951, and her second marriage, to Ambrose Alexander Cadogan, ended ten years later. She had two sons, Philip William Hope-Johnstone, an Army major who was born in 1943, and Charles Hope-Johnstone, born in 1948.

TWELVE

'SHUT UP RAMSEY!'

In eight seasons Ipswich rose from the bottom of the Third Division to earn promotion to the First Division in 1960/61. It was a good way to celebrate its twenty-fifth anniversary as a professional club. In the next season they won the Championship to outdo Tottenham Hotspur, the greatest club side of its time. The bar takings soared and the Cobbolds threw countless parties, even staging an extravagant dinner at London's Savoy Hotel to honour the champions. Cobbold came up with a new wheeze, inviting Bunnies from the Playboy Club, dressed in skimpy black and white outfits with tails. Unfortunately, they took offence with his use of four letter words and fled. Ted Phillips recalled 'They shot off but it was a great speech. He made the best speech I've ever heard. It was a scream.'

Alf Ramsey rose to speak, droning on in a monotonous tone, and a voice kept interrupting... 'C'mon Ramsey, stop boring everyone...

Enough's enough, Alfie.' It was the chairman, Mr John. 'Alf talks too
much,' he explained. Cobbold wore a black pinstripe suit because he
thought it was inappropriate to wear evening dress. The menu was
beautifully printed in French and the names were set out in full – such
as Horace Millward, Edward Phillips, Raymond Crawford and even
the groundsman, Frederick Blake.

Cobbold was not as animated as usual because he sat at the long top
table flanked by his enemy Bob Lord, the chairman of Burnley FC
(and known as the butcher of Burnley), and Alan Hardaker, secretary
of the Football League. Cobbold used to refer to Lord as 'Bollock
Chops' when he spoke of him in the Ipswich boardroom. Lord wore his
Burnley blazer, representing the League and the FA at the Savoy function, and Hardaker, a former Naval Commander, wore a sober suit.

Hardaker ran the League's Management Committee like an
Admiral, bullying the members, laying down policy and carrying it
through. He was variously known as 'the great dictator,' 'the Cagney
of the League' and 'the League's most celebrated enforcer.' He actually looked like Cagney and his language was often brutal. 'Most of
them are f——ing idiots,' he would say and Cobbold usually agreed.
Hardaker reigned as secretary for twenty-two years, from 1957 to
1979. He despised Revie, calling him a cheat. One of his truest comments, at a speech at another footballing occasion, was 'The first
priority of everybody in professional football should be to attract as
many paying customers as possible, and we are kidding ourselves if
we believe otherwise. Spectators are what professional football is all
about. Without them it has no point, no status and no future. I know
professionals who see the game as their own property and the fans as
people whose part in the ritual is a kind of privilege. The positions
should be reversed.'

He was opposed to the excessive amount of televising of football
and twenty-five years later he was probably proved right. Millions of
obese football watchers are now slumped into their armchairs, millions
of others are looking up to TV sets in pubs and fewer and fewer young
men have the inclination to play the game.

Lord was wearing his hearing aid at the Savoy dinner and feigned
deafness on a number of occasions when Cobbold tried to speak. It

was a convenient solution for both men. In his usual abrupt manner, Lord said in his speech 'Ipswich only won it because Burnley threw it away'. Cobbold and Ramsey declined to clap, or smile. Lord was not known as a joker.

Before the first course, Cobbold announced they had commissioned a photograph of the whole room, featuring every person there. A man climbed on a stepladder to ask the audience to face him. Not a single person smiled, or laughed, or gestured – even the Cobbolds. It wasn't quite the magnificent, uproarious celebratory event the Cobbolds planned. But they made up time later in the bar. 'These prices are a bit steep,' said Patrick. And as always, the Cobbolds paid the bill.

One writer, Geoffrey Green of *The Times*, described Ipswich Town's winning of the First Division trophy as 'the football miracle of the century'. Green, the doyen of sports writers, variously the cricket correspondent, lawn tennis correspondent, sports editor and the football association correspondent of *The Thunderer*, had a similar background to John Cobbold – educated at a public school, Shrewsbury, and brought up in a generation which espoused Corinthian principles. And he loved a drink. He had a huge capacity for spirits but it didn't affect his skill to put words together. He never used a typewriter, nor a laptop. He would pick up a phone and ad lib a thousand words to a typist at the office of *The Times* without a mistake. He was a gentle, much loved man and his autobiography was entitled *Pardon me for Living*. A man without ego, he declined offers from many publishers to write his life story but his daughter Ti said 'Papa, I want to know something about you when you were younger and some of the things you got up to'. So he relented. John Cobbold started his autobiography around the same time but he was too late. He filled only two tapes before he died.

The bohemian Green was a frequent drinking partner with Cobbold but, strangely, he never mentioned him in his book (he only made cursory mention of Alf Ramsey, whom he also spent much time with). He preferred to write about 'teams and players who have been touched by the angels,' not about normal people. Invited to speak at the annual dinner of the Football Writers' Association, a tipsy, swaying Green stood up and sang a song, *Over the Rainbow* to the delight of the 700 players, officials and journalists. He was definitely in the same drinking class as John Cobbold. Like Cobbold, he ate very little. But he made up with alcohol. He also dressed the same way as Cobbold, often wearing a shabby, ankle-length coat with fur-lined collar. Brian James, the former *Daily Mail* correspondent, spoke of a match in Moscow when Green mysteriously disappeared. 'No-one heard from him for several days and the rest of us covered for him, filing reports to his newspaper,' he said. 'We loved him to death but it was very difficult to get him out of bars.'

After the 1962/63 season, when Ipswich finished seventeenth, Cobbold was asked what was his biggest disappointment following the Championship success. 'Losing it again,' he said. In the 1963/64 season, Ipswich were relegated. A persistent interviewer asked him what he thought about Ramsey now that he had joined the FA. 'My opinion has never wavered,' he said. 'Alf is a remarkable little man for whom I have the greatest respect. He always seemed to find difficulty in making friends but I hope I am one of them. It is very nice to know he still lives around here, for the rest of the country regard us as backwoodsmen and we are very happy to be so. I'd like to see Norwich join us in the First Division – that would show that not all East Anglians have straw sticking out from behind their ears.'

An earlier party, celebrating promotion from the Third South Division in 1953/54, had been much more lively than the staid Savoy celebration. Mr Patrick was still recovering from his serious leg injuries and turned up for the party (held in a hotel in Sheffield) with his leg in plaster. He drank so much that he staggered onto a table and started throwing cutlery up to the ceiling. Plaster began tumbling down and he fell, hurting his leg. Most of the guests were also over exuberant, drowning the singing of the Italian singer who had been invited. Patrick shouted and screamed like a demented mental patient, prompting someone to say 'He's nutty'. Normally Patrick was the quieter of the pair and his behaviour on this occasion was very unusual. It was a rare instance of him losing control.

The Rt Revd Bishop John Waine recalled 'Patrick was gentle and generous and was interested in people, making time for the young and displaying a delicious humour. Despite his innate shyness, he had great charm. He rarely got upset when the team was losing. "It's only football," he would say. I remember he read out to me a letter he had received from a supporter. The man accused him "of smiling" after the team lost!

'John was a rougher diamond, but a wonderful character. I had been Bishop of Chelmsford and West Ham supporters lived in my parish. John told me "these West Ham fans are the same as ours, they like good football". He was very friendly with Len Cearns, the chairman of West Ham who used to live in Suffolk. Len was always touching his nose and that made John laugh.

'When I became Bishop of St Edmundsbury and Ipswich he rang me up and invited me to the boardroom. It was an open invitation and I loved my visits. They said I was the bookie's favourite but I don't know about that.' (Archbishops are not elected: their names are submitted to two officials who reach a consensus among the other Bishops before the name of the candidate is passed to the Prime Minister in Downing Street for approval. Her Majesty the Queen doesn't appoint them.)

The Bishop told an amusing story about his great friend Patrick. He said 'Patrick was a very compassionate man and when some supporters were calling for the dismissal of John Duncan as manager he told me "You know, it was so bad that at one stage I was chanting it myself!"' On a trip to Finland, Duncan and his staff were perturbed to discover that so much alcohol was packed into the luggage that Trevor Kirton, the man in charge of the playing kit, said 'There's not enough room for the last skip!' Patrick said 'Chuck out one of the skips with the playing kit!' One friend of a director said 'When Duncan went, Patrick cried.'

On a trip to the Ukraine, the local Communist hierarchy entertained the Ipswich directors before a European game and the President of the Ukraine, a fat man with a loud voice, said to Patrick 'I am the head of the local Communist Party'. Patrick said 'How splendid! Do you realise my uncle is Harold Macmillan?' The man laughed and said 'Oh yes, I have heard of him. A friend of Comrade Krushchev. Have another drink. We'll toast SuperMac. Ha ha ha!'

★

When Ipswich won promotion to the Second Division at Southampton, Alf's first professional club, Mr John organised an impromptu party at the Polygon – a hotel near The Dell which was used by transatlantic passengers before boarding liners at the Southampton Docks. The Polygon was closed near the end of the century and made way for a cluster of flats. By 2000, The Dell had gone the same way, except that the centre circle was preserved in the middle of the flats.

Cobbold called in a pianist and a violinist and drinks were served well into the night. He used to call Ramsey 'Old Stoneface' and he said 'At one stage I looked around I couldn't see Alf anywhere. Eventually I found him lying under a table singing "Maybe it's because I'm a Londoner". Alf hotly denied it saying "I'm not a Londoner, I was born in Dagenham" but it was true – and the way he looked at breakfast I wasn't surprised he didn't remember.'

On one of his visits to Switzerland, Mr John was in an accident while going down the Cresta Run. Some of his friends considered him to be an accomplished skier but he said 'I only pretend I can ski'. He loved his annual trip to St Moritz to go on the scary run. This time he crashed, smashing his face into the rock-hard ice. Blood spouted into the air and, as he came to a halt, nearby skiers came to his aid. He was helped to his feet and he was almost speechless, spluttering through his blood-soaked lips. He was carried to an ambulance and taken to a hospital where a surgeon inserted twenty-six stitches to the wounds around his mouth.

A few days later he set off for home. After landing at Heathrow, he had difficulty carrying his bags and his skis to a taxi rank and a taxi driver said 'You look as though you've been in a car crash mate.' 'I'm f——ing lucky to be still here,' came the reply. 'Came a cropper on the Cresta Run. That's the last time I'll do that.'

The taxi driver asked 'Where do you want to go?' 'Liverpool Street Station,' said the now retired skier. An hour and half later, with the rush hour traffic long gone, the vehicle stopped at the side of Platform 9 – the one where the Norwich train was about to depart. Cobbold started to search his pockets, then his wallet. 'I'm terribly sorry,' he said. 'I haven't got any cash on me.' The driver appeared to be upset. 'I know,' said Cobbold. 'Take my skis.' 'Okay,' said the taxi driver, 'that's a fair exchange.'

It was some weeks before he was fit enough to watch an Ipswich Town game. Later, he needed plastic surgery to rectify the scars. 'Can't lose my looks,' he said. He never skied again. 'I wasn't good enough at it,' he admitted. 'At one time I used to hurtle down the Cresta Run. I found it a very good cure for a hangover.' Several dozen competitors have been killed since it was inaugurated and he was unwilling to add to the number.

THIRTEEN

THE SAFE IS BLOWN!

The weekend Ipswich gained promotion to the First Division in the 1960/61 season, the club's safe was blown. The thieves broke into the office, seeking the takings of £3,000 after the 2-0 win over Sunderland. As Ipswich charged the lowest prices in the division, it wasn't a lot of money. The staff had followed their usual custom, removing the cash and depositing it at the bank. A few clubs still do that now and, as the briefcases full of cash are taken away in a car, the announcer says on the tannoy 'Mr Goodman has now left the stadium' or a similar coded message. This alerts the security and police staff that the money has left.

The thieves spread butter all over the safe on the night of 22 April 1961. David Rose, the secretary, said 'butter was everywhere, all over the walls, the ceiling, everywhere'. The only money remaining, £3 and one shilling, was the proceeds from the cycle park. Angry to find they had been thwarted, the robbers threw the coins on the practice pitch. The Cobbold brothers found it very funny indeed. 'Thankfully they missed the contents of the directors' stock of wine,' said Mr John.

Ray Crawford and Ted Phillips were the heroes of the season, sharing 70 of the 100 goals, earning Crawford an England recall – he was the first Ipswich player to be capped for England. Crawford scored 40 and Phillips 30, an incredible percentage. If there was any justice, Phillips should have been selected by England alongside Crawford. He was picked by Walter Winterbottom, the England manager, for a game against Austria that season only to drop out with injury. An explosive, brave player, Phillips played many times when he was in pain and paid a heavy price. In his fifties he found it difficult to walk. 'The pain was so bad in both knees that I couldn't sleep,' he said. 'I had operations but you can't improve a knee. I volunteered to pay for a knee replacement and I had a wonderful doctor. The first one was in 1991 and I didn't have any pain in that one. It was such a relief. Five years later I had a second artificial knee and that worked, too. It cost £9,500 each from the National Health. I could never have paid for it myself. I can bend the new knees up to 90 per cent, which is fine, but if I fall over, I'm in trouble. I've got to turn over my stomach to press myself up from my hands and try to lean up against a wall or a door. It's not easy to do it. That's the only problem. You've got to stay on your feet.'

Not every former footballer has been lucky enough to have expensive operations on the NHS. 'A friend of mine, Alf Marshall who played for Colchester, had a new knee and the Professional Footballers' Association paid half the bill,' he said. Thousands of ex-players are helped by the football union and it wasn't a surprise in November 2001 that 99 per cent of their members voted for a strike unless the Premiership League continued to pay 5 per cent of the money from the then TV deal to the players' union. The authorities soon gave in.

Phillips was born in Leiston, a small town in Suffolk, and was one of the few Ipswich players to have graduated from the county. He played for Ipswich between 1953 and 1963, scoring 160 goals in 269 matches for the club. 'The Cannonball Kid, that's you,' said Mr John. He bet on him to win a contest 'for the fastest shooter in the English game'. It was staged at Cheshunt, the Tottenham Hotspur training ground, and he won the prize, kicking the ball at 87mph. 'We used a leather ball in those days and if it was wet most of them had a problem to give it a whack,' said Phillips. 'Today's balls swerve around all over the place.

You can get more pace from them.' Phillips beat Tottenham's leading marksman Bobby Smith – who also ended up as a cripple (Smith has had hip and knee replacements).

Phillips achieved a unique hat-trick in terms of striking the ball through the goal net in matches. 'The first time was against Northampton in the Third Division,' he said. 'I hit it from about twenty-five yards and it burst through the net. Most of my goals came from outside the box. The only time I scored close in was with headers. These days they want to run the ball into the net instead of belting it. I always believed in power. I remember one goalkeeper jumped out of the way of one of my shots. He didn't fancy it any more.

'The second time I burst the net it was in a 2-1 win against Burnley in the 1962/63 season. That came from about thirty yards. The other time was in a testimonial game at Colchester and the goalkeeper was Ted Ditchburn, the Spurs goalkeeper who was a good friend. It went through the side netting and the referee signalled a goal. Someone complained it went in the side netting and I agreed. You don't take advantage over a mate!'

Phillips was a great admirer of Ramsey. 'The best I worked with and most people would say the same,' he said. 'He won the World Cup for England, no-one else. This latest fellow (Sven-Goran Eriksson) was never going to win it. Alf knew the game and he spoke sense. He used to say to Roy Bailey "make sure you fill the goal". He told him to stay up. "Too many of them throw themselves about," he said. Roy was the best goalkeeper Ipswich ever had, better than Richard Wright, and that Italian Matteo Sereni who was found out in English football.'

According to Phillips, Ramsey always kept calm despite any provocation. At half-time during a game against Bristol Rovers the Ipswich full-back Kenny Malcolm, who was brought up in a fishing family in Aberdeen, lost his temper and hurled his boots across the dressing room. Ramsey didn't react. 'He never said a word,' said Phillips. 'Carried on as though nothing happened.'

A journalist asked John Cobbold what was the most memorable moment in his twenty-three years as chairman of the club. Winning the League? 'No,' he said, holding his nose in the asphyxiating memory

of it all. 'No, my most vivid memory was travelling up a slow lift with
Ted Phillips one day after he'd had two boiled eggs and a plate of
baked beans for breakfast.'

In his role as chairman of Tolly Cobbold, he once went to perform
an opening ceremony of a revamped public house in Maldon, Essex.
The publican said to him 'I love your Cobnut' – Cobnut was a brown
ale. 'Oh,' said John. 'I don't. It makes me fart.'

Jimmy Hill, the long-chinned, pipe smoking, loquacious chairman
of the Professional Footballers' Association at the time, launched the
threat of strike action in 1961 after the Arsenal player George Eastham
took legal action over the £20 a week maximum wage. The Football
League finally conceded on the issue just two days before the deadline,
heralding the arrival of the £100 a week footballer in Johnny Haynes.
Trinder enjoyed recounting his stories to Mr John.

Trinder and his fellow director, Chappie D'Amato, called the players
in one by one to tell them the details of their contracts. Haynes was
the first and he left giving the thumbs up. One of the other players,
Maurice Cook, was told that he would be offered £15 a week in
the close season. Cook exploded. 'F——ing hell,' he said. 'Haynesy's
getting £100 a week and I'm getting £15!' Trinder said 'But Johnny
is a far better player than you are.' Cook replied 'Not in the f——ing
summer, he's not.'

Another player, Alan Mullery, rejected his contract and tossed it
along the oak table in the boardroom. Trinder threw it back, saying 'If
you don't like it, you can f—— off'. Trinder laughed, Mullery laughed
and they poured another drink. Ian Wooldridge, the much decorated
sports writer of the *Mail*, recalled 'There was an awful lot of industrial
football language, and plenty of drinking, at Fulham in those days.
There were no formal press conferences but reporters rarely left the
famous Cottage before 8 p.m. on a Saturday night, always with good
stories but sometimes with only a hazy recollection of the match
result.'

On one occasion a reporter named Vic Selwyn of the *Sunday Mirror*
interrupted what passed for a press conference with the manager
Bedford Jezzard. Somewhat tipsy, he said 'Beddy, can I ask a question?'

Beddy, a decent man, said 'Sure, what is it?' Vic said 'What was the score?' Jezzard was taken aback. 'Well, it was 2-1 but was there any doubt about it?' 'I just wanted to be sure,' said Vic.

The Ipswich boardroom was similar to the one at Craven Cottage, except that even more drink was consumed. The boardroom table dwarfed the room and the pinkish carpet was stained by alcohol and cigarette burns. One day someone mentioned the appalling state of the carpet and Robson, who was in charge of almost every aspect of the club, said 'I'll have to send for a patterns book to sort out a new carpet'. 'You don't know anything about patterns,' said John Cobbold.

A reporter from the *Daily Telegraph*, the late Robert Oxby, often competed with Mr John to drink the most wine and on one occasion he was in such a bad way that the chairman ordered his chauffeur to drive him home. He lived in Streatham, in South London. On a subsequent visit, Oxby was sitting in the Press Box when he leant forward, tripped over the ledge and toppled onto the spectators below. No-one was hurt.

Patrick Collins of the *Mail on Sunday* remembered a story about Oxby and Mr John. 'We were in Rome on a football trip,' he said. 'They'd been drinking rather heavily after dinner and Mr John told him "you must go to St Peter's, I'll book a cab at nine". Surprisingly, Bob Oxby turned up on time and the taxi driver took them as planned. The taxi driver said "You must go to the Sistine Chapel". 'How long will it take?' said Mr John. He was becoming rather thirsty on a hot day. "It won't take too long but it is a good walk," said the driver. The two men may well have set a record for rushing round the Sistine Chapel and were about to go when the driver said "You must see the Apostle. The bones are more than 2,000 years old." Mr John replied "will they be there tomorrow?" He was desperate to visit a bar.'

Drinking has always been a big part of football because there is so much time to fill. The Cobbolds used to entertain the opposing direc-tors for lunch and as kick-off neared, the directors began setting off for the directors' box on unsteady feet. Some had to be helped up the steps. After the game another hour or two drinking followed and those who drove their cars home would probably have failed a breath test had they been stopped by the police. The Cobbolds often invited a senior police officer to join them in the boardroom, ensuring that no-one was booked.

Once Mr John was stopped by a police officer after being caught driving at 60mph in a 40mph limit. He knew the policeman and stuttered a few words. 'Oh goodness,' he said. 'Seems I might have put the foot on the pedal a bit too hard.' The policeman smiled. 'Mr John, how many times have I told you, you've got to look in your rear window'. Like his brother, Patrick was also convicted of being drunk and lost his driving licence. He hired Billy Markham, a former employee of the Cliff Brewery, as his chauffeur. Patrick liked to be driven in an upmarket car: he had a Bentley, then a Jaguar.

Most of the Ipswich players were big drinkers, with the club providing a bar for them and their guests. Even now that custom is still maintained in some clubs – although more enlightened managers, particularly those from abroad, discourage their players from drinking alcohol or actually ban them from doing so. With the emphasis on physical fitness, it is anachronistic to continue the practice of awarding the best player a large bottle of champagne. But it still happens, introducing young players to imbibing.

With their exorbitant wages, modern young footballers are more likely to end up in court than previous generations of footballers. They are targets for opposing fans and hooligans and few learn the lesson. When they are drunk, the nastiest part of their personalities is sometimes accentuated, as the Leeds pair Lee Bowyer and Jonathan Woodgate showed in their two trials in 2001 and 2002. One of the Ipswich discoveries, England midfield player Kieron Dyer, took a long time to heed the admonishments of his manager Bobby Robson when he joined Newcastle.

When Ray Crawford first joined the club, John Cobbold often invited him out for a drink at the Station Hotel. Crawford was in digs and there was little to do in Ipswich at night. 'He never had any money,' said Crawford. 'He used to borrow £20 and pay it back later. He used to say "don't tell Alf".' Bill Baxter was another player who was tapped for a loan by the chairman. 'He usually wanted £20 to pay for a round,' said Baxter. 'He liked to shock people. On an away trip to Manchester United, he wore a smelly old coat to the boardroom to ruffle the United directors. I asked him "What's this, it smells horrible." "It's come from a sheep," he said. "It makes a great smell."'

John Cobbold's humour could be coarse, almost insulting, after a bout of drinking. But he was so well known and respected in the area that hardly anyone took offence. One friend said 'One day we were going into a restaurant, quite a posh place, when the restaurant manager asked him "do you have a reservation, Sir?" Cobbold replied "Oh Lord, do you think I'm a f——ing red Indian!"'

He overdid it on one occasion when the directors were having dinner in a hotel at Stamford on a trip back from a game in the North. 'He made such a racket that the manager asked him to leave,' said one. He could also be dismissive, almost rude, about women. At one of his dinners for visiting directors Ron Noades (the then Crystal Palace chairman) and his attractive wife Novella, a French teacher, were among the guests. Novella rose to leave the room after the meal and said 'I'm going to have a little walk up the road'. Cobbold said 'I imagine you do a lot of walking up and down streets for business!' There was a stifled laugh from some of the other guests and Cobbold was forced to cut short his fit of tittering.

One of the few occasions when Cobbold was short of a quip was when he invited the Ipswich players to a brief holiday at his Scottish estate. The goalkeeper Ken Hancock, who was signed from Port Vale in 1964, said 'We were on a long walk across the moor when this tall guy arrived carrying a billycan filled with tea. "Here," he said, "here's some tea for ya. It's steaming hot." He pushed it at Mr John and the chairman sniffed it and looked at it with suspicion. "There's some bracken floating on it," said Mr John, handing it back. "Never ya worry yoursel," said the man, "if ya drink it all it'll pass through your stomach and come out the other end, out your arse. That'll be no problem." That was the only time Mr John failed to respond with a witty retort.'

There were frequent family gatherings at the estate and the staff prepared huge meals with much of the food often going uneaten. 'Let the dogs have it,' John would say. And the children used to wear the same clothes for the whole week.

Cobbold had a serious side when he attended meetings of the Football League to discuss the state of the game. He often rose to speak in favour of encouraging clubs to spend more on younger players. Ipswich had developed their own young players, but other clubs preferred to go into debt and buy more experienced players. 'We have to be patient,' he urged. Not many clubs were prepared to wait. A couple of bad results and the manager would be asking for money for new players. Football is one of the few industries where bosses bring in new staff almost annually at enormous cost in an effort to add a small percentage of efficiency. Most times these panic measures only lower the standards. It creates more pressure and anxiety at a time when confidence is needed.

Graham Mackrell, former secretary of Sheffield Wednesday and West Ham, recalled 'John Cobbold made some useful contributions to these League meetings but he found it very frustrating, at all levels. Once we met in this old coaching inn on the A11 and after hours of talking, not much was resolved. He came into the bar and ordered some drinks. The waiter said "are you a guest at this establishment?" John was rather exasperated. "What's that got to do with it?" he said. "We need a drink."

'The waiter said "I'm sorry but I can't serve any drinks, only to those staying at the hotel." One of the other League representatives was staying overnight. "I'll get them in Johnny," he said. "Eight whiskies," was the order. "Make it f——ing large whiskies," said John.'

When Patrick worked at the Cliff Brewery he once ordered 35,000 bottles of wine with his own label and it went tolerably well, though much of it was drunk by himself and his friends. When he pioneered a new brand of lager called Husky, brewed in Hartlepool, it turned out to be a disastrous experience. For all his apparent knowledge and expertise, he never became a successful brewer.

With his plus fours, tweed jackets and twinkling eyes, he loved debunking important people. One day Sir Denis Follows, the secretary of the FA, turned up at the club wearing a bowler hat. Patrick had been shooting pheasant the day before and when he heard about Follows' bowler, he turned up on the following day with a pheasant perched on his head. Feathers fell everywhere. Follows saw the joke and laughed.

Burnley was the great rival of Ipswich and the club had a team full of internationals, whereas Ipswich had just one, Ray Crawford. Burnley was an industrial and mill town with a population of 91,000 at the time against the port and farming town of Ipswich, with a population of 119,000. Burnley had just one decent hotel. It wasn't a place to stay in. Ipswich had eight, three of them boasting that they had one of the finest dining rooms in Britain. The favourite phrase of Bob Lord, the dictatorial Burnley chairman, was 'I believe in calling a spade a bloody spade.' He was unpopular and lacked a sense of humour. Ipswich were the opposite, run by directors who never sought confrontations.

The obdurate Alf Ramsey never exchanged pleasantries with Lord. He didn't like him and it was a mutual feeling. Patrick once said 'The director's seats in the directors' box at Turf Moor was covered with elephant skin and Johnny thought it was the height of pomposity. Johnny refused to sit in them.'

In Ramsey's first two seasons as a player with Tottenham he won championship medals for helping his team to win the Second Division in 1949/50 and the First Division a year later. Now he had done it as a manager. He used only sixteen players to win the championship, one less than Tottenham's record in 1953/54. He was the fourth manager to win both titles along with Liverpool (1905 and 1906), Everton (1931 and 1932) and Tottenham (1949 and 1950). Ipswich won eleven successive victories between October and March, winning the League Championship by three points. Most of the goals came from Crawford and his partner Ted Phillips, who used to go shooting with the Cobbolds and their friends. The rustic Phillips was a fast bowler who loved playing village cricket.

The feud between John Cobbold and Lord started when the Ipswich directors turned up at the boardroom at Turf Moor and were ignored by Lord and his directors. John Cobbold was incensed. He said to his brother 'if those s——s aren't going to give us a drink, we ought to fetch our own.' So he went to the drinks cabinet and poured some white wine in a couple of glasses. No words were exchanged and the two groups ignored each other.

One Ipswich director recalled 'the story goes that Lord turned up in his chauffeur car at Portman Road, got out, marched up to the reception office and said to one of the girls "hand that to your chairman". It was his business card. Lord got back into his car and the chauffeur took him back to Burnley. One of the staff took his card to Mr John and John tore it up and handed back the remains. "Put that down the lavatory," he said.'

The dispute flared up later over some remarks Lord made following a game between Burnley and Leeds. Lord had implied that he was critical of the Jewish members of the Board at Elland Road. John Cobbold was so upset that he reported the matter to the Football Association in Lancaster Gate and filed a strong complaint. Lord was at the FA offices a few days later in his capacity as chairman of one of the committees and opened Cobbold's letter. He never spoke to Cobbold again. If they were in the same boardroom, they ignored each other and he refused to speak to Mr Patrick either. John Cobbold used to say 'he's a f——ing idiot.' He once said 'he's a f——ing butcher... and he's not a particularly good one. I hate racists and snobs. I won't have them in our boardroom. I would prefer a dustman to a snob.' One of his guests said 'he looks like a dustman himself!'

Founded in 1882, Burnley was one of the twelve clubs who started the Football League in 1888. Lord was elected on to the League's Management Committee and also the FA Council and tried to run both organisations. He failed to win the highest posts because he wasn't popular (similar to Ken Bates a generation later). Football always has its bullies. Lord sanctioned the Bob Lord Stand at Turf Moor and when he died his club fell like a meteorite. John Cobbold had a stand named after him at Portman Road but it wasn't his idea. Burnley lost their place in the top flight in 1987 and dropped down the divisions, only managing to preserve their place in the Fourth Division on the last game of the season.

One long-serving director said 'Bob used to miss the start of the game at home games because he was still in the office counting the money. He used to have his own turnstile.' That may or may not be true – but it was a fairly common practice at some clubs to devote the takings from one turnstile for a particular cause, or person, thus avoiding tax. Around this time football clubs were hit by entertainment tax and that caused a lot of mirth. 'What entertainment?' some directors used to say, including the Cobbolds.

Cobbold had good relations with every other club except Lord's Burnley and once bailed out Blackburn Rovers. Bill Fox, a bluff Lancastrian, was the chairman at the time and it was somewhat embarrassing to him because he was also President of the Football League – one of the most powerful positions in English football. John Howorth, the Blackburn secretary, went up to David Rose and said rather sheepishly 'We haven't got any money to pay the wages this week. I wonder if you could give us some on account.' Rose said he believed his directors would help, and after checking with Mr John, he came back with a cheque.

The Northern clubs usually served sausages in their boardrooms and Cobbold didn't like their texture: far too fatty. On one occasion he played a prank on Louis Edwards, the Manchester United chairman who had a meat business whose products were renowned for their low quality. (Louis was the father of Martin Edwards – who became chairman a few years later at Old Trafford.) Mr John ordered several pounds of fatty sausages and asked the cook to serve them in the Portman Road boardroom. Louis Edwards looked askance. 'That's all you'll get here,' said a laughing Mr John. 'You've been giving us that in your boardroom for years.' Ipswich's cuisine, like its wine, was envied throughout the League, except on that particular day when the United party arrived.

One chairman who was heartily disliked by the Cobbolds was John Smith, the long-serving chairman of Liverpool when they regularly won trophies around Europe. It wasn't jealousy but bad breath, however, that caused the ill feeling. The Cobbold brothers called him 'Mr

Halitosis' (the Greek word meaning abnormally foul breath – it may be caused by smoking, eating certain foods or infections in the tonsils, nose or throat but the main causes are gum disease and tooth decay). The Liverpool directors often dined with the Ipswich directors at the Copdock Hotel before matches and on one occasion John sat down at the dinner table and had some frozen sausages in his hand. He then put them on his head. Smith and his directors looked startled but said nothing as they carried on eating.

Cobbold kept chewing away, ignoring the bizarre headwear. Smith didn't have the same humour and panache as the Cobbolds. He was a serious man and a bit of a smooth customer. As the soup plates were removed, a waiter said 'Excuse me, Mr John. You appear to have some sausages on your head.' 'Oh, really,' said John. 'So I do. I must have forgotten to defrost them.' The chairman handed the sausages over with a jerky laugh. Smith struggled to summon up a half smile as the Cobbolds rocked back on their chairs, chuckling and chortling.

While eccentricity prospered off the field, the club's players were complimented on their behaviour on the pitch. Ipswich were one of the two clubs praised by the FA for not receiving an unfavourable report on the conduct of their players around that time. Matt Busby said of them 'they are one of the most attractive sides in the country' and Nottingham Forest sent a message 'we wish to congratulate you on showing that a team playing with skill and spirit can often achieve the kind of success which some imagine only money can buy, playing with a skill that your short career in League football belies.'

After another successful season, Ramsey summed it up, saying 'I think we did quite well'. While the League spent £10,000 on a PR company to find out why attendances dropped by 5.5 million over two years, Ipswich's average attendance rose to a record 23,000. Burnley's Turf Moor had a capacity of more than twice of Portman Road, the other challengers, whose White Hart Lane accommodated 63,000. Was Alf a genius? The people in East Anglia thought so.

FOURTEEN

ALF USES THE LONG BALL GAME

Some English managers have always been branded as long-ball expo-
nents and Graham Taylor, who took over as the national manager in
place of Bobby Robson in 1990, was the butt of much criticism for
this. But Ramsey was an exponent of it too, during his club managerial
heyday at Ipswich. Without money to buy players, Ramsey used a simple,
direct style, utilising his best passer, Jimmy Leadbetter. Leadbetter, who
wore the number eleven shirt, was said to be a left-winger. He played
on the left in the early days until Ramsey moved him into midfield. 'It
worked,' said Leadbetter, 'none of the rival managers cottoned on to it
and didn't try to do something about it until it was too late.'

Ramsey signed just one player in that season, Doug Moran – a
striker from Falkirk who cost £12,000. The goalkeeper Roy Bailey,
who came from a family of thirteen, recalled seeing an old looking
man hunched up in a wooden shed at the back of the stand smoking
a cigarette. 'Who's the old fellow?' said Bailey. 'That's the star player,
Jimmy Leadbetter,' said one of the staff. Bailey started out as a painter
and decorator in Croydon before joining Crystal Palace and then
Ipswich. He died comparatively young in South Africa.

Leadbetter, who was nicknamed 'Sticks' because of his spindly legs,
always wore long shorts, well past his knees. In his playing days the
other players wore reasonably short shorts, halfway down their thighs.
Ray Crawford used to pull his shorts up to show off his bulging thigh
muscles and one day he said to Leadbetter 'If you win the title, I'll
give you my shorts as a souvenir, they're unique'. He scored 33 goals
that season, just over a third of the 93 goals Ipswich scored in their 42
matches, with Ted Phillips scoring 28. 'I wore long shorts to hide my
knees,' said Leadbetter. 'They weren't a good sight. And I also wore
them to disguise my legs to fool defenders. They had less time to react
when I passed the ball.'

'Sticks' is now a non-smoker although in those days he was a heavy
smoker. 'I used to sneak off to the toilet at half-time to take a few

puffs to settle my nerves,' he said. 'They tried to get me to give it up
and one day I decided to stop and I played a bad game. Next week
Jimmy Forsyth, the trainer, came in before the kick-off and marched
up to me and shoved a Woodbine in my mouth. "Take that," he said.
"That'll get you going again." Well, I did have a good game and I
forgot about giving up. Mind you Alf had a few sly puffs. Everyone
thought he didn't smoke. He didn't want to set a wrong example. But
I saw him a few times round the back lighting up.

'I don't know why he bought me. I told him I was a has-been but he
told me "yes, but you can pass". He took me aside and said he wanted
me to play on the left wing. "I'm too slow" I told him. "I know, but
we need someone who can pass out there," he said. I was an inside
forward who hardly missed a game which was amazing really because
in those days the tackles used to fly around and the referees were much
more lenient than they are now. I agreed to shift and it suited me. In
the middle you're surrounded by opposing players and on the wing
you saw things better. I didn't have to keep looking back. I played deep
on the left and Roy Stephenson played the same way on the right. Alf
used that system of withdrawn wingers in the World Cup. He wasn't
a qualified coach but he was ahead of his time. He used a simple
idea – when we have the ball he wanted us to keep it. He aimed for
less, rather than more, passes. He wanted it up to Ray Crawford and
Ted Phillips as soon as possible. Ted loved a pass for him to chase. Alf
discouraged us from passing sideways and the few times he was upset
was when we passed it inside and gave the ball away.

'He was a very nice man. He never criticised anyone in public. If
he wanted to make a point he would call someone in to his office.
He was a gentleman. He had a team of has-beens and supposed no
hopers and none of us were big headed. It was a team with everyone
playing for each other. Alf used to love being on the winning side
against his old club, Spurs, and in that Championship side we did the
double over Tottenham, who had won the Double the season before.
We came back from 1-2 to win 3-2 at home and we won 3-1 at White
Hart Lane. Alf had a big smile on his face after those games. Our best
performance was at Turf Moor when we lost 3-4 against Burnley, the
other big rivals. Andy Nelson, the captain, shouted to the ref near the

end "Ref, give us another minute and we'll do it!" It was a game we wanted to last forever. Alf had a tremendous knowledge of matches. He could sit down and talk through games as though a video was being switched on.

'We beat Aston Villa 2-0 in the final game to win the League and we had shaken the footballing world. Stan Lynn, the Villa full-back, the toughest, hardest tackling full-back in the League, caught me and there was a loud crack as though my leg had been broken. It was the corner flag that cracked in two! Stan hit the ball as hard as anyone in the game and one of his shots hit Graham Vearncombe, the Cardiff City goalkeeper, and knocked him out cold. People called him "Stan the Wham" and he was a great lad. Came from Bolton. Sadly he died on 27 April 2002 at the age of seventy-three. Eight years before he sold his mementoes, including his FA Cup medal, for only £2,000.

'The Ipswich players covered for each other and we liked each other as people and it was a lovely feeling when we came out of the dressing room to go out on the pitch. Some of the teams had most of the play and we had to do a lot of defending. But our attacking methods were more potent than theirs and we had two great scorers in Ray and Ted.'

Two weeks after winning the Championship, The Royal Marines Band marched in front of the team's open-topped bus as they paraded through the town. Police reckoned that half the town's inhabitants took to the streets. Nelson held the trophy and later his players received silver trays, valued at £100. 'It was the time of the threatened strike,' said Nelson, who now lives in Havia, a Spanish village equidistant between Alicante and Valencia. 'The rules were that you couldn't earn more than £20 a week and £17 in the close season,' I said. 'I signed in 1959 and Alf offered me £17 and £14 and I told him I wasn't going to accept that. I was at West Ham and they'd offered Ipswich £8,500 for me.

'A day or two later I met the chairman, Mr John Cobbold. "I might have some good news," he told me. He went to see Alf and said to the directors that we're going to give a £3 rise. Well, we got the increase but the idea of me going to see him was that I wanted more, not the same. Anyway, it helped the team spirit that we were all the same money. Mr John was a lovely man but you couldn't take him seriously. He wanted to be one of the lads. When we went to the Savoy he picked up the tab for the drinks and we did plenty of drinking. The club kept that tradition going and when they organised the fortieth anniversary dinner, they still picked up all the bills. They paid for my fares for me and my wife Margaret and we had a fantastic time. I don't think many clubs would do that.'

Most of the players called Alf by his name. One or two called him 'Governor'. Later, Ramsey was to say 'Our success to win the League Championship with Ipswich was my finest achievement, even more than the winning of the World Cup.' Alf shook hands with the lady Mayor, Mrs Charlotte Green, and never attempted to kiss her cheek. One of the players' wives said 'I never saw him kiss a lady. I think he was too shy to do it. But he treated us with the greatest courtesy.'

Nelson, who was born in 1935 and was fifteen years younger than Ramsey, soon built up a close relationship with his manager. He came from Custom House in the East End and spoke the same vernacular as the manager. He was a strong, uncompromising defender and he was a junior at Upton Park when Bobby Moore was starting out his career. There was a cult of drinking in most clubs and West Ham's players were renowned for it. 'Bobby liked a drink,' said Nelson. 'He could go on benders and still hold his drink. You didn't see him drunk. He could return from a club and arrive at training and still put his training in. He used to drive his first wife Tina to the West End and when he came home, he donned a chauffeur's hat to make sure that he wouldn't be nabbed at the wheel by the coppers. He always did that.'

Another player tells a less amusing story about the great England captain. He said 'West Ham agreed to appear in a testimonial for one of the Ipswich players and when they turned up Bobby said "the lads want £10 per man to play". We were shocked. The custom was that the players played for nothing to help the beneficiary. We had to give him the money and in the end the proceeds were only £5,000.'

Moore was a very fastidious man. At home he insisted that his cushions weren't moved on the settee. He always did the washing up and Tony Palmer's video *Hero: The Bobby Moore Story* claimed that he used to dry himself while in the bath – a very difficult act to perform. 'He never shouted, he always looked immaculate and he made sure he wiped his hands before accepting the Jules Rimet trophy from the Queen.' *The Times* writer and amateur footballer Alyson Rudd said 'There was a mystical element to the film, as though all who knew him believe in some way that Moore was fulfilling his destiny. He suffered from cancer early in his career. He recovered and was then struck again. His daughter Roberta felt a surge of energy pass through her when her father died, lying next to her. She believes that represented Moore's soul. We can talk glibly about the spirit of '66, but according to this film, we cannot but underestimate the esteem in which Moore was held. He was kind, quiet and almost an obsessive. But he knew how to win with grace. When he was subjected to a nasty tackle, he would say to his opponent "well, that wasn't very nice, was it?"'

To celebrate Ipswich Town winning their first League Championship, the Cobbolds sanctioned a twelve day trip to Europe in early May. It was more of a tour of the beer cellars and bars than showing the skills of the new English champions. On the flight home Roy Stephenson was so drunk that he tried to open an exit door. 'We had to wrestle him back into his seat and strap him in,' said another player. In one game against Vejle Boldklub in Denmark the players were in no condition to last the ninety minutes and at half-time some of them found themselves locked in the dressing room, to their relief. Ted Phillips recalled 'we only had six players on the field and the game restarted. No-one knew the rule that the game was going to be abandoned if there isn't seven players. The game was soon called off. "What's going on?" I said. One of their officials said "it's a cycling race and it's about to start."'

In another game, against Offenbach Kickers, Phillips was appointed captain by Ramsey and asked to carry out a huge bunch of flowers to hand over to the German captain. 'We tossed up and I lost ,' said Phillips, who had a reputation for practical jokes. 'Toss up again,' I said. The German captain was surprised and asked the referee what was happening. The referee interpreted and I explained to him that in England the toss was the best of three. So we tossed up again and I won and I won the decider. I don't think the German understood what had occurred.'

Phillips had a habit of turning a hose on the players and sometimes the victim was Ramsey. The manager still kept his calm demeanour. Dermot Curtis, the Irish striker who came from Dublin, saw this happen once and he said 'Alf was so amazing. He took his tie off, said nothing and walked out to his car. His suit was soaking but he drove off as though nothing had happened.'

Curtis shared John Cobbold's love of music. 'He bought hundreds of gramophone records, high quality stuff, some classical. One occasion he brought his collection and his gramophone along to a game at Newcastle, except that he put it down on the platform at the station and forgot about it.'

In the following season after winning the League, Ramsey's credibility stayed intact despite having a desperately poor season. It was the freeze of 1962/63 and there was no football played between Boxing Day and 23 February. Ipswich failed to win a home game in four months. There were some drubbings administered to Ramsey's players, including a hat-trick in nineteen minutes by Denis Law; while Jimmy Greaves outdid Law, scoring a hat-trick in five minutes as Tottenham won 5-0. Ipswich finished seventeenth in the First Division, avoiding relegation by four points.

They had a brief appearance in the European Champion Clubs' Cup (known as the European Cup in short). In Malta, skipper Andy Nelson crashed into Alberto Cauchi, the Floriana of Malta centre forward and had his nose broken in two places. He went off to have his nose rearranged and soon returned. 'You look like a bleeding Bruce Woodcock!' said John Cobbold.

The chairman invited Brian Mears, son of Joe Mears, Chelsea's chairman, to accompany the trip as a guest and drinking partner. The team stayed at a hotel next to a beach and after leaving his cases, Mears went off to find Cobbold. The players were relaxing in the bar and one of the players told him that Mr John was in the sea. Mears looked out and was surprised to see Cobbold in a shirt and shorts standing in the shallow water. Mears shouted to attract his attention and Cobbold responded with a wave. Mears was wearing a suit and a stylish pair of crocodile shoes but soon joined his friend in the sea, with the water over his elegant footwear. 'Good morning John,' he said. Cobbold seemed taken aback. 'Oh, it's you,' he said. 'When I waved out I thought you were the wine waiter.'

The Maltese were a poor side, losing 10-0 at Portman Road with Crawford scoring five of the goals. Ipswich were drawn against AC Milan, Jimmy Greaves' old club, in the next round and they lost 0-3 at the San Siro Stadium. Nelson said 'We were babes in the wood compared with the Italians. They were up to all the cynical stuff, pulling your hair, spitting and treading on your toes. We were too naïve. We used to go forward with a cavalier spirit and not bother about the cautious side.'

FIFTEEN

THE GENERAL MOVES ON TO GHQ... AT THE FA

The FA wanted a new England manager and the man they wanted to take over from Walter Winterbottom as the manager of the national side was Jimmy Adamson, the Burnley captain and current Footballer of the Year. Adamson was born in the coalmining town of Ashington in 1929 and the cliché 'if you want to find a footballer, shout down a coal mine!' may well have started there: Jack and Bobby Charlton were born there as were five footballing members of the Milburn family, including Jackie Milburn (who was briefly manager of Ipswich).

Adamson rejected the FA's offer, citing his inexperience. He was a staff coach under Winterbottom in the 1962 World Cup but he hadn't managed a club at the time. So the FA turned to another Burnley centre half, Ron Greenwood, who was born at a nearby village named

Worsthorne on Armistice Day 1921. His father was a painter and decorator and his mother worked in a mill. He had started out his working career at the age of fourteen as a sign writer. He joined up as an apprentice for five years at five shillings a week and worked for several months at Wembley Stadium, working on signs around the ground. His first FA Cup final took place there in 1938 between Preston North End and Huddersfield – the game was famous for the George Mutch penalty. Thirty-seven years later he led out the West Ham side in the 2-0 win over Fulham. Two years later he was manager of England, a role he carried out between 1977 and 1982. Greenwood was a great football intellect.

In 1962, however, it was too soon for him to be England's manager. The year before he had left his job as coach at Arsenal to join West Ham. His career off the pitch had only just started. Greenwood was a scholarly, nice man – who was similar to Winterbottom in style and manner – and, he too, pleaded inexperience. 'It is a job which needs experience,' he said. 'I wasn't ready while Alf Ramsey certainly was.' So he turned down the FA's approach and Alf Ramsey was the new candidate. Alf was enthusiastically backed for the job by John Cobbold and, on 25 October 1962, the appointment was confirmed. Winterbottom, who also ran the FA coaching scheme, wanted to succeed Stanley Rous as secretary of the FA after being appointed President of FIFA and was the favourite to fill the post. The tall, imposing Rous, a lifelong friend of the Cobbolds, had played a big part in Ramsey's eventual arrival on 1 May 1963 as the second manager of England.

Known as 'The General' when he was a player, Ramsey was his own man. He could be a broody individual, strong and detached, and was awkward and stiff in the company of people he didn't know well. He was a private person, rejecting any overtures to discuss his private life or even his inner beliefs about the game.

Graham Doggart, the chairman of the FA, rang John Cobbold on 1 October asking permission to interview him. Cobbold made no effort to keep Ramsey and soon gave his blessing. He told his manager 'You are a silly s—— but we will not stand in your way. If England calls, we have to respond.' Doggart and Winterbottom entertained Ramsey to dinner in London and the appointment was soon sealed. Peter Hill-Wood said 'Johnny respected Alf Ramsey but he thought he was a bit of an odd fellow. He said he would be able to find someone as good but it didn't work out. Jackie Milburn was a great guy but he wasn't a good manager.'

When he arrived at the FA, by train and underground, Ramsey insisted on being solely in charge and his salary was confirmed at £2,000 a year, rising to £8,000 when he left eleven years later. He also made a condition that he would have the power of selection of players. Up until then the FA International Committee, numbering twelve elderly men (none of whom had played football at a high level), picked the side and their members used to push for the players who played for their clubs – which explained why so many changes were made and Stanley Matthews was often left out.

Before Ramsey became England's manager, Crawford was chosen for England by his predecessor Walter Winterbottom but only played twice, against Northern Ireland, laying a goal for Bobby Charlton, and scoring the first goal in a 3-1 win over Austria. Crawford was the first Ipswich player to be capped by his country. Ramsey showed no favours to him later, ignoring his claims to be kept in the England squad. Crawford, however, still remains a loyal supporter of Ramsey. And that goes for almost every player picked by Ramsey. They liked him as a person and as a manager. Alan Ball said 'we loved him. He stood by us through thick and thin. He often shunned the Press because he was worried what he might say if he really let himself go. He thought they should be as proud of the England team as he was and that they had no right to knock the side. He thought everyone should be happy just to wear a white shirt. Money should never be the motive. I think most of the players went along with him.'

One of Ramsey's hobbies was watching cowboy films. A footballer's life can be boring – enough to drive him to drink. Revie used to arrange carpet bowls and other games to fill the hours and Ramsey's answer to boredom was to take the squad to a cinema. 'He usually made the decision about which film they were going to see,' said Ball. 'And it was most times a cowboy film. He loved the guns, the shooting and the blood and the way they talked. I think the only other thing he loved doing as much was taking part in five-a-side practice matches with the team. I never knew a manager so keen to kick a ball.'

Jack Charlton was not a fan of Ramsey, possibly because they had similar, strong opinions. In his autobiography, he wrote 'I only had one conversation with him in six years. He was a very difficult man to get close to, not the sort to talk over a few drinks. He was a stickler for time. He would get up and say 'Bed... time to go!' One night he ordered us to go to bed and we were only halfway through the film *Butch Cassidy and the Sundance Kid*. I never caught up with the last scenes. He never shouted. If he thought you hadn't played well, he wouldn't speak to you.'

According to Ball, Alf was at his funniest when he didn't mean to be. 'We were on a trip to the Expo '67 international tournament,' he said. 'When we arrived at the stadium we discovered that it had previously been used by a circus and hadn't been cleaned up. He took one look at the pitch and said to the Canadian in charge in his poshest accent "it's covered with elephant shit and horse shit. My team cannot play on that. If it is not re-turfed we are going home." We were in fits of laughter but the Canadian was amazed. He couldn't believe that the mild-mannered Alf Ramsey could be so outspoken. But they re-turfed it.'

Ramsey was a bit of a racist, as Ball confirmed. 'He didn't like the Scots because he felt that they didn't like the English for no apparent reason except that we were English,' he said. 'And he didn't like the Argentinians and his outburst about "animals" during the 1966 World Cup proved that. But I don't think he disliked anyone else.' John Cobbold shared his xenophobia. 'Those f——ing Argies,' Cobbold said. 'They're worse than the Frogs.' Ramsey may well have been a victim of racism himself, because when he grew up in Dagenham the boys he played football with used to call him 'Darkie' because he had what they would have called 'a touch of the tar brush'. They thought he had descended from gypsies. Ramsey himself always declined to talk about his background.

At the end of the England *v.* Argentina game, which was held up for more than ten minutes because of the rumpus over Antonio Rattin's ranting, the amiable George Cohen, England's Cockney right-back, took his shirt off to swap it with an Argentinian. The player, named Gonzalez, was keen. Suddenly Ramsey appeared, grabbed the shirt and said heatedly 'Stop, don't give your shirt to that animal!' Cohen had handed over his shirt, but part of the sleeve was still around his left hand. Two yards away, Gonzalez held the rest of Cohen's shirt, as well as his own and was trying to yank it from the grasp of Ramsey. There was a celebrated picture of Cohen and Ramsey pulling one way and Gonzalez pulling the other way, like in a mini tug of war. 'I ended up with my shirt having an arm stretched four or five feet,' said Cohen. 'Alf was adamant that I couldn't swap it and that was it. Gonzalez let it go and I took mine with me into the dressing room.'

None of the England players exchanged shirts that day – which proved to be financially beneficial in years to come. Who wanted to buy a shirt of a little known Argentinian? Their own shirts were much more valuable. However, Rattin's shirt would have been worth a fortune had anyone swapped it with an England player. Afterwards Bobby Moore and his players weren't on talking terms with the Argentinian captain over his behaviour. The affair had started nine minutes from half-time, with Rattin complaining to the West German referee Rudolph Kreitlein that he had booked one of his colleagues without justification. The argument lasted an indeterminable time and finally the referee, a small man of five feet five inches tall, looked up to the six foot one inch-tall Rattin and produced a red card. In a TV programme years later, Rattin said 'I wanted an interpreter and I couldn't have one. The referee couldn't speak Spanish and I couldn't speak German. I had the right to speak to him but I was unable to.' The massively tall Ken Aston, at six feet six inches tall, similar in appearance to De Gaulle, came to the touchline to intercede and he couldn't interpret satisfactorily either. Aston was a former World Cup referee.

In a TV interview after the Argentinian game Ramsey said 'We still have to play our best football. It will come against the right type of opposition, a team who come to play football and not act like animals.' The last five words echoed around the world. FIFA leaders reacted angrily, condemning Ramsey. They wrote to the English FA saying the words 'were unfortunate and against good international relations in football'. The FA took no action against Ramsey. He wasn't even reprimanded. But the Argentine FA was fined and warned they would be banned from future World Cup tournaments if their conduct failed to improve. Rattin and two of his colleagues were banned.

Is it remarkable that many of the major controversies in big international matches involve small referees? They include Denis Howell, the referee who became the best Sports Minister the country has had, Roy Capey, Roger Kirkpatrick, Norman Burtenshaw, Alf Gray, Paul Durkin and others.

At the banquet after the winning of the World Cup, at the Royal Garden Hotel close to Kensington Palace, Howell and Harold Wilson joined Ramsey in the celebrations. The Prime Minister had his pipe in one hand and a glass of wine in the other. Ramsey allowed himself a few glasses of champagne. One of the first to congratulate him was John Cobbold. Wilson was the first Premier who courted the nation's football players, inviting them to 10 Downing Street to allow himself being pictured mixing with the stars. He saw it as a vote catcher and he was probably right.

He had a good sense of humour, knew the game and was able to speak to Ramsey almost as an equal in football terms. That picture of Ramsey when the final whistle was sounded at the end of the World Cup, sitting unsmiling on the bench at Wembley when he was surrounded by his excited members of staff, leaping into the air with their arms raised, said a lot about his character. One critic said he wore a straitjacket on his heart. But he did show his feelings later in the dressing room when he hugged the players as they stood on the stone floor home of the anaemic looking dressing room.

The day after, relaxing in an armchair in the hotel, he was asked by the *Daily Mirror* soccer writer Ken Jones if he could be interviewed. His answer was surprising in the circumstances. 'I'm not making any comment,' he said. 'Sunday is my day off.' Jones was as close as anyone to him but no-one in the press – even him – could claim he was a friend.

As he was about to drive off from the Hendon Hall Hotel, where England stayed, before departing to his home in Ipswich, a friendly English journalist said 'I just want to congratulate you, Alf, and thank you on behalf of all the boys for your co-operation'. Ramsey looked at him with astonishment. 'Are you taking the mick?' he said. On another occasion a South American journalist approached him and said jauntily 'I don't know whether you remember me,' he said. 'Yes,' said Alf. 'You're a pest.' In another knockdown to the journalists, he told them 'I don't need you. You ring me. I don't ring you.'

He was right, the journalists needed him more than he wanted to speak to them. But as he was representing the England football team, he had to speak up for it – and it wasn't his team, it was the nation's. You couldn't have too many secrets. A Ramsey-style national manager would not have survived these days. He rarely gave interviews. He emerged from the dressing room, came out with a few convoluted sentences which revealed little and walked off. Few journalists had his telephone number and when he was contacted he would often make his excuses and ring off.

The football journalists were powerful people in those days. Today they are even more influential. They can destroy England football managers, as Graham Taylor and Kevin Keegan discovered. Walter Winterbottom, the first England manager to be appointed by the FA, was a friendly, intelligent man who had been a Wing Commander in charge of PT at the Air Ministry and played a few games as a midfield player for Manchester United and Chelsea, where he guested with them in the Second World War. He was born in Oldham and was articulate, good humoured, and a natural teacher with vision and ideas. Sir Stanley Rous wanted to set up an FA Coaching Scheme under Winterbottom and there was opposition from the ninety-two FA councillors. When he suggested that Winterbottom should be appointed in charge of coaching as well as manager of the team the opposition wilted. 'It was a cheaper option,' said one councillor. 'Two jobs for the price of one!'

Winterbottom was friendly and helpful to the Press but whenever England lost, which wasn't often because the national side was one of the greatest ever, he would be castigated, even vilified. Ramsey decided that he would not cultivate friends among the Press and treated all the journalists the same. Sixty percent of his games were won, the same record as Ron Greenwood's, and he was more successful than most other national managers in the world, but it wasn't enough to save him.

When the critics wrote carping articles about him the FA councillors took notice and acted. Newspapers like controversy and dissension. They are not in the business of stability and good order. Joe Mercer, Uncle Joe, was the most popular when he was the caretaker manager in 1974. He wasn't long enough in the job to incur the anger of the writers. Don Revie was the most astute and cunning for he realised that a successful manager needed a few journalists on his side. He was friendly and put up a good front before the truth came out and he defected to Dubai, having sold his story to a national newspaper.

Greenwood was similar to Winterbottom, being principled and intelligent – they were professors of football like Arsene Wenger and Gerard Houllier. He would talk for hours about the game and its techniques – and many young journalists learned a lot from him – but he never revealed much about what was happening within the England camp. In the World Cup in Spain in 1982 he tried to keep secret the news that Kevin Keegan had left the party to visit a doctor in Hamburg. Keegan had suffered a back injury and the day before he decided to leave he was seen playing tennis at 2 a.m. on a floodlit court with Ted Croker. Asked how he was, he replied jauntily 'I'm fine!' Next morning he ordered a hire car and was driven from the Basque region in Spain, across France and through the North of Germany to Hamburg, an exhausting journey of many hours. Not exactly the best way of treating a sore back. The news soon came out from the Hamburg end.

In the 2002 World Cup, Eriksson and his press officers insisted that skipper David Beckham had been declared fit to play. But Beckham wasn't really fit. His ankle swelled up again after breaking a bone in his left foot six weeks earlier and it hampered the way he tried take his trademark, match-winning free-kicks.

In Ramsey's day there was no press officer to help him. Now there are several employed by the FA and their job is to shield the manager and his players from awkward questions. Press conferences are arranged for players who can say the right things and they are tutored to avoid being too frank and open. The coverage is controlled, like at 10 Downing Street and in other government departments. An industry of spin doctoring has emerged and sport is no different to government in the way news is manipulated.

Football has been called a substitute for war and the propaganda of warfare bears similarities to the pronouncements from football managers and officials who often want to disguise the truth. On one side, the generals and the football bosses are intent to release only news which suits them. On the other, the job of the journalists is to publish everything they can. Lies are told and journalists respond by writing what they see is the story. There are faults on both sides and this sporting conflict will always exist.

The Australian-born writer Phillip Knightley summed it up in his brilliant book published in 1975, called *The First Casualty, the War Correspondent as Hero, Propagandist, and Myth Maker from the Crimea to Vietnam*. It was prefaced with a very apt quotation from US Senator Hirman Johnson, who said in 1917 'The first casualty when war comes is truth.'

Bobby Robson was probably the most honest and the friendliest of the England managers. He would say 'I'm very busy, what do you want?' An hour later he was still talking. Some critics cruelly branded him a buffoon and he was harshly treated by the writers whom he helped. It was to his credit that he survived eight years among the landmines and the hand grenades and came out almost unscathed. Taylor also talked a lot and there has to be a balance between not talking too much and not enough, like Ramsey. Eriksson was guarded and was strong enough to say 'no comment' when he didn't want to answer a question, particularly about his private life. The journalists were restrained, partly as he was speaking in another language. Like all footballing honeymoons, it did not last too long.

Ramsey's image of being uncommunicative did not extend to his football contacts. Ron Tindall, the former West Ham, Chelsea and Reading forward who was also a Surrey county cricketer before becoming manager of Portsmouth, told a revealing story about when he worked as Portsmouth manager. 'I met him in the boardroom at West Ham and he asked me how I was getting back home,' he said.

"'I'm catching a train from Waterloo," I said. "I have a chauffeur outside taking me back to Liverpool Street," he said. "I'll get him to drop you at Waterloo." We got into the car for the next hour and he spoke about the England team, his hopes and what he planned to do. He was very expansive and I was very impressed. If he had been interviewed for a TV programme people would have got a totally different approach. But in those days the PR side was in its infancy.'

John Cobbold never worried about putting 'spin' on his words to journalists. He told them everything, and more – and it was usually enhanced by colourful language. He was so outrageous that few journalists dared to quote his comments. The Hill-Woods shared his love for a chat with the writers. Denis Hill-Wood spoke to them for hours and was always contacted for the issues of the day. Peter Hill-Wood will speak openly when he is telephoned. But there is hardly a chairman left who behaves like this. Even the ones who try to promote their own egos – and there are many – tend to be very circumspect about the whole truth.

SIXTEEN

'WOR JACKIE' FAILS TO SCORE WITH IPSWICH

Jackie Milburn ('Wor Jackie' of Newcastle fame) succeeded Ramsey as Ipswich manager in 1963. Colleagues when they were players, the two men had little contact after Milburn's appointment. Ramsey's comment as he left 'I've left a good side behind' upset the normally tranquil Milburn because it wasn't true. There were hardly any young players coming up through the ranks.

The Cobbolds should have realised he was the wrong man. He was simply too nice. He was player-manager of Yiewsley in the Southern League, aged thirty-eight, when Cobbold rang him to ask him if he wanted the post. There were sixty applicants and it was odd to turn to Milburn. He wasn't a coach, like Ramsey, and had minimal experience. A better candidate would have been the Wolves defender Bill Slater, but he turned them down. Slater was a teacher and he has spent all his life outside football as a teacher (he is also the only former Footballer of the Year who regularly turns up for the annual Football Writers Dinner).

A heavy smoker, Milburn was edgy and nervous and in his sixteen months at the club, he signed thirty-three players – one every fortnight. One of the Scots newcomers was Frank Brogan, who was signed from Celtic. He was twenty-one and not long out of boarding school after gaining a scholarship. On 11 June 1964, he arrived at Ipswich station and walked to the ground. 'They showed me to the decrepit old pavilion and introduced me to Jackie Milburn,' he said. 'There was a knock at the door and this odd guy came in wearing plus fours, a tweed shirt, his tie askew and a pair of brogue shoes. He spoke in a posh voice and said "Frankie, is that right you are signing for us?" I said "that's right". "Do you take a drink?" he said. I had been at Celtic for six years and the chairman, Sir Robert Kelly, frowned on drinking. So I said "sometimes I have a small stout". John Cobbold turned towards Jackie Milburn and snorted "he's no f——ing good for us!"

'When I got to know him I used to have a drink with him and I never met anyone who drank more. I reckon he drank up to four bottles of spirit a day. He was like the wild man from Borneo sometimes – but what a character. He was unique. They don't make them like that any more. He came from a world which has disappeared.'

In Milburn's first full season, 1963/64, the club was relegated after conceding an average of three goals per game. Cobbold's response the next season was to take the whole playing squad with their wives on a cruise to the Mediterranean costing £3,000. He said 'I think the players did a wonderful job and I am sure they will enjoy themselves. Football will not be mentioned and the players will be free to do exactly as they wish.'

He befriended the Greek captain, regularly inviting him to join in shooting at seagulls when they were spotted close to the vessel

SS *Fiesta*. He was not a crack marksman and neither was the captain. Unfortunately the weather was bad and most of the party spent the time in their cabins trying to recover from sea sickness.

Cobbold loved indoor games, particularly cards and chess. Often he turned up at his pubs to watch the players taking part in darts matches. Larry Carberry, the Liverpool born full-back, said 'he wasn't much of a darts player. He liked to come along for a sociable drink… or two or three.' One player, Joey Broadfoot signed from Millwall, recalled 'He prided himself on not losing. He was always betting on the result of these games. He was ultra competitive. Jackie Milburn summed it all up when he told me that I hadn't seen him before I was signed so if it didn't work out no-one would put the blame on me.'

Broadfoot was one of the more interesting characters at Ipswich: cheeky, outspoken and likeable and he had a great relationship with John Cobbold during his two spells. He was always short of money and, when he first arrived, Cobbold lent him £20. Cobbold also gave him a signing on fee of £2,500 – which was then illegal under the Football League regulations. Broadfoot, a fast and speedy right-winger, rarely trained because he had a knee problem. He used to travel up to Ipswich by train. Later, he owned his own taxi.

He was twice imprisoned, once for running a brothel (which he strenuously denied), and once for buying foreign cars and changing their documents to sell in England. 'I was guilty as tried over the cars and served my sentence,' he said. Broadfoot was a non-conformist and while attending a banquet in Sweden he suddenly put his feet on the table, took out a Mars Bar, and proceeded to eat it. He still attends the club's annual dinner for former players. He now has an arthritic knee, however, which hampers his movement and these days is finding difficulty putting his feet up. And he has given up Mars bars.

On Boxing Day 1963 Ipswich recorded their heaviest home defeat, with Fulham's Graham Leggatt scoring a hat-trick in three and a half minutes in a 1-10 rout. It was the fastest hat-trick ever scored in the First Division. Interviewed by a radio reporter, Cobbold said 'It could have gone either way'. One of the directors recounted the story later when Robson took over and Robson said 'That's the sort of manager you need. He'll do for me!' Cobbold ordered a celebration dinner at the end of the season at the Great Eastern Hotel next to Liverpool Street Station, with all the staff and players attending.

Milburn sold Crawford to Wolves, which was seen as a mistake, and by September of the following year he was complaining of stress and told Cobbold he wanted to resign. Cobbold liked him and tried to persuade him to stay on but, after a 2-1 defeat at Norwich, the bitter rivals from forty-five miles up the road, he quit. Most clubs, realising that the manager was on his way out, would have a new man lined up. Some of them appoint new managers before the previous one is sacked or forced to resign. But Cobbold handled the change of manager according to the rules and it took him a month to find a new manager. The fresh incumbent was Bill McGarry, born at Stoke in 1927, who played for Port Vale, Huddersfield and Bournemouth and was capped 4 times by England. If Ramsey had been a hard man, this man was harder... much harder.

The *Official History of Ipswich FC* said of him 'he was an aggressive character who always gave 100 per cent himself and expected nothing less from everyone around him'. He introduced a Spartan training scheme to improve the fitness levels and those who failed to meet the standard were omitted and treated like outcasts. Joey Broadfoot described him as 'A moaner and a hard guy to deal with. I told him "you're so miserable". He said "you'd be miserable, if you were manager of this lot!" But he was okay.'

Cobbold and his directors left it to McGarry and there were frequent rows among the players, often leading to fisticuffs. One of the more explosive characters, Scotsman Bill Baxter, asked for a transfer but was talked into staying. He was one of the outstanding defenders in the Football League, although he was a man of only medium height. He shared McGarry's philosophy of playing it hard, with the emphasis on stopping the opposition. The players didn't like McGarry, but they had great respect for him.

Born in 1939, Baxter came from Broxburn, a village near Edinburgh, and was signed by Ramsey in 1960 when he was serving as a sapper at Aldershot. He was paid £15 a game – which was good money compared with the maximum of £20 a week. 'I remember we were playing a practice game in pre-season and I kicked Reg Pickett and Reg complained to Alf,' said Baxter. 'After training Alf called me up. I thought he was going to tell me to cut it out but to my surprise he said "go in harder".

'I never saw him lose his temper. He was like a school teacher. People ask me how he motivated us, but I suppose he had the right, self motivated players and he got the best out of them – the whole eleven.' Baxter spent ten years at Portman Road and averaged 40 League appearances out of an available 42 in each of those seasons. 'I hardly missed a game,' he said. 'I never had a bad injury.' But in 1997 he contracted athlete's foot, a simple complaint for sportsmen. 'My toes started turning black,' he said. 'I was in holiday in Croatia, I can't remember the name of the place, down on the right side some-where. I had diabetes and was advised to return home. I was living in Dunfermline, and I still live there now, and I saw a consultant and he said I ought to have my right leg amputated below the knee. I had no choice so I had it done in the Queen Margaret Hospital nearby. It was a big shock but you couldn't do anything about it. You just have to get on with it and deal with it. I'm the same weight as I was playing which is lucky and I still play bowls and golf. I used to work for British Telecom, but I've had to stop that. Now I'm enjoying my life in retirement.' His golf handicap was thirteen… and now he has time to maintain it.

Harold Smith, a director of the club between 1964 and 1995 and now vice president, recalled a board meeting during which the subject came up about McGarry's salary. 'Someone suggested that a pay rise ought to be in order after his impressive start,' he said. "Nonsense," said John Cobbold. "He wouldn't accept it." But McGarry told him "don't be daft, I'll take it." I think he got his rise.'

Smith described an incident on a ferry trip back from a game in Holland, 'Johnny was in second class and the pilot, who looked rather bad for drink, was in first class,' he said. 'In those days the club had to try to save every penny. The purser invited us over for a drink and he asked if we wanted to see the docking of the ship into harbour. We agreed and joined him on the bridge. I was astonished to see the pilot, with his cap askew, in charge. "Don't worry about him," said the captain. "He is incapable of piloting anything. Most of it is automatic now and we take no notice of him anyway." It was one of the few occasions when John failed to out drink the next man.'

Baxter recalled another cruise when Cobbold arrived at the ship only to be told his cabin didn't have a porthole. 'He was very upset,' said Baxter. 'He refused to take it and instead, persuaded some crew members to lend him a huge net which he suspended over a tiny swimming pool. He lay back in it, knocking back the wine.'

The relations between the chairman and the fiery McGarry varied from cordial and enthusiastic to resentment and, sometimes, rudeness. McGarry lost his temper when things went against him. 'F—— off,' the chairman usually responded. The two men were born within a few weeks apart and were opposites. Cobbold was a dilettante: McGarry was a single minded, ultra professional who was obsessed with his work. He was still coaching in his late sixties in Bophuthatswana after divorcing his long-standing English wife and having made a new home in Africa with a much younger, local woman. He was then seventy-five but was slowing down.

'Bill McGarry was one manager I could compete with very well because my knowledge of certain Anglo-Saxon words was as good as his,' said Mr John. 'He did a good job for us, getting us into the First Division again and I was sorry when he decided to go to Wolves. I saw him many times and he often admitted that one of his biggest mistakes was to leave Ipswich. Soon after he left he was pleading to me to come back and said "I've got more bloody scouts working under me at Wolves than Baden Powell ever had."

'When McGarry first arrived at Portman Road I got all the playing staff together in the dressing room to introduce them to the manager. It was so packed you couldn't breathe. I heard later from the players that as soon as I had left McGarry told them "That was your f——ing chairman and it is the last time he will come into this dressing room." It was the first time I had been into the dressing room and was certainly the last.'

Ipswich never had a fines box for swearing. 'I would soon be broke,' John said. Swearing and cursing is an intrinsic part of football and most players, even foreign players, still use swear words in every sentence. Managers set the tone and young players copy their example. The Cobbolds were set apart from the cursing classes on the work floor. They did it to shock or surprise, but few who knew them took much notice of it. 'With no women in the boardroom and in the directors' box it was looked on as a male preserve,' said a director. 'It was part of their eccentricity and their old world charm, if you could call it that.'

Doug Moran, the Scots striker from Falkirk, said 'Alf never swore. I think the worst thing he ever said was "that was bloody awful" if we hadn't played well. That's unusual in a dressing room. Alf never lost his rag. I can understand why people regarded him as aloof, but that wasn't how the players saw him.'

Under McGarry's hard-swearing regime the club finished fifth in the 1964/65 season and there were few laughs in the dressing room and on the training ground. However, there was a hilarious 'buckets of salt' incident in a game against Norwich, the traditional rivals. Kevin Keelan, the long-serving Norwich goalkeeper, complained that he lost his footing on an icy surface when he let in two goals and at half-time the referee asked the ground staff to spread salt in the goalmouths. Seeing the salt being tipped on the ground at the end where Ipswich was to defend, the Norwich fans objected, leading to scuffles. 'Pick it up!' they shouted but it was melting as they spoke.

At the time hooliganism was developing into a major problem and the FA issued a ten point directive, banning the throwing of toilet rolls and other missiles, stopping managers from coaching from the line, prohibiting criticism of referees and among others, telling the clubs to concentrate more on entertainment and less on winning at all costs. Ipswich rarely infringed and McGarry had to make the best of his resources. For the first time supporters had to watch dour, unimaginative football and his exasperation was often expressed by kicking down doors. A carpenter was regularly brought in to effect repairs.

Cobbold ordered pictures of himself and the other directors to be put up in the directors' toilets to relieve the dreariness. There were five photographs reproduced in a framed picture and it still hangs on a wall. Top left features a snapshot of Patrick Cobbold as a baby wearing a cheeky smile, sitting on a donkey with a caption 'saddle sore'. On the other side is a photograph of his brother John, also an infant, twiddling his fingers. The caption reads 'this little pig went to market'. John had a peculiar fondness for pigs.

Ray Crawford remembered an incident many years earlier: 'We were travelling on a train and Jackie Milburn and Mr John and some other directors were having a reasonably serious discussion about the youth scheme, as serious as you can when Mr John was about,' he said. 'Mr John looked out the window and suddenly shouted out "look at those pigs, look at the size of those bollocks!" Everyone roared and that was the end of the serious discussion.'

Two other photographs in the picture hanging on the wall were of directors who died, Willie Kerr and Murray Sangster. Kerr is portrayed as a baby with an appealing quiff and, as he was a Scot and a reader of Robbie Burns, the caption reads 'oh would some power the giftie gie us to see ourselves as others see us'. Sangster's picture was less attractive and the caption says 'even his father was sore about this picture'. The only living director on the picture is Harold Smith and the picture shows him dressed as a baby girl. The caption is 'Thank Heaven for girls'.

Patrick Cobbold still had that smile up until he died. It was a diffident, almost apologetic smile. He looked the same on the day he was elected as a director of the football club in 1964, eighteen years after his brother John joined the board. His mother, Lady Blanche, was appointed the first President in 1965 and she may well have been the first female President at any of the ninety-two Football League clubs. As a former Master of the Hunt, she was well equipped and she took her duties very seriously. She was a fearsome lady but loved and respected by those who knew her well. She never forgot a name. Robson said of her 'she was a very distinguished lady and didn't come often to the ground. They didn't allow ladies in to the boardroom. Johnny wouldn't allow that.'

On another trip to Holland by ferry to play a match the Cobbolds forgot to arrange a ticket for Lady Blanche. They arrived at the ground and Lady Blanche wasn't there. 'Christ,' said Johnny. 'We'll have to send out a search party.' An hour before kick-off Lady Blanche turned up – the Dutch were more liberal about women being in special areas – and Johnny said 'I'm terribly sorry mother. How did you get here?' 'I got a ticket like everyone else,' she replied.

Around that time the club was in financial difficulties and Mr John paid the wages for a few weeks himself. With Ipswich finishing in fifteenth position in the 1965/66 season, equalling the points tally of Norwich, McGarry was tempted to leave. Wolves wanted him and the directors blocked the move. Cobbold said 'Wolves can have me if they like, but not McGarry. I am dispensable. He is not.'

Ipswich were close to an outbreak of hooliganism in the 1966/67 season when the players, staff and supporters of Huddersfield were incensed by a penalty decision in a Second Division match at Portman Road. Their protests were so vehement that the home supporters were furious. Those standing near the dugouts shouted 'Shut up!' and one of a political bent, clearly a Conservative, said loudly 'Clear off back to Huddersfield and take your Gannex coat with you!' This was a reference to the garment the Labour leader Harold Wilson used to wear. Wilson was born in Huddersfield and a large statue of him stands near the railway station.

When the spot-kick was converted by Frank Brogan, an Ipswich fan ran on to the side of the pitch, picked up the trainer's bucketful of water and tipped it over the Huddersfield manager Tom Johnston and the substitute. The FA had just introduced substitutes and there was a limit to one per team. It was the turn of Johnston to be enraged, jumping to his feet and shouting and waving his arms. The linesman tried to placate him and it took some time to calm him down. Johnston, a Scot born in 1918, managed a host of lower division and relatively obscure foreign clubs, including Valdokoski Harka in Finland, and had three spells in charge at Huddersfield. He was described as 'a shrewd strategist who ruled his clubs with a rod of iron'.

Except for Tom Johnston, the soaked substitute, and a few angry supporters, the rest of the football fraternity in England were generally euphoric following England's winning of the World Cup. Attendances rose sharply with 3,000 extra customers turning up at Portman Road at every home game and a grateful nation gave deserved honours to

Ramsey and his captain. Prime Minister Harold Wilson bestowed a knighthood on Ramsey – or Her Majesty the Queen did to be more accurate – and in the New Year's List Bobby Moore was given the OBE. Later in their lives, Ramsey and Wilson shared the same distressing illness, Alzheimer's. Both had remarkable recall of facts and figures when they were in their prime. It was tragic that they should be struck down. Long before England's triumph at Wembley, the players were already calling Alf 'Sir Alf'. He kept his promise that England would win the Jules Rimet trophy and Cobbold postponed his holiday to Nassau by a day to call in on the new knight to congratulate him in person.

The fortunes of Ipswich Town FC improved dramatically in the following season and McGarry's stern demeanour switched to broad smiles when Ipswich won the Second Division title in 1967/68. Out came that old open-topped bus and the parade was led by the band of the Green Jackets. It was the club's fifth championship in fifteen seasons and vast amounts of alcohol were drunk – with John Cobbold leading the way. McGarry presented his chairman with an £8,000 Rolex watch on behalf of an appreciative club, modestly inscribed 'From the greatest to the great'. A few weeks later, Cobbold was walking along the concourse towards the main stand at Stamford Bridge when his watch was snatched off his wrist in a crowd. 'I wasn't quick enough off the mark,' he said. Maybe he was unsteady on his feet by this time and was in no position to resist. (Even though a fit, young footballer like Gary Mabbutt had his Rolex snatched a few years ago.)

A new Second Division trophy was handed over by League President Len Shipman, a jovial man who liked a tipple, because the original silver one had previously melted in the heat of a fire at Coventry's Highfield Road ground. In 1968 the Football League appointed a banker and part-time referee, named Graham Kelly, as assistant secretary and his first job was to visit a group of clubs to inspect their financial records. Cobbold was quite shocked. 'We've got nothing to hide,' he said. 'He's wasting his f——ing time.' After a quick look at the books, Kelly joined Cobbold and some of his friends and plenty of wine was consumed. Kelly recalled in his book *Sweet FA* that 'John Cobbold was one of the game's great characters. He owned a white

Rover at the time and when we came out he saw his driver sitting in the backseat watching TV. 'Shift your arse, f——face!' he shouted. Before we were driven off to a hotel for lunch, he went over to the practice ground and peed all over the grass. He said 'that shows you, I've got absolutely nothing to hide!'

Back in the First Division, Ipswich sank towards the bottom of the table and McGarry, despite signing a new contract a few weeks earlier, announced he was joining Wolves in succession to Ronnie Allen, the former England forward. Allen, a longstanding manager, was yet another footballer who spent a lot of time as a player heading heavy leather footballs and died of Alzheimer's Disease in 2000. Only now has serious research been undertaken into the subject of brain damage.

McGarry had been in charge for only four years when he resigned. John Cobbold said in a statement 'The Board has decided to release him with disappointment and reluctance, bearing in mind that his contract was only signed a few months ago and the Board went out of their way to meet his demands. We felt that to bind McGarry to his contract would create difficulties and embarrassment and would not be in the interests of the club in the long run.' It was couched in polite language but you could imagine Cobbold coming out with a few oaths under his breath.

SEVENTEEN

THE CASE OF THE RELUCTANT GARDENER

In the months after England won the World Cup there were hardly any foreign players playing in the Football League. One of the first was Colin Viljoen, a South African who made his debut for Ipswich against Portsmouth in March 1967 and scored a hat-trick against Portsmouth. But unlike now, the barriers were still up to prevent overseas players appearing for English clubs. Jobs were jealously guarded and newcomers were held at bay.

The son of a plasterer from Doornfontein, a poor suburb of Johannesburg, the slightly built Viljoen was seventeen when he was spotted by an English coach named Gordon Edelston, who knew McGarry well. 'He's very quick and skilful and scores goals,' said Edelston. McGarry reported to John Cobbold 'I've got a kid who looks like being an exciting one. We ought to get him over here for a trial.' It hadn't occurred to Cobbold, however, that the boy wasn't eligible to play. He would need a work permit. 'I'll get that sorted out,' said the chairman.

For a seventeen-year-old to be sent on his own from Johannesburg to London was daunting enough, but there was a strike by British Airways staff and instead of arriving at Heathrow, Viljoen found himself in Basle via SAA, the South African carrier. He had to stop overnight, lodging with a friend of a stewardess, before flying on to London. It was 82 degrees when he stepped off from the aircraft in London. 'It was like being home,' he said later. In 1965 it was a very hot summer. There was another mishap on his long and tiring adventure – Reg Tyrell, the Ipswich scout, was supposed to have picked him up but mistook the right day. Tyrell thought he was coming the following week.

Most seventeen-year-olds would have panicked, but the mature Viljoen rang the parents of his sister's husband who lived in Stratford in East London. They offered him a bed for the night and, carrying his small bag, he journeyed on the District Line to Stratford and spent a day there before Tyrell collected him. Tyrell, a kindly man who specialised in discovering young talent, drove him on to Ipswich where he stayed for the first few weeks.

Once Viljoen started training, McGarry realised that Edelston was right: his trialist was going to be a star. 'He could be the key man in our side,' he said. 'And he's the quickest at the club.' Viljoen was timed at 10.2 seconds in the hundred yards, beating everyone in the squad by yards. He had to be in the first team. The secretary, David Rose, wrote to the Home Office seeking a work permit, only for the request to be turned down. Britain's employment rules at the time barred professional footballers from abroad playing for English clubs.

It was a closed shop. McGarry saw Cobbold and said 'What can we do?' Cobbold thought for a while. 'I know,' he said. 'I'll tell them we're given him a job as my assistant gardener at Capel Hall. He doesn't actually need to do any gardening…'

The work permit was granted for two years and he was given permission to play as an amateur, except that he didn't pull up any weeds. He never even went to Capel Hall in this period. 'I didn't like gardening,' he said recently. 'I've got a fairly big garden in Edendale, one of the nicest parts of Johannesburg, and I employ a very good gardener. He does it. I was paid £45 a week for being the phantom gardener at Ipswich. Mr John thought it was very funny!'

Viljoen had to wait five years before he was granted naturalisation papers. Cobbold won the concession over a work permit by enlisting the services of Sir Dingle Foot, MP for Ipswich (who beat him in a by-election in 1957 by 26,898 votes to his 19,161 and also lost to him in the 1959 General Election). Foot had become a close friend and Cobbold often took him as a guest to Ipswich Town's home games.

Tyrell also recommended a future England international, Mick Mills, from Portsmouth in the same week that Viljoen arrived and they grew up in digs in the town. Mrs Lockwood, the lady in charge, rationed them to one electric fire in the front room in her old, tiny house. There was no heating in the bedrooms. Viljoen's fellow teenage guest was Derek Jefferson, a defender from Morpeth who was three months younger. 'He was a killer,' Viljoen recalled many years later. 'McGarry trained him to whack people and was often sent off. He was a madman on the field, always being booked. He was short sighted and that was his excuse. Now he's a born-again Christian.

'McGarry was good for me. Training was all about getting fit and maintaining a very high standard of discipline. I didn't mind that. Everyone was wary of him because he could whack you if he thought you were slacking. He had total control in the club. The chairman accepted every word he said.

'I used to get in first at 8.30 in the morning and cleaned the boots of McGarry and his assistant Sammy Chung. McGarry used to play in the practice games and tackled opponents like he wanted to hurt them, or toughen them up. He liked me and I think Pat Godbold and some of the staff liked me because I used to say "Good morning, how are you?" and be polite. A lot of footballers don't have any manners. They think they are stars and they are rude to waitresses and secretaries.

'One of my favourite characters was Bobby Hunt, one of three brothers who all played for Colchester. He was a very funny man and in one game, against Manchester City, the referee was about to blow the whistle to start the match when he shouted out "Hey ref, how long is there to go?" When I told Mr John he laughed like a drain. He kept repeating it to his cronies for the rest of the week. I thought Mr John was a bit of a nutcase when I first met him. He used to spend a lot of time with the apprentices, laughing and joking with them and buying them drinks. He was very generous and he spent money like water. They were kids from all round the country, away from their homes for the first time, and he made a big effort to settle us in.'

Danny Hegan, another player, nicknamed Viljoen 'Ace' and he loved it – although some of the older players were slightly jealous. By the time of the 1978 FA Cup final that feeling of resentment bubbled over and his thirteen years at Portman Road ended with bitterness.

Two summers after his arrival, Viljoen went home to Johannesburg and told the new manager Bobby Robson that he wasn't coming back. 'I said I wasn't earning enough money,' he said. Robson banned him from the team but, realising that he had great talent, he persuaded the directors to increase his weekly wage. 'Bobby was a great motivator and still is,' said Viljoen. 'He talked you into almost anything. I remember we were short of players before a big game and I was injured. After training he called me into his office overlooking the pitch and he said "You've got to play, if you play, we'll win". He went on for an hour and a half. He likes a talk. So I played. And we won.

'He's an amazing man. He has conquered cancer twice and still keeps going on at the same pace in his seventies. He never stops. He's got this great passion for the game and I can't see that ever ending. He's a fantastic communicator. He always had time to speak to anyone, from the top to the bottom. I won't say he was the greatest tactician. He used to set his team out in a straightforward way, usually 4-4-2, and asked them to get plenty of crosses in. I once asked him "what's the best advice you could give anyone?" He said "never hold grudges. Once it's happened, it's gone." He had lots of rows but always forgot about them afterwards. The other piece of advice he gave me was that the best players don't make the best teams. You've got to get players to gel and make into a good, all round team. Alf Ramsey said the same thing.'

On one pre-season, Robson had the team quartered in a hotel in Magaluf, Majorca and someone noticed that water was cascading through a room above. 'Who did that?' said one of the players. No-one owned up. Later one of Robson's assistants confessed that Robson had forgotten to turn the taps off. He was forgetful even in those days.

Viljoen made his two appearances for England in 1974 in a hectic week of the British Championship, a 0-0 draw against Ireland on Saturday and 2-2 against Wales the following Wednesday. 'It was the proudest moment of my career,' he said. 'I lined up with ten English players and me and it was a time when England had a surfeit of outstanding midfield players, like Trevor Brooking, Tony Currie, Alan Hudson, Alan Ball, Gerry Frances, Stan Bowles and Colin Bell. Someone as good as John Hollins couldn't get in.'

At his large, beautifully appointed bungalow in Johannesburg he still has his England shirt and cap framed and hung on the wall of his lounge. The shirt looks odd by modern standards. It was made of airtex material with red and blue edging. He was awarded only one cap for the British Championship. That was the procedure until the Championships were abolished – that accounted for the fact that many players of the day ended up with far fewer caps than they should have had.

Normally players wear lightweight suits in the summer for international duty, but Don Revie set up a committee among the squad to help design a heavy duty off-white suit with six inch lapels and velvet lining. 'The material was so stiff it looked like a tent,' said Viljoen. Most of the players discarded theirs and one FA official of the time said 'The suits were unwearable and they threw them away. Oxfam wouldn't have taken them.' Viljoen still keeps his suit but never wears it, not surprisingly.

Alan Hudson, the Chelsea forward who was thought unlucky not to have more than two caps, played a key part in designing the suits. 'I think he was taking the mick,' said the FA official. Under Ramsey there was no committee of players. He made all the decisions himself and when members of the FA International Committee, his bosses, raised the matter of sponsorship and exploiting commercial opportunities, Ramsey replied 'What do we need to do that for? The players are playing for the honour of their country, that's enough.'

Revie took the opposite view and seized every possible chance to bring in extra money, not just for the players, but for himself. Sven Goran Eriksson found himself in a similar position in the 2002 World Cup campaign, letting the players wear boring dark navy blue suits and hideous brown shoes. They were given goody bags containing £10,000 worth of laptops, electronic games and videos to stave off boredom during their visit to the Far East. Eriksson was criticised for taking part in an advertising campaign for Sainsbury's, for which he was paid £200,000. TV adverts showed him leaning over a plate of fried egg, bacon, chips, bread and tomatoes – the traditional English breakfast which has been banned by modern football coaches and managers!

Viljoen was out of football during most of the 1977/78 season through injury and was desperate to regain fitness in time for the FA Cup final. The week before he was picked to play against Aston Villa and Ipswich lost 4-0, with some of the players appearing not to be trying. He was very angry. 'They didn't want me to have the ball,' he said. 'They wanted Roger Osborne to be in the cup final side. Roger was a workhorse of a player and Bobby Robson chose him ahead of me. I didn't go to Wembley and I didn't watch the game on TV. Roger scored the winning goal, so they were right. Everyone thought I was still injured.'

After the Wembley victory Viljoen went to see Robson and told him 'It's time for me to go'. Robson didn't talk him out of it and said 'OK, QPR want you and I'm asking £100,000.' Rangers were unable to match the fee so he went to Manchester City instead. His medical examination at Maine Road lasted just five minutes. 'I couldn't believe it,' he said. 'With my injury experiences in the previous season they should have checked things thoroughly but they didn't.' He played only 25 matches for City and departed to join Chelsea.

That was another unhappy period for him and, after 19 appearances between 1980 and 1982, he retired to take up a pub near Heathrow. He had a recurring hamstring injury and the chairman Ken Bates said to him 'You're finished. Hamstring.' Viljoen said 'Horrible man. He wanted my insurance to be paid up, but I resisted and saw an expert, Dr John Williams. He diagnosed a snapped hamstring and eventually I left, on my terms, not Bates's.'

Viljoen went through two unhappy marriages and now is happily living with Judy, an Afrikaans girl who is twenty years younger. He is a football agent now, running his own business from his home. 'I married too young,' he said. 'The second one didn't work either. It's not easy in football. Footballers pick up girls and they rush into these things.'

He specialises in handling young African players, moving them on to Europe and he takes only his 10 per cent cut. He will never be a millionaire. Most of his fellow agents are very rich men, shifting professional footballers from club to club around the world. There are three kinds of football agents – the honest ones, the sharks who push players into changing clubs to make obscene sums of money, and the crooks. The Cobbolds would have hated the majority of them. The Ipswich creed was to encourage their manager to find young players and teach them how to become international players. It was a family, based on stability.

Clubs like Ipswich have now found it very difficult to stay at the top without overspending and joining the pack. As Ipswich dropped back into Division One from the Premiership in 2002, the successors to the Cobbolds had to try to re-establish normality and living within their means. It wasn't easy. Football at the highest level in England has been totally distorted by the excessive payments to clubs by television and there were signs that the boom was slowing down. But the market was still absurdly overheated.

EIGHTEEN

COBBOLD APPOINTS
MICKEY MOUSE!

John Cobbold took his time to appoint a new man and thought he had a good candidate in the studious Frank O'Farrell from the West Ham stable, renowned as a gentleman. Cobbold and his directors Murray Sangster and Ken Brightwell met O'Farrell in London and they agreed a deal. A day later the chairman of Torquay, where O'Farrell had been the manager, rang to say his manager intended to stay. Cobbold was livid, especially as O'Farrell left Torquay to join Leicester a few days later. At the end of the season, Leicester was relegated and Cobbold chortled 'Serve him right you s——.'

The new contenders were Jim Scoular of Cardiff, Bob Stokoe of Carlisle, Billy Bingham, from Plymouth, and Bobby Robson, unemployed. Robson's name was added because Dave Sexton, the Chelsea manager, wrote to Cobbold pleading his friend's case. 'He wrote saying Bobby should be given a chance,' said Cobbold. 'They'd been on FA coaching courses and they were the same age.' Bingham, a loquacious Irishman, was asked to attend at the Great Eastern Hotel, the hotel closest to the end of the railway line from Ipswich, along with Robson. Bingham was offered the job but changed his mind, saying he was happy to remain at Plymouth. Cobbold was heard to say 'Christ, we're down to Robson'. After a few more drinks, he joked to a drinking colleague 'we're going to give the job to Mickey Mouse!'

Cobbold didn't seem to rate him. Robson had been sacked by Fulham after nine months and was forced to sign on the dole. The day he was told the news he had to go, by the chairman Eric Miller, he burst into tears. Miller, a shady financier, later committed suicide, shooting himself in the head. Robson put up such a convincing performance with his passion and enthusiasm, that Cobbold took him on a salary of £5,000 a year without a contract, which was soon changed to a three-year contract. Cobbold said 'We could tell he was the type for us and that he would never let us down. If we kept faith in him he would keep faith in us. I told him "We're a Cinderella club and your job is to keep us in the First Division. We don't have any money. Good luck.'"

Next day Cobbold told the *Evening Star* 'I was very impressed by him and there is no doubt he is the man for the job. We're not giving him a contract, but I realise no manager can be judged in less than two years. I sincerely hope Bobby stays with us considerably longer than that.' Just short of his thirty-sixth birthday, Robson was starting out on an adventure which was to last almost fourteen years.

When Robson took over, Ipswich were eighteenth and, after several stormy months, he took the club to twelfth in his first season. His second game, against Manchester United (which featured George Best on his first visit to Portman Road), ended in a triumphant 1-0 win. He recalled 'Johnny didn't say a lot early on. He called me Bobby and I called the brothers Mr John and Mr Patrick. He didn't put any pressure on me and let me get on with it. I was a teetotaller when I started but he always invited me into the directors' sanctum and insisted I should have a drink. I drank sweet sherry.

'The directors were great people. Posh really, with their tweeds and check suits. I can honestly say they were unique. I've never known directors like that then or now. Directors are different people these days. They want results, otherwise they try another manager. Mr John's approach was that if we lost he would ring me the next morning, commiserate about the defeat and invite me and Elsie out for lunch. If we won, he never bought lunch. After a win he used to open a bottle of champagne. If we lost, he'd open two bottles.'

Cobbold joked 'There is no truth in the rumour that Bobby Robson runs the Ipswich Town team alone. On the contrary, I am a ruthless dictator. I telephone him every morning and say "What's on your mind, Bob?" He tells me everything and then I bark out my orders. They are the same every day. They are "Right, carry on."'

Robson needed plenty of support from the directors because a stream of dissatisfied players left the club and two of them, Baxter and Tommy Carroll, were never picked again after a fight with Robson, supported by his coach Cyril Lea. Baxter ripped down the team sheet on the door and Robson responded angrily. Baxter threw punches and the two men grappled on the ground before another player, Geoff Hammond, intervened. Baxter and Carroll were sold for £31,000. Cobbold liked Baxter, but he and his directors backed his manager. Baxter never returned to Portman Road until he attended the fortieth reunion for the 1961/62 Championship side in the spring of 2002. Thirty-three years on from the fight in the dressing room, Baxter now has no bitterness. 'That's all forgotten,' he said. 'These things happen sometimes in football.'

Before Carroll was sold there was an interesting insight into Cobbold's style of business management. Carroll, a full-back from Dublin, kept pestering Robson about his salary. Robson kept turning him down and Carroll insisted on a meeting with the chairman. 'I'm telling you,' said Robson. 'There's no more money and the chairman leaves these matters to me.' Carroll pressed for a meeting with Cobbold. Eventually, after Carroll gave a damaging interview to the local newspaper, Cobbold relented. 'Let him in,' he told Robson. Carroll was invited into the boardroom and Cobbold said 'I understand you want to see me. Well, here I am and you are looking at me. I am the chairman of this club and this is the manager, Bobby Robson. Mr Robson handles the wages of players, not me.' With that, Cobbold walked out, leaving Carroll dumbfounded. Carroll was sold to Birmingham City and lasted there only a further season in professional football.

Bespectacled Derek Jefferson, a defender from Morpeth who was short-sighted, was the club's first player to be sent off at Portman Road in the Robson era and only the second player to be sent off in Ipswich colours in a League match. He was Ipswich's answer to Nobby Stiles (who was also short-sighted). 'I was a bit of a nut case,' he said recently. 'I was lucky. God came into my life and I remarried and now I'm coaching and working with kids in inner cities in Birmingham and London on a grant from the Football Foundation. I'm in with a group whose aim is to take kids off the streets and get them into meaningful activities. Football is a start for them and they learn about standards and how they and their parents can improve standards. It's very rewarding. If I hadn't become a Christian, I don't think I would be alive now.'

Robson was like Brian Clough in that he insisted on sportsmanship on the field. If players infringed the rules, he would say 'that cost a suspension, it's not worth it'. On another occasion Robson wanted to buy players – the club had earned extra money from improved attendances – and the directors told him there was £100,000 available. After his usual long days on the training pitch, Robson and his scouts drove round the country looking at talent. 'Before I bought Allan Hunter we drove a 500-mile round trip to Blackpool and back, and that was before the M1 was finished,' he said. 'It was well worth it.'

Robson fixed on two players, Jimmy Robertson from Arsenal for £55,000 and Frank Clarke from QPR for £44,000. He signed them and rang Cobbold afterwards with the news. 'He didn't even know the names,' he said. 'That was the type of chairman he was. Can you imagine one of today's chairmen allowing the manager to sign a player who he hadn't spoken to himself or hadn't heard of?'

After Robson's first season he was told that McGarry had promised a holiday in the sun for the whole playing staff and their wives. Robson was against the idea, saying the wives – as well as the players – did not deserve it. He was aghast. Cobbold explained 'They've got to go. We gave our word.' A three-match tour was fixed in Cyprus to cover the costs and a group of fifty-seven people, including some of the directors, went off to Heathrow. The trip was a disaster, with the wives arguing with each other and complaining to Robson about their rooms, the food and other trivial matters. 'It's impossible to please them,' he told Cobbold. Cobbold sympathised. 'That's the last time I do that,' said the harassed manager. Cobbold said 'Next time we'll leave the wives behind.'

Arsenal went on several summer tours, with the players taking their wives along, but they also found many unexpected problems. 'It's amazing how wives can fall out,' said a former player. 'There's plenty of jealousy and pettiness. It was a good reason to leave your wife behind. Some wives didn't go and the single players often picked up other women and it was reported back. You'd soon find a marriage breaking up!'

Robson's patience was also tested in 1971 when Chelsea's Alan Hudson shot into the side netting. As the ball rebounded back into play from a stanchion, referee Roy Capey signalled a goal. A furious Robson went to see the referee. 'He was shaking,' he said. 'He realised he'd made a mistake. The linesman was right there. He had a better view. But he didn't do anything either. The club didn't really want a fuss about it so we accepted it.' In these days the TV cameras would have righted such an injustice but Ipswich's muted appeal was rejected. Ipswich lost 2-1.

A new stand, seating 3,700 at a cost of £180,000, was built that year in place of the old wooden 'Chicken Run,' opened by Sir Alf Ramsey. Robson also completed the signing of Hunter, the Blackburn Rovers centre half, for £90,000. A tough, uncompromising defender from Sion Mills in Northern Ireland, he had the same birthday as Mr John. The chairman always sent him a birthday card signing 'from my loving brother.'

Hunter looked like a character in the film *Zulu* – upright and moustachioed. Despite his unsmiling appearance, he usually led the singsongs on the coach or on a plane trip. He recalled 'when we were on plane trips Mr John always insisted on a round of drinks once the aircraft took off. Most other clubs never offered drinks until the plane set off for home after the match, and only if the team had won.'

The Ipswich fans called for Robson to be dismissed after the home side lost a League Cup tie against Manchester United. George Best destroyed the Ipswich defence with a brilliant hat-trick and Robson tried to explain it away by saying Best was the difference between the sides. 'I feared for my job,' said Robson. 'It was the first time the fans turned on me and it wasn't nice. It was the first time I'd heard cries of "Robson out!"'

Next day Cobbold called a board meeting and sent for his manager. 'I was very anxious,' said Robson. The chairman called the Board to attention and said 'Gentlemen, the first business of the day is to officially record in the minutes the apologies of this Board to the manager for the behaviour of the supporters last night. Agreed? If it ever occurs in this ground again, I will resign as chairman. Forthwith. Right, on to the next business.'

One of his players, Irishman Bryan Hamilton, said 'He wasn't known as a clever businessman. He wasn't that sort of person. But one decision showed that his heart was in the right place and it was

a fantastic gesture. He was incredibly generous and he revered Bobby
and I think it was reciprocated.

'When I was signed in 1970 I came into the office and a jovial looking man, shabbily dressed, was sitting there eating ice cream. He was
a strange looking fellow and he offered me some. I went to Bobby's
office later and after a chat he said "I'll introduce you to the chairman". In came this man… it was Mr John. He talked to anyone and
treated them all the same, the highest and the most humble. And like
his mother, he never forgot a name. One day a couple of parents had
brought their sons from Ireland for trials and he invited them to Capel
Hall. He opened the champagne and poured it and he was still wearing
his dressing gown.'

Later that season, when the club had slumped to the bottom of the
table, Robson was again called in, this time to offer him an improved
contract. Cobbold said 'Our managers do not come and go at this
club. Our manager's name is not written in chalk on his door with a
wet sponge nailed by the side.' In Robson's early years, the crowd was
lukewarm about him. Brian Talbot, the midfield player who signed for
the club a week after his seventeenth birthday, said: 'For his first three
seasons he used to get a lot of stick but Mr John wouldn't hear a bad
word about him. He told Bobby "ignore them, it's me who counts and
I'm right behind you."'

Talbot, who was born in Ipswich in 1953, made his debut seven
months later at Burnley's Turf Moor. He said 'We used to have a lei-
surely coach ride up there and all the directors went with us. The chairman always booked a room in a hotel on the way up there on a long
journey and on the way back for a proper dinner. Except him. All he
had was three whiskies. He wasn't a big eater.' Trevor Kirton, the driver
known as 'Wheels', recalled 'Mr John wasn't a great lover of travelling
in the coach and often he used to ask me to stop in London in heavy
traffic and get out. He would disappear down the underground and
finish the journey by public transport. On one occasion, on route to
the Midlands, we stopped for a toilet break at Cambridge. After a short
time, I was told to drive off, although he was still in the toilets.

'The directors used to come up the night before and they would
always have a sweep to guess the time the coach arrived. The person

who picked the furthest time away from the exact time would buy the first round of drinks. If the chairman lost, which he did much of the time, he would announce that I was sacked. The other directors also cottoned on to it and I was sacked every journey.

'One of my other jobs was to look after the bar in the Directors' Lounge. When I first started, keen to please, I asked the Cobbold brothers if it was a good idea to bring in some different drinks. Mr John said "Don't bother. The drinks we serve here are proper drinks. It's not a party, if they don't like it, they needn't come." Malcolm Allison was the person who started the ban on cigars. There were always boxes of cigars and on one occasion the box of big Havanas had run out. Allison was a kind of person whom the chairman didn't warm to. Allison started moaning, complaining about the size of the cigars, and Mr John told me "this is the last time you put cigars in the boardroom". And I don't think any were brought in again.'

Hamilton, who signed from Linfield in 1971, said 'I had the happiest five years of my playing career at Ipswich. The quality of life was different to any club I'd encountered and I played with, and managed or coached, thirteen clubs. The Cobbolds were fans and they loved the club and never criticised anyone. It was such a relaxed place.'

In his football career, Hamilton and his family moved house fourteen times. 'It put a great strain on your wife but you had to do it,' he said. 'And we're still married! A lot of marriages broke up and I'd say the percentage of divorces are even higher now than those days. Players had to make the best of it from their careers. I was sad to leave but I went to Everton because I wanted to join a big club. Ipswich wasn't a big club.'

The Cobbolds used to entertain their players who attended the annual dinner of the Professional Footballers' Association dinner in London and paid for their rooms in a hotel. Talbot said 'We called them Mr John's pyjama parties. The Cobbolds paid all the expenses for the players, laying on a bar at their room and he always presided in his pyjamas. It could go on for a few hours. There was no expense spared. He saw it as a reward for their efforts over the season.'

Cyril Lea, the softly spoken Welsh wing half who was born in Moss, had an extraordinary story about the Cobbolds. Lea, who was at the club for almost fifteen years as a player and coach under Robson between 1964 and 1979, was soon inured into the Cobbold drinking habit. 'Just after I signed I was invited in to the boardroom and was handed a large whisky,' he said. 'It was a huge one and I had to drink it. I think he was trying to get me sozzled.

'The night before a game we were having dinner at a hotel, drinking champagne. You can't imagine it happening these days. Mr John asked a waiter to bring in another ice bucket. There was a bottle in it, presumably champagne. Mr John got up, picked the bottle up and walked round to Patrick, emptying the bottle over his brother's head. It transpired it was water, not champagne. Everyone treated it as a big joke and Patrick sat there as though nothing happened. Then he rose, slowly took his coat off and handed it to a smiling waiter. "Can you take this to the oven in the kitchen to warm this up?" he said. They were like overgrown schoolboys.

'John was the more eccentric of the two. Bobby Robson gave the okay to most of the changes at the club and one day it was decided to tart up the front of the directors' box. A carpenter fitted some veneer, a thin strip of wood in front of the visitors' part of the box. Mr John saw it and sat in front of it. He started to kick it, making a hole. By the time he had finished, there wasn't much left of it. "I don't want to be different from anyone else," he explained. "We're not show offs."

'On another occasion he invited a coach party to look round his home at Capel Hall. It was mid-morning and Patrick was still in bed. "Come along" said John. "This is the best bedroom in the house. Don't worry about him." As the startled guests came into the room they saw Patrick in his pyjamas in his bed. "Oh that's the time," said Patrick.

'John was always up to tricks. He thought Bobby was on the serious side and did his best to ruffle him. We were organising sprints along the track at the ground one day and, as Bobby was about to shout "go" with three or four players on their marks, there was a voice from the back of the stand shouting "go!" Bobby was furious. He turned to a muffled figure and said "Cut that out. I'm the bloke giving the signal, not you. Keep quiet." The players got ready again and as Robson was about to start the man called "go" again. "I told you," said Bobby. "You do that again and I'll have you thrown out. That's your last chance."

The players got down, Bobby was about to give the signal and this fellow piped up again. "Go" he shouted. Bobby went puce in the face. He stormed over to the man, whose face was partially covered, and said "that's it, you're out". The man said "I can't go, the chairman told me to do this. I've got my orders." He was a member of the ground staff and Bobby didn't recognise him.'

John Cobbold wasn't a buffoon, although some people thought he was. Lea said 'At many of our night outs, he would sit down at the piano and play the piano like an accomplished musician. The first time he did it was at a hotel in Belgium on one of the tours. The locals were entranced. He would sing, but he wasn't the best singer in the world.'

NINETEEN

PEEING ON THE BOARDROOM CARPET

There was a special bond between the directors of Ipswich, Southampton and Arsenal – the Cobbolds, the Southampton directors Lt-Col. Sir George Meyrick (Bart) MC, TD and John Corbett and the Hill-Woods (Denis Hill-Wood and his son, Peter). Most of them were Old Etonians with the same background, and with a love for good wine and good cigars. They also shared the Cobbolds' beliefs about the Corinthian spirit.

One day, as the two sets of players were about to start the contest on the field, Arsenal's honorary padre, the Revd Noel Bone – a gentle and inoffensive man – said 'Best of luck, may the best team win'. Mr John responded 'F—— good luck! We WANT to win.' 'I think Noel was rather shocked,' said Peter Hill-Wood. 'There were boozy affairs and his language could be rather strong.'

Ken Friar, the long-serving secretary of Arsenal, said 'He was a man's man, a great man. And he was a very honourable man. He used to have his spaniels in the boardroom racing around and some visiting directors were a bit uneasy. John used to explain he couldn't find dog-sitters so he had to bring them. Sometimes they used to relieve themselves.

'I was told he left Glemham Hall to live in Capel Hall because he left the water running in his bath and the ceiling collapsed. Lady Blanche was very upset and gave him his marching orders.' The Cobbolds used to recount the story about the time when one of their bigger dogs attacked and killed a chiwawa at Capel Hall. The lady who owned it was mortified and John Cobbold tried to commiserate and failed. "I'll buy you another one!" he said. She burst into tears. But later she accepted his offer.'

Hill-Wood was once invited to stay in Capel Hall. 'It was a very good night,' he said. 'He brought out a large bottle of whisky and the only thing was that he left the French windows open and the donkeys, "Alka" and "Seltzer" keep wandering around the house. He didn't mind. By ten at night I was pissed and suggested we should have something to eat. "Great idea," said Johnny. "Let's see what we've got in the fridge." I followed him into the kitchen and he opened the fridge door to reveal half a bottle of fresh orange and one egg. "Ah well," said Johnny, "let's get another bottle of whisky opened!"'

'We went together on trips to Europe to attend European draws. Once we were in Monaco and he invited every member of his board and we were well represented. Our delegates went to the function to see the draw being made but the Ipswich party remained in their hotel drinking. They didn't know the draw until we got back.'

When Arsenal played at Portman Road their visiting directors used to stay at the Copdock Hotel on the previous night. Cobbold, who presided over his frequent lunch sessions with his cronies at the same hotel, invariably turned up to join the Arsenal party for dinner. It didn't matter that he was on the opposing side. 'Who are you signing now?' he would say. 'Fetch another bottle of champagne,' he'd shout. He rarely had dinner.

He didn't know too much about the intricacies of football. At a game at Filbert Street he congratulated the side that was leading 2-0 at half-time. Leicester were in blue shirts, the same as the Ipswich players in matches at Portman Road, but on this occasion Robson's players appeared in yellow. The chairman told Robson 'I congratulate you for the way the team are playing such entertaining and enterprising football today. Have you come up with some new routines in training?' An exasperated Robson said 'You've got the teams the wrong way round. We're losing. Leicester are winning, not us.' Cobbold said 'Oh f——!'

The Cobbold family still has close links with the Ipswich Show and they used to own horses known as the Suffolk Punch, a breed that was renowned for great strength. They were bred to carry knights in armour and in later years they were recognised as powerfully built agriculture horses, which were well suited to hard work. In 1972 the club arranged a competition for a new motif for the club and 1,000 entrants took part. John Gammage was the winner, using a Suffolk Punch as the focal point, with a horse resting one of its front feet on a football. A castellation theme was incorporated into the design, representing the ancient buildings in the town and around the docks and wavy blue lines represented the nearby sea.

A new, effervescent talent emerged in the 1972/73 season – eighteen-year-old Kevin Beattie from Carlisle who was called 'the new Duncan Edwards' by Robson. Three years earlier, when Beattie had just left school, he should have signed for Liverpool, not Ipswich. One of Liverpool's scouts saw him and told Bill Shankly to sign him. Beattie was given a rail voucher and his instructions in a letter to travel by train to Liverpool. He got a bus to Anfield and, when he arrived, there was no-one to meet him. So he went home.

John Carruthers, Robson's scout in the North, heard about Beattie's misfortune and fixed him up to go to London to take part in a trial game against Fulham. Robson was warned that Beattie was 'a bit wayward' and told Ron Gray, his chief scout 'when you pick him up off the train, don't take your eye off him!' Beattie takes up the story. 'Ron booked a room for me in the Great Eastern Hotel and it was the first time I'd been away from home. I was fifteen, right out of school. There were two beds, one for him and one for me. I woke up in the night I saw this apparition sitting in a chair alongside the other bed, all in white. I thought it was a ghost. Then I saw it was Ron's grey hair and he was sprawling out in his white Long Johns. I asked him about it at breakfast and he said he was keeping guard on me to make sure I didn't get away. He was a great character. He was a big lovable teddy bear of a man who would brighten up any room he walked into. He was full of little quips and was so down to earth. He loved bright, colourful clothes and we all loved him. He would always tell me "you're the greatest". The next young player he would meet, he'd say the same thing. They were all the greatest to him.'

Born in South Shields, Roland Gray (his proper name), was renowned as a fine judge of talent but he wasn't a great manager. He had Graham Taylor, Jim Smith and Ray Harford under him at Lincoln between 1966 and 1970 before he had two spells as manager at Millwall. During one worrying season he answered criticism of his players, saying 'The morals of the boys have never been better.' A journalist said 'you mean morale, not morals.' 'You know what it means,' he said.

There were frequent demonstrations outside the old Den and, sitting in his office one day, he heard the noise of another group advancing towards the club offices. Suddenly the demonstrators started to bang on the corrugated tin outside. Ron looked at the journalists and said 'they're right you know.' And on another occasion he looked out to see a large group carrying a coffin. 'Christ,' he said. 'They're coming for me.' One of the staff members reassured him. 'It's the chairman, not you,' he said. Mick Purser, the chairman, owned a car business in the Old Kent Road and the windows were regularly smashed by bricks and other missiles.

Ron Gray was chief scout at Portman Road between 1970 and 1987 and died at the age of eighty-two in 2002. As one of the players said at his funeral 'They don't make them like him any more.' Two days before he died several of the Ipswich players turned up to see him and one of his signings, Allan Hunter, was there. Ron saw him and his eyes lit up. 'Big Al!' he said. 'I always had you in the World XI.'

Another of his signings was George Burley. 'He came to my home in Ayrshire to sign me and it was done in the kitchen when I was fifteen,' he said. 'He always described it as a kitchen sink signing. He was a legend.' John Wark, another of his signings, recalled 'My favourite story was about when he gatecrashed into schools in the London area. The head teacher at one school wasn't keen on professional clubs' scouts attending games, although there were one or two lads who had been identified as potential stars of the future. Ron wasn't going to be put off that easily. He turned up at the school and slipped the janitor a few bob. When a figure appeared in the playground, sporting overalls and with a cap pulled down over his head, no-one batted an eyelid. And to make himself look even more inconspicuous, Ron even had a broom in his hand, sweeping up near the football pitch as he kept one eye on the game taking place.'

In those days scouts were important people. They discovered the stars and were paid commissions, nearly always in 'readies' – money which wasn't declared to the Inland Revenue. They were poorly paid but they loved their work. The successors to people like Gray, the legendary Chelsea scout Jimmy Thompson and Jack Hixon (the man from the North East who discovered Alan Shearer), are still working but they have been largely supplanted by agents. The agents run big businesses with an annual turnover of millions of pounds. A high proportion are millionaires. No scout has yet ended up as a millionaire.

Some clubs have now dispensed their scouts, sending their coaches and other members of staff out to assess players. Burnley, the club that found so many stars in the 1960s, is the latest to disband their scouting staff and other clubs who pruned their staffs include Sunderland, Crystal Palace, Fulham and Watford. 'It used to be a twenty-four-hour-a-day job,' said one scout. 'You'd watch a kids' game in the morning, a reserve game in the afternoon and a League at night. Nowadays managers buy players from abroad without looking at the player. The agent shows them a video and they take that as gospel. The managers often have a percentage of the fee – most of them have got it in their contracts. It's a lot of money involved.

'These days the chief scouts earn between £30,000 and £50,000 a year, which isn't a fortune compared to what top players get. There aren't many in the £50,000 bracket. Some can get 2 per cent of the resell value of players, which can be a good sum. This is one of the reasons the players go from club to club – the managers make money from it, too.'

One of the biggest earners from the transfer market used to be the late Brian Clough and, in one six year period, he admitted that he made £1.2 million from player transactions and had to repay £600,000 to the Inland Revenue. Other high fliers were George Graham, Ron Atkinson and several other managers still working. Behind the scenes, there was a significant number of managers who took 'considerations' and the FA still can't stop them. Some managers have a clause in their contracts allowing them to be paid by agents as a percentage of transfer deals. The bigger the deal, the bigger the number of agents involved, with their payouts hidden away in offshore accounts. It is difficult to prove that regulations have been breached.

Beattie was put into a youth game in a public park in Fulham the day after Ron Gray took him to London. John Chandler, one of the physiotherapists with Ipswich, was walking around the ground with Gray and after half an hour Gray nudged him in his arm. 'We've struck gold,' he said. Beattie had the assets to become a great player but injury brought him down.

He had an excellent relationship with Mr John after he went into digs and was soon taking part in a donkey race in the grounds of Capel Hall. Cobbold wasn't a natural horseman and Beattie and Hunter were first-timers. When they eventually mounted the donkeys, 'Alka', 'Seltzer' and 'Burp', no-one was able to start the race. 'Get the game-keepers to give them a whack on the rear,' shouted Cobbold. The donkeys broke into a gallop and after one lap Cobbold's animal suddenly stopped, tipping the chairman into a small lake. As he staggered to his feet he said 'I won it! That's the first time I've won anything in my life.'

Beattie won the Player of the Year in his first full season and was soon picked by England. His impetuosity led to a series of injuries and, after damaging his left knee while playing for his country at the age of nineteen, he was never properly fit again. When he quit at the age of twenty-nine he was plagued by problems mainly relating to drink and almost died from pancreatitis at the age of thirty-seven. 'I was four hours away from leaving this world,' he said. 'I was given the last rites.' He had his ninth operation to his knee in 2001. 'I had too many cortisone injections,' he said. 'But I'm not bitter. I love football and I would never live anywhere than Ipswich. They are special people. Bobby Robson treated me like a second dad.'

Some players go through a career without injury, others are plagued with it. Bobby Charlton spoke about the subject on the day that Manchester United beat Ipswich 1-0 at Portman Road at the end of the 2002/03 season when Ruud van Nistelrooy's controversial penalty condemned Ipswich to Division One. 'I never have an injury,' he said. 'Not even a hamstring strain, which is the most common muscle strain. The only injury I had was a hernia and I did that playing golf. I was out for two weeks.' His career started at Old Trafford in 1954 and ended at Preston in 1974, after having appeared in 642 League matches. Sir Walter Winterbottom, the first manager of England, once said that Charlton had the elasticity of muscle of the Brazilians – who generally avoided muscle strains. Pele was probably the finest example.

The Ipswich players never poked fun at the stern, disciplinarian Ramsey – but they did it with Robson. On a trip to Scotland before a Texaco Cup game against St Johnstone, Robson and a group of players were walking a golf course and, with Robson immersed in a newspaper, he was heading for a particularly deep bunker. Beattie was the first to spot the danger and Hunter was about to warn him. But Beattie held his finger to his lips. Robson tumbled into the bunker throwing up a cascade of sand and the players roared with laughter. As Robson climbed to his feet, he carried on his walk without a word. Over a drink later no-one mentioned the incident. Later, when the players retired to their rooms Robson sought out Beattie. 'Look matey, let me know where the bunkers are next time,' he said.

Former England left-back Mick McNeill, who played for the club between 1964 and 1972, recalled the occasional visits to the Cobbold estates at Rannock, in Perthshire. The large, bleak house had no central heating and had to rely on wood fires. During the football season the place was freezing. 'Mr John ordered a huge side of beef and it was delivered by a van,' he said. 'He didn't know how to cut it up so I was called upon. He sat on a massive leather settee with sweat rolling off his face. As I was serving it up I said to him "what would you like to have to drink, Mr John?" "I'll just have a beer," he said. After the meal he and Patrick sat on the back of the settee, facing each other, and bashing each other with cushions. It was like a kind of pillow fight. They specialised in that.'

On the outside, they appeared to be successful landowners. But the family had been trying to sell their estates for generations and they were finally sold for relatively small sums. In 1930 the *Daily Telegraph* reported 'One of the largest Highland estates which has come into the market for some years is the Rannoch property, a huge area of nearly 67,000 acres, or well over a hundred square miles, which Captain Ivan Cobbold, the Duke of Devonshire's son-in-law, is selling. It sounds grand to be the owner of a territory like this, but the area is only moor, forest, lochs and rivers and fit for nothing else by grouse and deer. The late Captain Dudley Coates had a large adjacent estate of a similar character and it realised, about eighteen months ago, something in the neighbourhood of a sovereign an acre.

'Captain Cobbold is disposing of Rannoch, so it is understood, because of the heavy death duties which he has to meet consequent on the death recently of his father Mr John Cobbold, a member of the rich Ipswich brewing family. At the same time Captain Cobbold must be a wealthy man, for when he married Lady Blanche Cavendish and entered the ducal family of Devonshire, his father made very handsome settlements indeed on the couple.' They were rich and no-one disputed that. But after he died in 1944 his bachelor sons were unable to hold on to the family fortune. They were too generous.

In his heyday, Captain Cobbold was rated as one of the best shots in Britain and it was estimated that he fired 40,000 cartridges in a season at his grouse estates. It was a costly business. In 1938, 21,000 acres of his Craganour estate were sold for an undisclosed amount and in 1943 another 20,000 acres were sold off from the Rannoch estate. 'Cappy' was also an outstanding cricketer and was a member of the Eton first team. Lord Cranworth, his lifelong friend, said of him 'Ivan Cobbold was a man of many talents, great abilities and infinite charm. He was a patriot with every fibre of his being.'

The personable Frank Brogan recalled one of Ipswich Town's most hilarious visits to Rannoch. After drawing 2-2 at Newcastle in

February 1965, the coach took the party on to the hunting lodge to get ready for a friendly game on the following Tuesday against East Stirling Clydebank. 'My landlady gave me a heavy cardigan, ideal for tackling the cold weather,' said Brogan. 'The house was perishing cold and you needed something like that. The rooms were very large and none of the bedrooms had heating. There were log fires downstairs but the only room that was really warm was the kitchen, so we used to crowd into it. Mr John laid on plenty of drink and signed for everything. The players took the mick out of him all the time and on this occasion he put his drink down to go out to go to the toilet. One of the players peed in it and when he came back, took a big gulp and spat it out into the fire. Flames shot up into the air and I was showered with soot. I looked like a coalman.

'Up to thirty people were staying there and there was a big staff of ghillies, gamekeepers, cooks, butlers and so on. It was like being in the 1920s, with the lackeys touching their forelock and being subservient to the chairman. He used to organise these singsongs and dances, except that there were hardly any girls to dance with. Most of the men wore kilts and he made them tie their hankies around their heads to pose as girls. This would last into the night and most of the players had hangovers when they got up the next morning. No wonder we lost that game. Bill McGarry was the manager then and he was a strict disciplinarian. But he'd given up. "You f——ing well do what you like." he said.

'I remember one murky day when the squad went for a walk to clear our heads. There were miles of peat bogs and trees and deer but it had a special aura about the place. I quite liked it. One of the players said "Mr John, what's that over the mountain beyond?" Cobbold replied "f—— all!". And he was right.' Douglas Alexiou, a former director of Tottenham Hotspur, went to occasional dinners with the Cobbolds and said 'They were like a couple of naughty prep school boys. They were wonderful people, so warm and friendly. They used to swear all the time. Patrick would get up from the dinner table and say "that's it, I'm f——ing off for the night. Goodbye!"'

TWENTY

ALF WAS SACKED

And he never told his closest and nearest footballing mate

Alf Ramsey was sacked as manager of England on 21 April 1974 and he asked for his employers, the FA Executive Committee, headed by the chairman Sir Andrew Stephen, to delay the news until 1 May. He wanted time 'to enable me to notify my family before they read it in the newspapers first.' That was typical of him. He did it his way, right up to the end (at his funeral Frank Sinatra's 'My Way' was played – it was his favourite song).

The decision to remove him was effectively taken on 14 February, St Valentine's Day, and the FA International Committee had minuted from the previous meeting 'On behalf of the members of the committee on 5 November Mr Dick Wragg, the chairman, expressed sincere regrets to Sir Alfred Ramsey that the England team had been eliminated from the World Cup but wished to place on record that Sir Alfred Ramsey had the unanimous support and confidence of the members of the senior committee.' It was, of course, the dreaded vote of confidence that preceded the sack.

Ramsey had no confidence in the elderly members of the International Committee right from the day he started his job at Lancaster in 1963. Dr Neil Phillips, who worked as the England doctor during Ramsey's reign, said 'When Alf became manager at Ipswich, John Cobbold and the directors gave him a free reign. He was secretary of the club as well as the manager and he was used to making the decisions. At the FA he was excluded from most of the decision making and he found it hard to adapt.

'He won the concession to pick the side but that's about all. It was ludicrous that a committee of about ten people picked the England team. They were all directors of clubs and they wanted to pick their own players. Walter Winterbottom, his predecessor, was always frustrated by that. When Alf took over he was very upset to be told that

Lady Ramsey wouldn't be allowed to sit in the directors' box, or the Royal Box at Wembley. She attended a few games and had to sit outside and that irritated him. They were very close. Their marriage was a great love story and for her to be slighted in this manner was very upsetting to him. Particularly when the FA allowed Don Revie, his successor, to let his wife Elsie sit in the directors' box.'

Ramsey called his wife Victoria 'Vic' and she called him 'Alfred'. They shared the same interests, including gardening, visiting friends around the country and abroad, walking and skiing in Austria, which he loved. While he was working for the FA, he still lived in their house in Ipswich, travelling to and from London by public transport and Lady Ramsey still lives there now. The immaculately maintained detached house has many treasured memorabilia, paintings and books. She is a remarkable, cheery lady and has a full life including working voluntarily at a local hospital.

Ramsey was given three months notice from 30 April and was paid £8,000 tax free. 'I felt desperately sorry for Sir Alf,' FA secretary Ted Croker at the time, 'because he was an honourable man who had done his best for his country for more than ten years. But I felt the committee had made the right decision. It was time for a change. Sir Alf's style had been successful but when change was needed he didn't seem to adapt enough. England's failure was only partly due to the lack of co-operation of some clubs.' Croker was a charming, well liked man who survived an air crash in his younger days. He also had the advantage of playing the game, appearing briefly for Charlton, and not many FA committee members now have played the game.

Croker was shocked at the mean minded approach of the FA Councillors and tried, too late, to repair the damage. Dr Phillips said 'The story of the dinner mats always rankled with Alf. Some time after England won the World Cup some of us, Harold Shepherdson, Les Cocker, Alan Bass and myself were rummaging around of the basement at the FA offices in Lancaster Gate and Alf saw these blue boxes covered with dust. "What's that?" Alf said. Denis Follows, the FA secretary at the time, said "That's the World Cup dinner mats. They are from aerial photographs of the venues for England's games." "They're beautiful pictures" Alf said. "We'd like to have some to give to my staff. It would be a nice souvenir for them." Denis said "they're only for the FA councillors." We sounded off and let Denis know what he thought of it. But we didn't get our mats. Les Cocker, the assistant trainer who worked closely with Revie at Leeds, never forgot it. He was quite a fiery character and after Alf was sacked and Joe Mercer took over as caretaker, Ted Croker organised a meeting of the England staff in Sofia to try to establish a better relationship with the FA. When Ted asked them what was upsetting them, Les said "I'll tell you, the dinner mats". Croker looked mystified. "What dinner mats?" Cocker explained heatedly and Croker said "I know where these boxes are. They're in my garage at Lancaster Gate. I'll get them out and make sure you'll all get one." I think Harold Shepherdson and Les Cocker got theirs, but I don't think Alf got his. He ought to have had one.' Sadly, Croker died on Christmas Day 1989. As his wife Kathy said, 'special people die on Christmas Day'. He did a lot to improve the FA's old fashioned style of operating.

Ramsey experienced many snubs in his reign. One of these came in Mexico during the 1970 World Cup. Most experts thought the England team was better than the 1966 side and the players felt the same way. But they believed it was a major mistake to stay at the Hilton Hotel in the centre of the sprawling, smoggy city of Guadalajara, where the players were packed in three to a room. The night before the Brazil *v*. England game the players were kept awake by rowdy Mexican and Brazilian supporters accompanied by a band. Despite protests from England officials, police took no action. Bobby Charlton and Gordon Banks, key players, were forced to change their rooms, moving to the rear of the hotel. England lost 1-0. Nowadays England players are given single rooms.

Ramsey insisted on the FA bringing their own food and drinks with them to ensure that the players remained free of stomach problems. But the night before the game against West Germany, Gordon Banks went down with the runs and was forced to drop out. Peter Bonetti took over and made the mistake, diving over a long shot, which put England out. Ramsey said to another *Daily Mirror* journalist, Nigel Clarke 'I was convinced it was a CIA plot to stop Banks playing'. But there was no evidence to suggest that there was any chicanery. When the players left in the coach for the stadium back to the hotel, Ramsey sat next to Bobby Charlton and apologised to him for taking him off prematurely. Next day on the flight home he sat alone, glum faced and the only words he spoke on the whole journey was 'We would have won if Gordon had been fit to play.'

Ramsey was only middle aged as the preparations started for the 1974 World Cup tournament and wanted security from a better contract. His annual salary at the time was barely higher than today's stars' weekly wage. But the committee had no intention of giving him another term. Professor Sir Harold Thompson, the vice chairman of the FA, was the most powerful figure at Lancaster Gate at the time and insisted that Ramsey should go. Unpopular, boorish and bombastic, the Oxford professor carried the rest of his colleagues and appointed the popular Joe Mercer as a temporary manager until Revie, the Leeds manager, was confirmed. Revie's appointment was a disaster – one of the worst in the history of English football. Revie lacked principles and most people in the game knew it but the FA deliberately chose him because they thought he was a winner. He was a success at club level, but not at international level. He was banned for ten years from working in football but his appeal was later quashed: perhaps because Sir Harold Thompson had served on both committees – the one that appointed him and the other one that banned him.

The Cobbold brothers had a brief exchange of words, five to be precise, with the Professor in 1978 and Johnny counted it as one of his greatest successes. The game was Ipswich *v.* West Bromwich Albion in an FA Cup semi-final game at Highbury. Thompson, renowned for his rudeness, barged into the Arsenal boardroom, interrupting a discussion between Cobbold and Ken Friar, the Arsenal secretary, about plans to hold a joint banquet after the Arsenal *v.* Ipswich cup final that year. 'What's going on?' said Thompson. Cobbold shouted 'F— off, you f—face!' Thompson looked shaken and retreated down the corridor. 'Open another bottle of champers,' said Johnny. 'Delighted,' said Friar. Thompson failed to appear at Highbury for the next two years. 'I've got him banned for two years,' chortled Cobbold later. And when Denis Hill-Wood, the Arsenal chairman who missed the semi-final to attend another game, heard the news and sent a crate of champagne to the Cobbolds as a thank you gesture. In these days, a man like Thompson wouldn't have survived. He was well known for being a groper and, on a flight taking the England squad to a match in Europe an air stewardess reported that he had fondled her while serving drinks. The FA mounted a cover up operation and nothing emerged. He was fortunate to stay in his job.

Ramsey was very bitter for the rest of his life about his dismissal. 'I was never given a reason for the sack,' he said. To be abandoned in favour of a footballing felon, Revie, was a cruel snub and he never forgave the FA's rulers. Revie pushed gamesmanship to the limits, often leaving friendly notes to referees to encourage them to give decisions in favour of Leeds. Around that time the level of violence on the field was at a peak. But Revie also had a sense of humour. In an international game between England and West Germany (as it then was), Norman Hunter – known as 'Bite Yer Legs Norm' – had a boot yanked off his foot after crashing into a German player. Most players would have handed it straight back. Instead, the German player picked the boot up and hurled it into the crowd, preventing Hunter from putting it back on quickly and carrying on playing. Cocker, Revie's long-serving trainer, reacted angrily, screaming at Revie 'that b—— is a cheat!' A smiling Revie said 'I admire what he did. We'll have to do it next time.'

Ted Phillips often met Ramsey on the 5.30 train from Liverpool Street to Ipswich and on 1 May he bumped into him again. 'Come and have a drink,' said Ramsey. 'I've been laying cables and I'm a bit dirty,' Phillips said. 'No, I'll do it,' said Alf, making his way to the refreshment car. Subsequent England managers always travelled first class. Ramsey always travelled second class. He came back to the carriage carrying two lagers and a couple of miniature scotches. 'You've pushed the boat out,' said Phillips. Ramsey smiled.

They chatted amiably and, as the train passed Chelmsford, Ramsey disappeared to return with two more miniatures. Phillips lives in Colchester and got up to leave the train as it came to a stop. 'Thanks for the drinks,' he said. 'See you on tomorrow's 5.30.' Ramsey smiled again. As Phillips was greeted by his wife Margaret outside Colchester

Station, she held up a copy of the local newspaper. The front page headline was 'Ramsey sacked by the FA'. Phillips was astonished. 'He didn't let on, not a single dickey bird,' he said. 'But that was Alf. I tried to get him to attend the annual reunion of the Ipswich players. We always have a dinner and everyone enjoys it. Several years I tried to talk him into it and one year he started to give me the impression he might come. I told him I'd pick him up and take him home. He wouldn't get any hassle. He said he'd go and I went round to his house to collect him. Lady Vicky came to the door and she said "I'm sorry Alf has gone out". I never tried again. The old boy didn't fancy it.'

Ramsey was never given a medal for winning the World Cup. He was a bitter man after his removal and never forgave the men he felt responsible. He snubbed them and turned his back on them. However, he acquired presents and souvenirs in his career and after he died in 1998 some of his memorabilia fetched £83,188. It was the first time his family had come into money. He never attempted to cash in on his fame. He had no agent, no advisor. But in his later years he allowed himself to put his name on articles in the *Daily Mirror*. These articles sometimes contained criticism of other England managers, including Bobby Robson, and that upset Robson. It didn't help to mend what appeared to be a rift between the men.

If Ramsey had been in charge in the 2002 World Cup he probably would have refused to copy the example of Sven Goran Eriksson, who became a multi-millionaire from his activities both on and off the field. Ramsey's retiring personality would have prevented that happening. His friends said that he suffered a lot of Press criticism. Much of it was plainly untrue but he never responded, never threatened to sue anyone. He kept his own counsel and his dignity.

Geoff Hurst, who scored the first and only hat-trick in a World Cup final, sold his memorabilia, including his hat-trick shirt, for £91,750. The late Bobby Moore's collection was sold by his widow to the West Ham museum for £1.8 million and Ray Wilson released his in 2001. His full-back partner George Cohen sold his privately in 1998. Gordon Banks, who sold his for £124,000, expressed the resentment towards the treatment of the World Cup heroes. 'We got £1,000 each

for winning the World Cup,' he said. 'We'd won it for our country
and it got a pittance. Nearly all the members of the squad never made
a fortune.'

At fifty-three, Ramsey was comparatively young as a manager when
he left the employment of the FA, but those who knew him thought
his spark had dimmed. He had no desire to seek another top football
job and stayed at his house, with its beautifully maintained garden,
in the posh end of Ipswich. Twice a week he went to play golf with
three trusted friends.

Cobbold thought he might get offers. Ramsey's record of 69 victories in his 113 internationals, with only 17 defeats, was unparalleled.
But except for a couple of token directorships outside of football, there
were no overtures. Cobbold made no effort to persuade him to launch
a comeback. A chairman of a First Division club said 'I don't think he
was as close to Alf as he was with McGarry and Robson. Alf was his
own man and Cobbold was a bit apprehensive about tackling him. He
left Alf to himself. You thought Cobbold might have given the biggest
party ever. He never missed the chance to have a party. But he didn't
have one for Alf. He told the directors that Alf can come back as a
guest here but he never pushed it.'

Harold Smith, who lived nearby, was delegated to see Ramsey to
invite him to games at Portman Road. 'We shared the same gardener,'
said Smith. 'But he was a difficult man. He didn't make a big effort to
make friends. I told him an open invite was there for him but he rarely
followed it up. He would say "they didn't invite me" but we did.

'On another occasion I met him in a boardroom at another club and
invited him to come back to Ipswich on the coach. But he declined. By
the time he was sixty-five he wasn't a well man and I was on the FA
Council and we took up the question of his financial state. He wasn't
rich and I was asked to see him to talk about a pension. Ted Croker
rang me to say that the Executive Committee wanted to give Alf a
more comfortable life. When I saw Alf the next time I advised him to
hire an accountant and then get back to Croker. I believe he did and
when I saw him again he said "Thank you for what you have done.
It's been satisfactory." I saw him a few times later in the boardroom at

Ipswich and when he saw a journalist, he would walk out. He wasn't a forgiving man and that was the way he was made.'

One of his best and most trusted friends was Len Barnes, a former fitter mechanic in the Royal Artillery who played golf with him in a foursome right up to his final months. 'He was a gentleman, a wonderful man' said eighty-four-year-old Len. 'But he was a bit of a bandit on the golf course! He wasn't an outstanding golfer. His handicap was 22 to 24, never got any better. He loved the game and played in all weathers, even in the worst of the winter. There were four of us who played at Rushmere Golf Club: Alf, me, the late Eric Abbs, who worked at Ransomes and Phil Chapman, a farmer who also died. My handicap was 14 and I still play the game. When we played with Alf, the pair who lost paid for the tea in the club house. We did that every time, never varying it.

'I first met him when I was on leave from the Army and he was manager of Ipswich. I remember Vicky drove him to Rushmere when he started playing. He was a one-man band in terms of marriage and he never looked at another woman. He had his own sense of humour and rarely talked about football. He never boasted about his job and when he talked about players, not very often, he never criticised them. He didn't like going to functions and didn't like to speak in public. He was a private person. No-one tried to pester him at Rushmere but there was an incident in his later years when a photographer chased after him and he lost his temper. He struck out with a club and I think the fellow was given a fright.

'The last time I played with him he was about to play his drive on the first tee and tripped over a box for wastepaper and stuff and collapsed to the ground. I tried to lift him and couldn't. I managed to turn him over on his back and pumped his chest. After a while, he started to get up. "What do we do now?" he said. He was anxious about being seen. "Anyone seen me?" he said. "No, you're all right," I said. Two days later he was fit enough to go to America to see his daughter Tanya.'

But while in America he suffered a severe stroke and he didn't have the money to pay for treatment. He was flown home and taken to hospital in Ipswich and placed in a public ward, along with patients of both sexes. Those who visited him were shocked to see England's greatest footballer manager – the only Englishman to win the World Cup in the game which England invented – in a common, public ward. There was a move by FA officers and councillors to have him moved to a nursing home but he died on 15 May 1999 and the death certificate mentioned the effects of a stroke, prostrate cancer and Alzhiemer's.

A few days earlier, Bobby Robson was so upset that he rang the FA and said he would offer £10,000 to pay his private expenses if the FA would match his offer. It was too late. Alf Ramsey partly succumbed to dementia – and an increasing number of footballers of his era have died from it. The subject of damage to the brain caused by heading the ball was highlighted by the death of the England and West Bromwich Albion centre forward Jeff Astle. On 12 November 2002, Andrew Haigh, the South Staffordshire coroner, ruled that Astle died of an industrial disease after twenty years of heading a heavy leather ball. The inquest was told that he suffered from degenerative brain damage, mostly to the front of the head. He died at the age of fifty-nine, unable to recognise his family. Ramsey was in a similar position, being unable to speak, and he, too, headed heavy leather balls countless times in his career. Another England manager, the caretaker Joe Mercer, also died of the same illness, along with Danny Blanchflower – who claimed he rarely headed the ball – and seven members of the Port Vale side which reached the 1954 FA Cup semi-final were said to have suffered from senile dementia. There must be hundreds more.

Ramsey had three brothers, Albert, Len and Cyril. Albert, the oldest, looked like him. He helped Lady Vicky to arrange the memorial service at St Mary Le Tower Church in the centre of Ipswich, the same church where the memorial services were held for a number of members of the Cobbold family, including John Cobbold on 13 September 1983. She wanted to invite the World Cup players and so many former players, officials and FA people turned up that the church was packed to overflowing. Sir Bobby Charlton spoke and so did George Cohen. Geoff Hurst, the man who did so much for Ramsey to win the World Cup, said in his 2002 autobiography: 'I went to the funeral but I was disappointed not to see more people from the footballing establishment'. When the new Wembley Stadium is finally built the FA might well want to make amends and name it 'The Alf Ramsey Stadium'. It is unlikely that another England manager will win the World Cup again. The FA leaders have brought the game into disrepute over recent years. This would be a suitable occasion to reverse the trend and honour a man who was shabbily, disgracefully treated.

The Rt Revd Richard Lewis, Bishop of St Edmundsbury and Ipswich, conducted the service. There might have been a memorial service at one of the great London churches, to celebrate an outstanding football life. But his family and friends respected his wife's feelings. He may not have had much money in his life, but he had great wealth of a different type, which few people are lucky enough to possess – a truly happy marriage which was the most important part of his life. Love is better than money and it always will be. It makes the world go round.

TWENTY-ONE

ALF HAD A GREAT SENSE OF HUMOUR, SAYS GEORGE COHEN

Only one Prime Minister has been assassinated in this country – Spencer Perceval in 1812 – and not one England football manager has been shot and killed. But on 21 April 1970, forty-five minutes before the kick off in a match between England and Northern Ireland at Wembley a warning arrived from the police that provoked a crisis. 'We have been told that the IRA are intending to assassinate Alf Ramsey,' said a senior officer. 'We think it may be a sniper.' According to someone in the dressing room at the time the players appeared shocked.

Soon, the teams were due to leave the dressing rooms and walk up the tunnel. Should the game be called off? An FA official named

Dickie Bird (no relation with the garrulous former Test umpire) always led the teams out. Before internationals and FA Cup finals, the two managers lined up behind him with the players in an orderly queue behind. Ramsey would be an easy target as he came out of the tunnel at the east of the stadium, although there were few obvious parts which could shield a potential assassin.

The ground was filling up rapidly and the attendance was later given as 100,000. There was no sign of a sniper, or a rifle. In major matches at Wembley there were around 800 police on duty and they fanned out around the stands, making an obvious deterrent to any potential killer. But in the time it would have been impossible to search the whole ground.

Back in the dressing room, Ramsey called for silence. 'It will be all right,' he said. 'As I walk out I will have Harold Shepherdson on my left and Les Cocker on my right. They will protect me.' Laughter erupted. And the order was given to proceed. England, fielding six members of the 1966 World Cup side, won the game 3-1 and the British Championship match finished without any dramas. The news was suppressed, according to Neil Phillips, England's doctor. 'We were soon going to Mexico for the World Cup and there was a lot of publicity about guerrillas in Mexico,' he said. It was one of the great untold stories of English international football.

The Troubles – the IRA bombing and shooting campaign – had started in Britain in the previous year and there were hundreds of hoax warnings almost every week. At Test matches there were up to forty a day. Police had to take action if a certain code was passed and it led to hours of fruitless searching of buildings, railway stations, bridges, sports grounds and anywhere which could be attacked by terrorists. The policy of the police was to withhold any information to the media. No-one leaked the news. But if a code word had been passed on, the police would have had to give the order for evacuation.

One of the few occasions when a major sporting event was interrupted by an evacuation was in 1973 at the Lord's Test between England and the West Indies. Dickie Bird, the umpire, said in his first book *Not Out* 'The ground was full to capacity, more than 30,000, with thousands sitting on the grass. Just before lunch, a warning was telephoned claiming that a bomb had been planted in the ground. An IRA campaign was going on in London at the time. Not long before, a bomb went off in Oxford Street. It appeared that this call was genuine. There were many more that summer which weren't and which were ignored. But the police advised that the ground should be cleared and at 2.40 p.m. Billy Griffith, the secretary of the MCC, made the announcement. Few wanted to go home so they all came on to the playing area. Thousands of people were milling around and it was a most confusing situation.'

Dickie said 'I was sitting on the covers which had been wheeled out to protect the playing pitch, thinking that was the safest place. It was most unlikely that a bomb would be under the covers! West Indian supporters wearing colourful shirts and holding bottles, laughed and joked with me. "Don't worry Mr Dickie," said one. "The bomb has gone off. It was under the English batsmen. We put it there."

'After half an hour, Griffith came on the tannoy again and told us the police wanted both teams off the field. We were escorted off in small groups and the England players and the umpires went to a tent in the gardens behind the pavilion. The West Indies players were sent back to their hotel. It was a very frightening, confusing position to be in. After a break of eighty-five minutes, during which time the police searched all the buildings and the stands, it was announced that play could resume immediately. There had been no bomb after all but the authorities couldn't take any chances.'

Geoff Hurst later gave an insight into Ramsey's hold over the players. In his book, written by Michael Hart, he said 'Alf had absolute power. He was the boss and his authority was never questioned. His word was law. If he said "Don't talk to the Press" no-one talked to them. He dealt with some strong characters – including Jack Charlton and Nobby Stiles – and you might have expected that some players broke rank, but no-one did.'

Any student reading the period of the early nineteenth century would know about the fate of Spencer Perceval. On 11 May 1812, Perceval was shot in the heart by John Bellingham, a disaffected commercial agent, as he entered the House of Commons. Bellingham's business had been ruined and his appeal to the authorities to be compensated was rejected. Perceval was popular in the House and the Speaker said 'In most faces there was an agony of tears and neither Lord Castlereagh, Ponsonby, Whitbread and Canning could give a dry utterance to their sentiments'. But around the country there were demonstrations in favour of Bellingham and the police was needed to clear the streets.

George Cohen, probably the best liked member of the 1966 World Cup squad, has vouched for Ramsey's sense of fun. 'He had a great sense of humour,' he said. 'Pretty dry but it was always well timed. He used to call you by your full name, like Geoffrey Hurst and Robert Charlton. My favourite story was about the time when we were playing in Sao Paulo for a little World Cup. We were at the stadium and the Brazil *v.* Argentina friendly, so-called friendly, erupted. The locals went mad, they started fires, fireworks went off, the police waded in with their truncheons and it was all hell let loose. Very calmly Alf got up and announced "Gentlemen, I am ready to go. You are advised to join me." He stepped on to the pitch and started running and we sprinted after him across the pitch and out to our coach. I've never seen us leave a ground so fast.'

Dr Neil Phillips treated Alf with a broken toe in Toronto in 1967 and he said 'He was taking a training session and stubbed his toe. I looked at it and recommended he should go to hospital. The verdict was a fractured toe and it was strapped up and he had to walk on sticks. He turned up on sticks for a press conference and when the journalists saw him hobbling about one said "what happened, Alf?" Alf replied "The earth moved!"'

'Alf used to make a habit of shaking the players' hands when they departed for home after a tour and thanking them. But he never made it clear they would be picked for the next squad. One of Gordon Banks' best games was against Brazil and we got a good result for a change. But for Gordon's brilliance, Brazil would have won by five or six goals. Gordon went out to buy all the papers and read the back pages. When Gordon was about to leave, Alf shook him by the hand and Gordon said "see you in two weeks time". Alf stared at him and said "maybe".

'Alf liked to chide the Charlton brothers. One occasion, Jack was pumping him about the intricacies of the game and how he picked his side. Alf told him "I don't pick the best players. I pick the best men to fit the system." That was a bit deflating for Jack. Near the end of a South American tour in 1969 some of the players were moaning about the altitude in Mexico, the weather and the food and Alf asked Bobby what he thought about it. Bobby said "I'll be happy to get back home as soon as possible". Alf responded "well if that's the case, I won't pick you again".

'Alf was one of the most kind and thoughtful people I've ever met. He always asked about my wife and son Michael and before one England *v.* Scotland game he said he'd like to have a day out for Michael at the game. Michael was eight at the time and he was very excited at the prospect. He arrived in London and Alf sent the team coach to pick him up at the station and took him back to the England hotel, the Hendon Hall Hotel, near Wembley. There was just one passenger, Michael. At the hotel he sat between Jimmy Tarbuck and Bobby Charlton at lunch and was so excited that he couldn't eat anything. He went to the game in the coach, walked onto the pitch before the start, sat in the dugout during the game and came in at half-time to listen what was said. Alf said he wanted to make it a day, a special day. Michael never forgot that day.'

Ramsey was loyal to those who were loyal to him. Said Phillips 'Alf loved Nobby Stiles and Nobby was booked for a foul on Jacques Simon in the game against France in the 1966 World Cup finals. Alf asked him about it and Nobby said it was an accident. "It was a mis-timed tackle and there was no malice," said Nobby. Alf accepted his word. Training at Highbury a few days later a senior member of the FA International Committee came up to Alf and told him that the Committee had ordered him to leave Nobby out of the side. FIFA didn't like the way Nobby played. Alf didn't hesitate. "If Nobby is banned, I'm resigning" he said. It was incredible. The members of the Committee soon changed their minds.'

TWENTY-TWO

TIME TO GO, SAYS BOBBY

Bobby Robson had fourteen momentous years at Portman Road, including ten years in Europe and the winning of the UEFA Cup in 1981. He had absolute power within the club. Hardly anything was decided without him being consulted. 'They used to ask him how many toilet rolls were needed,' said one member of the staff. Robson often said 'I've got the best job in the world'. Patrick Cobbold always had the same reply when anyone asked whether his manager would be moving to another club. 'The only way Bobby Robson will leave this club with our blessing is to become manager of England,' he said.

Barcelona (three times), Atletico Bilbao, Everton (twice), Derby County, and the Saudi Arabian FA all tried to prise Robson away from Portman Road. He showed immense loyalty to the brothers Cobbold, because they were the only people to give him a job when he was out of work in 1969. But from the day when he was called up for the national side in 1957 under Walter Winterbottom his greatest ambition was to be an eventual successor of the revered manager. He was a Winterbottom man through and through.

It was, after all, Winterbottom who persuaded him to join his FA coaching course in Paddington Street under Jimmy Hill, Ron Greenwood and an abrasive but funny coach named Jackie Gibbons. Greenwood first worked with Gibbons in 1949 when he was playing with Brentford. Christened Albert Henry, he was known as Jackie and he was one of the great characters in English coaching circles. He served in the RAF and his loud voice was rarely silent. A right-winger at Brentford and Tottenham, he cursed more heartily than the Cobbolds and he specialised in geeing up his coaches. And he liked a glass of whisky.

In his final days he was the compère at the annual dinner of the London Coaches Association at Highbury and, upset with the background noise when the chief guest was speaking, he screamed into the mike 'Shut up your f——ing mouths you f——ing c——s. Your speaker is a better coach than you lot put together. Give him a f——ing chance. If you don't like it, f—— off!' Noticing that some of the waitresses were in hearing distance, he then said 'Sorry ladies, but you can see that some of these f——ing people haven't been brought up properly!'

Winterbottom launched the FA Coaching Scheme in 1948 and Greenwood, Robson, Hill, Dave Sexton, Malcolm Allison, Terry Venables and others were his graduates, with Gibbons in the role of encourager in chief. They started their playing careers on £20 a week and one of the reasons why they took up coaching was that it enabled them to earn extra money. Today's players are earning so much money few are interested in learning such skills and this is why managers like Robson, Lennie Lawrence, Dario Gradi and Dave Sexton, who is still involved with the England setup, are still working in football. They did the courses, they learned the game and with their vast experience they can survive.

Unfortunately, too many ignorant football club chairmen are still appointing unqualified players as managers, purely on their name. UEFA have now forced England to conform and it is compulsory for prospective English managers to pass examinations. English football was twenty years behind the Continentals until recently. Without Winterbottom's vision, however, it would have been fifty years behind.

Robson passed his FA Full Badge Coaching examination in 1961, being one of fifty taking the examinations, and it started a lifelong love affair with coaching. He coached the Oxford University side to two successive wins in the Varsity match, not so much for the money but the experience. After training he drove to Oxford to take the training and returned home late in the evening. He was paid two guineas, two pounds and ten pence per session. By the time he took over at Ipswich he was one of the most respected coaches in the country and he made a point of retaining his links with the FA after becoming an FA Staff Coach.

After taking Ipswich to second place in the First Division championship in 1982, four points behind Liverpool, he was appointed manager of the England B side and acted as a scout for Greenwood, when he became England manager at the age of fifty-five. His great friend Greenwood set up a line of succession and it was no surprise that Robson would be his eventual replacement.

More money was coming into football since the publication of the Lord Justice Taylor Report in the early 1980s, forcing clubs to rebuild their decrepit, unsafe stadia. Ipswich FC soon added their name to the lengthening list of clubs putting themselves into crippling debt, paying out £1.4 million for a new stand – named after the sponsor Pioneer. It was built without frills. Three of the six directors voted against it and three in favour. Robson had the decisive vote and he was in favour. John Cobbold was aghast to learn that a Japanese company was going to invest in the club. 'I'm not going to invite a Jap into my boardroom,' he said. Robson spent a long time convincing him it was necessary. The meeting was duly arranged and Cobbold, dressed in his usual style, was introduced to the Japanese leader of the deputation. Cobbold was reluctant to linger, saying 'I'm off to London for a drink with the Duke of Kent.' The Japanese director said 'You know the Duke of Kent?' 'Yes,' said Cobbold. 'We're old mates. He's the President of the FA.' The Japanese were very impressed and the deal was quickly completed over a handshake.

Neil MacFarlane, the Sports Minister, opened the stand on 5 February 1983. The Cobbolds were not admirers of MacFarlane – or indeed any of the Sports Ministers. 'They don't understand the game,' Patrick once said. Sir Stanley Rous, who did know the game, was one of the guests and he cut the tape at the ceremony. The FA had a short list of five to find a candidate to replace Greenwood and the names were Lawrie McMenemy, Jack Charlton, Joe Royle (the present Ipswich manager), Robson and Brian Clough. Robson thought Clough would be Greenwood's successor. The forthright Clough had built an admired, ball-playing Nottingham Forest team, winning the European Cup in 1981, but he had upset a number of influential councillors at the FA by walking out as coach to the England Youth side only a few months after he agreed to take the post.

Robson had a good relationship with Clough and he recalled how he knocked on Clough's office after a match and, when he entered, was astonished to find that Clough was lying in a dark room on a settee, appearing to be sleeping. While Robson spent most of his time coaching his players, Clough let his trainer, Jimmy Gordon, take the training. The two men did, however, share a common love – taking their dog for a walk. Robson named his spaniel 'Roger' after Roger Osborne who had scored the only goal in the 1978 FA Cup final.

Nottingham was never his favourite city. In the FA Cup sixth-round tie at the County Ground in 1981, Ipswich earned a replay which they eventually won by a right-footed goal scored by Arnold Muhren (possibly the first he had scored with his 'wrong foot'). The team coach was vandalised with 'Forest' etched along its side and a wing mirror was smashed. A year later a brick was thrown into a window of the same coach. Team coaches are still being attacked now, even though most of them are unmarked.

Robson, the FA loyalist, was the first to be approached in February as England manager. FA secretary Ted Croker rang Patrick Cobbold and he responded with his familiar response – he will only leave here for the England job. Croker saw it as an act of approval and offered a lower salary than the one Cobbold was prepared to offer his manager. 'I like the sound of the job,' said Robson, 'but I don't like your terms.' At another meeting at Luton's Chiltern Hotel, just as the England squad was about to depart for Bilbao in the World Cup, the FA increased the figure. Still it wasn't enough and a higher figure clinched his agreement at a meeting in Madrid.

Patrick Cobbold kept fighting, offering his manager a ten-year contract, but it was a futile gesture. In a final, despairing bid to retain Robson's services, he said 'What about doing both jobs, working for us when you weren't on duty with England?' Serving as a national manager is not a wholly full-time job. With an indulgent chairman, a Premiership manager could do both jobs. Robson said later 'I knew I had to take the England job. If I didn't, I would regret it for the rest of my life.' The directors and staff raised enough cash to buy him a Cartier watch as a farewell present.

But there was a doubling up factor, because the FA made him England manager and the national coach – just as Winterbottom had been. It didn't work. Robson, the sixth England manager, soon discovered that running the coaching department was a full-time job. He left much of the work to Charles Hughes, the controversial head of the department. Hughes was disliked by most of the football journalists, who kept up a vendetta against his advocacy of the long ball. Robson knew that he had many qualities and used them profitably, although he questioned the risk of losing the ball by overusing long passes to the front players. In his first match as England manager, he invited the Ipswich directors and his secretary, Pat Godbold, as his guests in Copenhagen, as well as his father Philip and his four brothers. It was a typical gesture by Robson.

When he was appointed as manager of Ipswich in 1969 the local newspaper sent a photographer to Ipswich Station to take a picture of him with John Cobbold, his chauffeur and the local football correspondent. Almost fourteen years later, when he left for the FA, a similar scenario was re-enacted. John Cobbold was greyer, more stooped and less ebullient – as cancer advanced through his body – but he came out with a typical comment as the photographs were completed. 'P—— off so I can get on with the real business,' he said to Robson.

The Robson family had five brothers, but one of them died. Like his father, who started work at fourteen and was still working in his late sixties, Bobby Robson began work at fifteen and is still working. The family was brought up in a small, mining cottage in Sacriston, County Durham, without a bathroom, and four boys slept in one bedroom, using two double beds.

Robson was soon under attack from the tabloid newspapers when he took charge of his first England game, against Denmark. Peter Shilton was a saviour and the match ended 2-2 with Jesper Olsen equalising near the end. The critics blamed Robson for not retaining Kevin Keegan and the Keegan affair rumbled on for a few years.

In his eight years in charge, Robson was hounded by certain sections of the Press and twice Sir Bert Millichip talked him out of resignation. He blamed his unfair treatment on the circulation battle between the *Sun* and the *Mirror* and he was probably right. When the loudest voices start wailing, others follow and the England manager

– whoever it is – faces an onslaught unless he can produce a side which keeps winning.

Unfortunately for Robson, the hysteria reached its peak in the 1980s. He was such an accommodating man that he tolerated the antics of the critics. If someone like Sir Alex Ferguson, Brian Clough or Jack Charlton was in charge he would have retaliated and refused to speak to those who upset him. Ferguson has always intimidated the Press and conducts his press relations in his own way. If a journalist upsets him, he is banned. Robson couldn't ban anyone and always answered all the questions put to him.

In his era there were no spin doctors and no team of PR staff. There was just one press officer. Now the present incumbent is shielded from the excesses and conferences are carefully staged to avoid rows. Robson, an honest man, met the controversies head on. In the build up to the World Cup in Mexico in 1986 he invited his predecessor Ron Greenwood to talks about how to prepare the squad. Greenwood was happy to co-operate, but Robson knew that he couldn't make the same request to Sir Alf Ramsey. 'He knew the problems and I would have loved to talk to him but I couldn't,' he said. 'At the time his articles in the *Mirror* were full of vitriol and I didn't deserve that. They were scurrilous.'

In those eight years Robson lived every headline, every drama and every controversy. His passion for football kept him afloat and his record of 47 wins and 29 draws out of 95 matches was a worthy one. His percentage of wins (49) compared to Ramsey's (60) suffered because his World Cups were played abroad, whereas Ramsey's first one was played at home. Taking England to the semi-final in the World Cup in Italy was a colossal achievement and he did it knowing that he wasn't wanted for the 1994 tournament. Graham Taylor had already been lined up for the job.

Whenever he went back to his home in Ipswich, he met Patrick Cobbold or spoke with him on the telephone and Cobbold always had encouraging words for him. He knew all about John Cobbold's cancer and understood it – but it was hard for him to accept his own illness when he was diagnosed with a cancerous tumour in the colon in 1992. He took over as coach at PSV Eindhoven, the Dutch club which has a similar background to Ipswich, after the 1990 World Cup and he prided himself on his fitness. He claimed he never missed a day's training and boasted that he was as fit as some of his players. His father had a record of not missing a shift down the mine when he worked at the coalface. His genes were sound.

Robson took PSV Eindhoven to the Dutch championship in 1991/92 and his subsequent failure to win the Champions League to Anderlecht should not have been a reason for concern. One day he noticed that he was passing a little blood and went to see the PSV medical consultant Artur Woolf. The doctor came up with confirmation and the tumour was removed in the St Anne's Hospital in Geldorf. PSV announced that he had a medical problem and he was given three months off. But no-one knew it was cancer. Typical of him, he started working again without the necessary convalescence and had to go back to hospital to eliminate a blood clot. Back at Ipswich, a small number of friends knew the real facts but kept them quiet.

Somewhat harshly, PSV decided not to renew his contract. His craving for football management, despite his illness, led him to join Sporting Lisbon, the near-bankrupt second club in the Portuguese capital. It was not a good place to work in, racked by scandal and financial problems, and in December 1993 he was sacked by the President, Sousa Cintra, although Sporting were top of the League. 'I'm the first manager to be fired when I'm top of the League,' he said with a grimace. Within six weeks he was back at head coach with FC Porto, winning the title in 1995.

Robson is a tough character who fights back against adversity, on and off the field, but the news that autumn was enough to scare him. He knew that he had a problem about sinusitis dating back to his early days as manager of Ipswich. But now it was worse, affecting his sense of smell. His wife Elsie constantly told him he needed a check up and finally he relented and saw his local doctor in Ipswich while on a brief visit to London with the Porto squad. They were there to play for a testimonial match to raise money for Paul Elliott, the former Charlton, Luton, Aston Villa, Bari, Celtic and Chelsea player whose career ended with a sickening tackle by Dean Saunders, the much travelled Welsh international striker. Elliott sued Saunders and lost the case, incurring huge costs. Robson did him a favour to let his club take part and his generosity was rewarded. If he hadn't been in London, instead of flying back to Porto from his side's pre-season in Sweden, he wouldn't have met his doctor and his illness might not have been diagnosed. 'I might have died,' he said. It's an old cliché but one good deed leads to another.

Dr Keeble, Robson's GP in Ipswich, referred him to his local ear, nose and throat specialist Ian Lord and Lord carried out a scan on an area between his nose and his left eye. Robson felt no pain and still maintained it was a simple clean up. But later in the day Mr Lord rang and said he was coming round to see him with the verdict. Ten minutes later he arrived and said 'You have a malignant melanoma in the face and it will spread to the eye and then to the brain. It is very serious.'

Still uncertain that it was life threatening, Robson asked for a second opinion and went to see Mr Dan Archer at the Royal Marsden Hospital in London. Archer agreed with the first diagnosis and the surgery was performed within forty-eight hours. To reach the tumour, which was almost as big as a golf ball, the surgeon had to remove his top teeth, cut through a bone and go through his mouth. The operation was a total success but it took several weeks before his face returned to its normal state. Again the news was suppressed and although many people suspected he had a problem, only his relatives and close friends knew the facts and they kept quiet about them.

Elsie tried, unsuccessfully, to persuade him to retire at the age of sixty-two – well beyond the normal age for a top football manager. Instead he opted for the biggest, most pressurised job in football, at Barcelona. And he had two great seasons at the Nou Camp, winning the European Cup Winners Cup and the Spanish Cup. But he didn't win the Championship and was relegated to technical director under Louis van Gaal. By the end of his second season, after turning down offers from Everton, Celtic, Besiktas, Sporting Lisbon, Benfica, the Nigerian FA and the Saudi Arabian FA he accepted the post as manager of Newcastle. It was going back home for him. His last mission was to win the League. Ramsey had won a Championship and he hadn't. 'That hurt,' he said. 'If I would have matched that it would have been a fairytale. I won the title in Portugal and Holland and I should have won it in Spain too. I almost won it at Ipswich. I lost it twice on the last day of the season, 1980/81 and 1981/82. We were at Middlesbrough and at half-time we were 1-0 up and about to be Champions. But we lost 2-1. Aston Villa lost at Highbury and still won the title.'

He was, however, a lucky man to still be alive. John Cobbold's illness wasn't diagnosed early enough, his was. Twice. Now he spends some of his time raising money for cancer equipment at the Ipswich Hospital. Each unit saves hundreds of lives each year. Most cancer patients are diagnosed too late. When he was dismissed by Newcastle at the start of the 2004/05 season Robson was an angry man. He believed he had been the victim of a conspiracy to undermine his position at a club which he took from the bottom to the top six in his five years in charge. He left without a settlement and had to wait for his compensation. He, and Newcastle chairman Freddie Shepherd, knew he would be back.

TWENTY-THREE

'ARE YOU A DUTCH BULB?' ASKS THE CHAIRMAN

Arnold Muhren was twenty-seven when he joined Ipswich in 1978, the year that foreign players were allowed in. His full name was Arnoldus Johannus Hyacinthus Muhren and, when John Cobbold first met him, it was purported that he said 'Are you a Dutch bulb?' Muhren, a serious, studious man wasn't offended. 'He was a comic,' he said. 'He was always joking and telling stories, sometimes dirty stories. He could laugh at himself.

'He said to me "Don't worry about the results as long as we've got enough booze to keep things going."' Muhren was a teetotaller so he never accepted Cobbold's offer for a glass of wine. 'He was a great man,' said Muhren. 'He gave us the impression that he was honoured to be with us. He was always very generous. Most chairmen are unhappy if their team lose and if it keeps losing they want to sack the manager.

'Mr Cobbold was the opposite – so friendly, so kind. He never panicked. It was a family club, so well organised and everyone knew everyone else. It was the happiest years of my football life. Today it is about business and it is dominated by television. They want big names and clubs have spent far too much money and some are in trouble all over Europe. In Holland there are matches almost every day. It is too much and it is turning people away. Mr Cobbold used to say to me "you can't stop it". But I think you need to otherwise it will destroy itself.'

Tottenham signed Ricardo Villa and Ossie Ardiles in 1978 and it was hailed as the best foreign pairing ever signed by an English club. But Ipswich's purchases of Muhren and Franciscus Johannes Thijssen ran them close. They were signed by Sir Robert Robson from Twente Enschede a few months apart. Enschede is one of the most boring towns in Holland and twice in Robson's reign he took Ipswich there to play UEFA matches in 1973 and 1974 and knew the club and their players.

He recognised that Muhren and Thijssen were totally different to the average English player. They were highly skilled artists who treated the ball as a friend. Alf Ramsey would have loved working with them. Muhren's passing was almost idyllic and Thijssen's expertise on the ball was mesmeric. They balanced each other on the flanks and Robson was forced to turn his side into a passing team. 'Before that he told the defenders to get the ball quickly to the front men,' said Kevin Beattie. 'Afterwards they got us to use Frans and Arnold and it was better to watch. Frans could turn on a sixpence. He was the last piece in the jigsaw.'

Between 1978 and 1982 Ipswich reached the heights, winning the UEFA Cup in 1981, with Thijssen winning the Footballer of the Year Award – the first foreigner player next to Bert Trautmann in 1956. In the 1980/81 and 1981/82 seasons they finished second to Aston Villa and Liverpool in the First Division. 'We were the second best team in the country to Liverpool,' said Robson.

Thijssen was a worthy winner of his award and really should have gone down in the records as the first foreigner to win it. Trautmann was considered foreign, but the former German prisoner of war had been living in England for years and was qualified as English. In the Football Writers' Association vote, Mills came second, John Wark third and Muhren sixth. Wark was also awarded the PFA 'Player of the Year' trophy. No other club has ever monopolised the voting before or since. In a consolation prize, Paul Mariner was presented with the 'Roy of the Rovers Centre Forward of the Year' award by Sir Alf Ramsey. Cobbold told him 'I used to win that every year before I became chairman.'

By this time Cobbold was looking ill, though he attended the banquet at the Grosvenor Hotel in London. He hired a suite and stocked the bar with every conceivable drink. He invited the players to his suite and the drink flowed all night. He was in his habitual pyjamas. 'What a f——ing party!' he said. 'Better than the f——ing football writers dinner! They're a tight lot!'

Villa and Ardiles cost Tottenham £800,000, but the Ipswich pair cost £350,000 (Muhren £150,000 and Thijssen £200,000). Ipswich made £100,000 profit by selling Brian Talbot to Arsenal for £450,000. 'Good business,' said Robson. Muhren, who weighs the same now as when he first started out in his career, works as a coach at Ajax and has produced some outstanding Dutch footballers. Thijssen, thicker in build, is also a coach in Holland. 'English clubs tended to be insular and Bobby Robson and Keith Burkinshaw were the first to go outside for players,' said Thijssen. 'These days it's gone too far the other way with too many foreigner players being signed by the big clubs in Europe. In the 2000/01 season Ajax fielded nine overseas players in their first team and that was far too many. It stopped giving our own young players a chance. The quality has suffered and Holland has not been so successful.'

In England the financial downturn in 2002 pushed the pendulum back again, forcing clubs to spend more time and money to develop their own players. Outside the big Premiership clubs, the emphasis is now on using coaching expertise to improve players instead of rushing out to buy expensive players from around the world. Agents were controlling the market, making fortunes from it. The FA leaders were weak, being powerless to stop the corruption which has riddled the game, right to the very top. Big name managers were still taking bungs.

Ipswich were pioneers in rearing their own players and still are – but for a brief, mad moment when they joined the stampede, buying £15 million worth of foreigners in the 2000/01 season. Most of them turned out to be duds. The outlay was financed by money from Rupert Murdoch's BSkyB TV company and the family club found themselves being prostituted by the riches from television. Sky thrives on exciting news like big money signings and controversies. Its influence on football has many good sides to it, like promotional activities and high quality coverage at prime time, but football has been overexposed and that led to a fall off of interest. TV demands rapid change, not things which slowly evolve. To succeed with running a football club the owners need to be patient. Under the Cobbolds, Ipswich FC was like a backwater, fed by a slow-moving river which usually got there in the end. And they had a lot of fun.

The huge sums from TV helped turn the river into a torrent and being relegated at the end of the 2001/02 season was a crushing setback. The highly esteemed Burley found himself being sacked. The experienced Joe Royle took over and soon found it a tough task to revive the club. It was difficult for any football club to stand back from the rush. Nearly all the other clubs overspent as well and they were driven by the fear that if they went down to a lower division, that may well be the end for them. Now a new cycle is re-emerging, with clubs reverting to the similar policy employed in Ipswich, Burnley and a number of other medium sized clubs. If foreigners are signed, they have to be the right characters who can fit into the side like Muhren and Thijssen did and are not overpriced.

About the only thing Ramsey and Robson agreed on was that you don't necessarily have to buy the best players to produce a winning team. You need sound, self-motivated players with character to make a team that works; players who like and understand each other. You don't need mercenaries. Hiring foreigners was the reason why England lost the colonies in America, employing a predominantly German army which served ultimately under the mad King George III. History would have been totally different but for that mistake.

When John Cobbold was approaching fifty he became a member of the Good Samaritans. Some of the Ipswich group approached him to become chairman of the Friends of the Samaritans and surprisingly he agreed. Michael Stowe, one of the group, said 'He was a lovely chap and we were delighted to have him. He had a directness which we admired and at the same time, he also had a laid back approach. He had a great sense of humour.

'He wasn't going to drive himself into a nuthouse. He said that if the meetings were lasting too long he would have to say "I said at the start we were finishing at 9.30 and at 9.30 I will sound the final whistle!" He preferred to discuss plans over a glass or two of wine after the meetings broke up. He would say "you get better results over a glass of wine." He was clever at delegating and getting people going.

'He didn't do any "befriending work" answering calls himself. But he would help at fund raising events. One was a wine and cheese party at his home, Capel Hall, and on another occasion his mother, Lady Blanche, helped organise an exhibition of historical costumes and robes and regalia. It raised £1,200 – and that was a lot of money in those days. He was very generous with his time and with his money. After the 1978 FA Cup final he talked to the FA about making a donation to the Good Samaritans from the proceeds of the Charity Shield match at the start of the following season. The opening game of the season is still the League champions against the FA Cup holders and it raises a lot of money. I think he persuaded the organisers to give a decent donation to the Samaritans.'

In 1964, Ipswich faced financial problems and there was immense pressure on the directors. John Cobbold wrote out a cheque to cover the next month's wages for the players and staff. David Rose said 'It was a difficult time and Mr John came to the rescue. He got his money back later.'

When Cobbold was the Good Samaritans' chairman, the Ipswich group took 6,200 calls in 1978. In 2001 the total was 28,800, with 16,440 speaking contacts. The difference was explained by the fact that 12,360 rang and hung up before someone answered. 'That 28,800 appears to be much higher, but when other areas are busy, calls can be switched to Ipswich,' said Stowe. The number of suicides in England in the late 1970s was around 4,300 each year. In 2001 it was 6,400 and, in a macabre way somewhat reassuring, there are around twice the number of road deaths. With the increased pressures of modern life it might have been assumed that the figures were much higher. The 18,200 volunteers offer support in 49 languages and in 2002 it received nearly 5 million calls, nearly all of them between 10 a.m. and 2 a.m.

The Samaritans were founded by the Revd Chad Varah and took its first call on 2 November 1953. They were given its name when the *Daily Mirror* referred to 'a Good Samaritan telephone service'. The biblical story of the Good Samaritan is in the Gospel of Luke. It tells how a 'certain Samaritan' helped the Jewish victim of a robbery lying beside the road. The man had earlier been ignored by a priest and a Levite. Jesus said that it was the Samaritan who proved 'neighbour until him that fell among thieves'. Jesus then urged his questioner 'Go, and do thou likewise.'

John Cobbold died in 1983 and in his will he said he didn't want flowers but wanted money donated to the Good Samaritans. The sum donated in lieu of flowers came to £2,500. It paid for hundreds of return calls to men and women in distress. A fellow member of the Samaritans claimed that Cobbold left £100,000 to the organisation, but Stowe said he wasn't aware of it.

Cobbold was a giver all his life. He was unique. There will never be another John Cobbold as chairman of a football club. The way the game is going, some chairmen might need to dial the Good Samaritans' number for help. David Sheepshanks for one. Late in January 2003 he accepted an invitation to become Patron of the Ipswich branch of the Good Samaritans. Shortly afterwards he was forced to call a Press conference to announce that the club was going into administration, for rescheduling debts and keeping the club in business.

'We have no benefactor,' he said. 'With the transfer market collapsing we had no alternative.' The club owed more than £30 million and there were tough times ahead. The club captain Matt Holland, a loyalist who used to do a lap of the pitch at the end of games clapping the fans, had to be sold to Charlton, a similar club, for less than £1 million because Ipswich couldn't meet his wages of £20,000 a week. For several weeks an administrator presided over a fire sale and eventually the stricken club was allowed out of its financial straightjacket to resume business. Dozens of creditors were left short changed and included former manager George Burley, who finished up receiving 5p in the pound on the remainder of his contract, which was originally worth more than £2 million. Burley, who became manager of Derby County, was due to receive a further 10p from the pound if Ipswich were promoted in the 2003/04 season. He was disappointed but he managed to keep Derby up.

Sheepshanks presided over a meeting of creditors and other interested parties. If it had been a normal club, the people there would have been very angry, calling for resignations. Not one person objected at the meeting and Sheepshanks was thanked for his efforts. If you treat people decently they respond in the same fashion.

For a while, even journalists were charged for alcoholic drinks in the Press Room. John Cobbold would have rebelled against that. He would have insisted that the white wine should still be poured out in the boardroom.

If you are interested in purchasing other books published by Tempus, or in case you have difficulty finding any Tempus books in your local bookshop, you can also place orders directly through our website

www.tempus-publishing.com